Contents

Part 1: Introduction

Part 2: Lesson Plans

Suggested Timetable for Jolly Phonics: STEP 1

<table>
<tr><th></th><th>Daily Teaching</th><th>Week 1</th><th>Week 2</th><th>Week 3</th><th>Week 4</th><th>Week 5</th><th>Week 6</th><th>Week 7</th><th>Week 8</th><th>Week 9+</th></tr>
<tr><td rowspan="2">Letter Sound Recognition</td><td rowspan="2">• Lesson pages and actions
• Flashcards and games
• Sound books
• Jolly Phonics Wall Frieze
• Jolly Songs</td><td>s a t
i p</td><td>n ck
e h r</td><td>m d
g o u</td><td>l f b
ai j</td><td>oa ie ee
or z w</td><td>ng v oo
oo y x</td><td>ch sh th
th qu ou</td><td>oi ue
er ar</td><td>Continue to review the letter sounds.</td></tr>
<tr><td colspan="7">• Introduce the sounds, letters, and actions through stories, at a rate of one sound a day.
• Review the letters and sounds so that the students know them well.</td><td colspan="2">• Learn the sounds of the capital letters in preparation for reading sentences.</td></tr>
<tr><td>Letter Formation</td><td>• Multisensory practice:
- pencil grip
- correct formation</td><td colspan="9">• Feel the letter shapes: air writing / grooved letters in the Finger Phonics books.
• Learn the formation of the new letters. Review the formation of recently learned letters.
• Practice neat letter formation: lesson pages, dry-wipe boards, lined paper.</td></tr>
<tr><td rowspan="3">Blending (for reading)</td><td rowspan="3">• Hear the word after the sounds have been spoken by the:
a) teacher b) students
• Letter games / activities
• Word-blending boxes
• JP Little Word Books
• Decodable readers</td><td>• Aural blending: the teacher says the sounds in a word / the students listen for the word.</td><td colspan="5">• Blend words with:
- initial and final consonant blends, e.g. <u>st</u>op and mi<u>lk</u>.
- double letters, e.g. duck and hill.</td><td colspan="2">• Start using the JP Little Word Books with students who can independently blend simple regular words.</td><td>• Introduce decodable readers:
- JP Readers, Orange Level for hesitant readers.
- JP Readers, Red Level for confident readers.</td></tr>
<tr><td colspan="9">• Frequently blend simple words that use the taught letter sounds, including words with digraphs.</td></tr>
<tr><td></td><td colspan="8">• Introduce the reading of phrases (Week 2) and simple sentences (Week 5), using suggestions from the lesson plans and/or JP Word Bank. Demonstrate how to adjust the pronunciation of certain words, such as a and is.</td></tr>
<tr><td>Identifying Sounds in Words (for writing)</td><td>• Segment regular words
• Dictation</td><td colspan="9">• Identify the sounds in a word: Is there a /s/ in nest? Is it at the beginning, the middle, or the end?
• Call out simple words, e.g. dog, clap, sheep. The students respond by saying the individual sounds and holding up a finger for each one: /d-o-g/ (3 sounds, 3 fingers); /c-l-a-p/ (4 sounds, 4 fingers); /sh-ee-p/ (3 sounds, 3 fingers). Write the sounds on the board as they are called out and blend them with the students to read the word and check it is correct.
• Dictate letter sounds and simple regular words, including words with digraphs.</td></tr>
<tr><td>Tricky Words</td><td>• Read tricky words and identify the tricky part
• Write tricky words, remembering how the tricky part is spelled.</td><td colspan="6"></td><td colspan="2">• Teach the first 12 tricky words:
/sh/ lesson: I
/th/ lesson: the
/qu/: he, she
/ou/: me, we
/oi/: be
/ue/: was
/er/: to, do
/ar/: are, all.</td><td>• Continue to review the tricky words.</td></tr>
</table>

Suggested Timetable for Jolly Phonics: STEP 2

Weekly Units	1	2	3	4	5	6	7	8	9	10	11	12	13
Alternatives	‹y› as /ee/	short vowels	‹ck›	double letters	long vowels and ‹a_e›, ‹e_e›, ‹i_e›, ‹o_e›, ‹u_e›		‹ay› as /ai/ ‹oy› as /oi/	‹ea› as /ee/	‹y› and ‹igh› as /ie/	‹ow› as /oa/ and /ou/	‹ir› and ‹ur› as /er/	‹ew› as /ue/	‹aw›, ‹au›, ‹al› as /o/
	• Use flashcards to review the 42 basic letter sounds, short and long vowels, and alternatives that have been taught. • Use dictation to review the alternative spellings taught so far. • Listen for the short and long vowels in words and introduce some of the spelling rules associated with them (e.g. using ‹ck› after a short vowel). • Read a variety of words, phrases, and sentences as frequently as possible (as a class or in small groups/individually), and use blending for unknown words.												
Handwriting	Capitals SATIPN	Capitals CKEH RMD	Capitals GOULFB	Capital J	Caps ZWV	Caps YXQ	Review the alphabet: upper- and lower-case letters	Review formation: • ‹b› & ‹d› • capitals A–M	Review: • ‹r›, ‹n›, ‹m›, ‹h› • capitals N–Z	Review: • caterpillar ‹c› letters • alphabet order	Review: • tall letters • alphabet order	Review: • letters with tails under the line • alphabet	Review: • ‹e›, ‹z›, ‹s›, ‹v›, ‹w›, ‹x› • alphabet order
				Review ‹ai›, ‹oa›,‹ie›, ‹ee›, ‹or›	Review capitals: Groups 1&2	Review capitals: Groups 3–7							
	• Practice correct letter formation for both upper- and lower-case letters. • Introduce the letter names through reciting/singing the alphabet, starting in Unit 1. • Review the lower-case letters and corresponding capitals that have been taught (Jolly Phonics Alphabet Poster / flashcards / upper- and lower-case letter matching / capital and word dictation). • From Unit 7: Introduce the alphabet in four color-coded sections: A–E; F–M; N–S; T–Z. Each section represents roughly a quarter of the words in a dictionary.												
Words and Sentences	Discussion pictures for each lesson:												
	the hen	in the park	on the pond	the fox	the fish	in the dark	the noisy ducks	the queen	digging for gold	the shark in the ship	fixing the car	the statue	having a picnic
	• Use pictures for discussion and vocabulary building. • Model how to write words, phrases, and sentences with the students, including capital letters, periods, and spaces between words. • Encourage independent writing about the pictures, using words, phrases, or sentences, according to ability.												
Tricky Words	you, your	come, some	said, here, there	they	go, no, so	my, one, by	only, old	like, have	live, give	little, down	what, when	why, where	who, which
	• Read the tricky words and identify the part(s) that are tricky. • Practice writing the tricky words by looking for the tricky part(s) and following the tricky word spelling routine. • Use flashcards and dictation to review reading and writing the tricky words that have been taught. • From Unit 5, sufficient teaching has been covered to introduce the Jolly Phonics Readers, Yellow Level. Only give to confident readers at this stage.												

Suggested Timetable for Jolly Phonics: STEP 3

Weekly Units	1	2	3	4	5	6	7	8	9	10	11	12	13
Alternatives	‹ph› as /f/	soft ‹c›	soft ‹g›	Review the main alternative vowel spellings.				‹ue›, ‹u_e›, ‹ew› as /oo/	Review the main alternative vowel spellings.				‹air›, ‹ear›, ‹are› as /air/
				‹ai›, ‹a_e›, ‹ay›	‹ee›, ‹e_e›, ‹ea›	‹ie›, ‹i_e›, ‹y›, ‹igh›	‹oa›, ‹o_e›, ‹ow›		‹ou› and ‹ow›	‹oi› and ‹oy›	‹er›, ‹ir›, ‹ur›	‹aw›, ‹au›, ‹al›	
	• Use flashcards and dictation to review the alternative spellings that have been taught. • Use the "vowel hand" regularly to review the short and long vowel sounds. • Identify short and long vowels in words and reinforce the spelling rules associated with them (e.g. the alternative vowel spellings ‹ay› and ‹oy› are nearly always used at the end of a word). • Read a variety of words, phrases, and sentences as frequently as possible (as a class or in small groups/individually), and use blending for unknown words.												
Read, Write, and Review	Review capital letters and the four color-coded alphabet sections.						Review letter formation and using digraphs in words and sentences.						Review: alphabet order
	ABCDE	FGHI	JKLM	NOPQRS	TUVW	XYZ	‹oa›, ‹ng›	‹oo›, ‹or›	‹ie›, ‹ee›, ‹ue›	‹sh›, ‹ch›, ‹th›	‹er›, ‹ar›, ‹ai›	‹oi›, ‹ou›	
	• Continue to practice correct letter formation, especially of capital letters and digraphs. • Regularly review the letter names through reciting/singing the alphabet without prompting. • Review the lower-case letters and their corresponding capitals, encouraging neat and accurate handwriting (Jolly Phonics Alphabet Poster / flashcards / upper- and lower-case letter matching / capital and word dictation). • Practice writing words with digraphs, using model sentences.												
Words and Sentences	Reading comprehension for each lesson:												
	out at sea	yes or no	at the park	read and match	read and draw	sentence matching	read, write, and color	in the zoo	having a party	the bad-tempered goat	crossword clues	on the beach	the mid-night feast
	• Use a range of activities to improve the students' blending abilities and develop their reading comprehension skills. Include text that uses the alternative letter-sound spellings and tricky words that have been taught so far, as well as longer and more challenging words. • Write independently in various ways: on a chosen theme; retelling stories; writing about pictures; describing their own experiences. The students' spelling will not always be accurate, but their work should be readable.												
Tricky Words	any, many	more, before	other, were	because, want	saw, put	could, should, would	right, two, four	goes, does	made, their	once, upon, always	also, of, eight	love, cover, after	every, mother, father
	• Encourage the students to read the tricky words and identify the tricky part(s). • Use various strategies to practice writing the tricky words. • Use flashcards and dictation to review reading and writing the tricky words that have been taught. • Write sentences from dictation using regular words and the tricky words already taught. • From Unit 1, sufficient teaching has been covered to introduce the Jolly Phonics Readers, Green Level, for confident readers who have finished the Yellow Level. From Unit 10, sufficient teaching has been covered to introduce the Blue Level for confident readers who have finished the Green Level.												

A Brief Overview of the Program

What is Jolly Phonics?

Jolly Phonics is a multisensory program that teaches young students the skills they need to read and write fluently in their first year of school, although the basic principles of the program cover the skills needed for learning to read and write whatever the age. The teaching is divided into three parts or "steps," the timetables for which are shown on pages 2 to 5. There is a write-in Student Book for each semester and a Jolly Phonics Teacher's Book, which provides step-by-step lesson plans and an in-depth introduction to the program. This structured approach is suited to whole-school, whole-class teaching but it also works well with individual students.

At the heart of the program is the teaching of the English alphabetic code, which expresses the relationship between the sounds that can be heard in words and the letter(s) that are used to represent those sounds. When students read a word, they are decoding: They look at the letters, recognize the sounds they represent, and blend the sounds to hear the word. When the students write a word, they are encoding: They listen for the sounds in the word and write the letters that represent those sounds. English has a complex written alphabetic code (see the chart on pages 34 and 35), which is why it needs to be systematically and carefully taught. Step 1 teaches the students one way to write each letter sound and Steps 2 and 3 introduce and review the main alternative spellings.

The principle aim of Jolly Phonics is to teach students the five key skills that they need to apply the English alphabetic code successfully in their reading and writing. Once the students have mastered these skills, Jolly Phonics continues to extend and consolidate the learning, introducing the students to alternative letter-sound spellings, new tricky words, basic sentence structure, pre-dictionary skills, and reading comprehension. Step 1 teaches the five key skills, while Steps 2 and 3 consolidate and extend the learning. The next important stage in the students' literacy development is to hone their writing skills by giving them a structured, systematic grounding in spelling, grammar, and punctuation. This is provided by Jolly Grammar, a six-level program that builds and extends the teaching in Jolly Phonics.

Jolly Phonics has been developed by classroom teachers and has a tried and tested record of success in many different places and settings around the world. Teachers following this method can be assured that their students will read and write independently much more quickly. Case studies and links to research can be found on the Jolly Learning website. A summary of two U.S. case studies can be found on pages 7 and 8.

The five key skills taught in Jolly Phonics

Jolly Phonics Step 1 teaches the five key skills for reading and writing:

1. Learning the letter sounds
2. Learning letter formation
3. Blending (for reading)
4. Identifying the sounds in words (for writing)
5. Tricky words

The first four skills are taught simultaneously. Each lesson introduces a new letter sound and teaches the students how to write the letter(s) that represent the sound. The students then practice blending and segmenting words which use that sound.

The tricky words are taught by saying the word, blending the sounds, and encouraging the students to identify the tricky part of the spelling. As a result, they are not introduced until the sound /sh/ is taught. By then the students have had plenty of blending practice and know most of the letter sounds.

There are 40+ sounds in English, which is considerably more than there are letters in the alphabet. Step 1 introduces them at a rate of one sound a day. Most students are very capable of coping with this fast and stimulating pace. However, the rate of introduction can be adjusted according to the number and duration of lessons available and the age of the students. Audio for the main letter sounds is available from the Resource Bank on the Jolly Learning website, along with many other useful resources for teachers and parents, including videos, activities, and worksheets.

How does Jolly Phonics align with the Science of Reading?

Since it was first published in 1992, Jolly Phonics has always focused on direct, explicit instruction of phonemic awareness and phonics for both reading (decoding) and writing (encoding). Phonemes – the smallest units of sound – are taught from the start, and the students practice blending and segmenting, as well as letter formation, to connect the phonemes to their corresponding graphemes (the letters that represent sounds). Students are taught to blend all through the word, with no guessing or memorizing of whole words. Each lesson in Step 1 begins with a story to strengthen phonemic awareness and encourage vocabulary development. As their letter-sound knowledge increases, the students are able to blend and segment more and more words automatically, leaving more working memory available for comprehension skills. There is also an extensive library of decodable books, including fiction, non-fiction, plays, and poetry to increase fluency.

What is the Science of Reading?

The Science of Reading is a term that has come to encapsulate all the scientifically based research compiled over the last fifty years that shows us how students master reading and writing skills. Linguists, cognitive psychologists, neuroscientists, and other specialists across many nations, languages and disciplines have concluded that to create competent readers, we must understand how reading develops in the brain and teach and assess our students accordingly.

One such study by The National Reading Panel (Teaching Children to Read, April 2000), analyzed hundreds of research studies and reached a consensus that, for the best results, students need explicit instruction in phonemic awareness and systematic phonics teaching, with a focus on improving fluency, vocabulary acquisition, and reading comprehension.

Jolly Phonics and the Science of Writing

The Science of Writing is the term being used to bring together the existing research on the teaching of writing. Although this body of research is not as extensive as that for reading, it indicates that writing instruction is most effective when it is taught systematically, alongside reading. The success of Jolly Phonics supports these findings. The program teaches the students to say the individual sounds and blend them into a word for reading; for writing, the students listen for the sounds in a word and then write the letter(s) that represent those sounds and so spell the word. From the start, the lesson plans provide explicit direction and practice in letter formation and introduce segmenting and writing words at an early stage. Then, as the students progress, they are taught to write phrases and sentences in scaffolded and independent writing, as well as dictation. The students continue to improve their writing throughout kindergarten with Jolly Grammar: a comprehensive, six-level program that teaches spelling, grammar, and punctuation, and which covers the main spelling patterns for the various sounds in English.

Jolly Phonics in the USA: Two Case Studies

Iowa

In 2003, Valley Elementary School in Elgin, Iowa, realized their kindergarten classes were falling behind national standards for literacy and that they would have to make changes. They assessed the students using DIBELS (Dynamic Indicators of Basic Early Literacy Skills), a set of standardized, individually administered tests, and found they were below the benchmark in two key skills for reading and writing: blending and segmenting. After adopting Jolly Phonics, the kindergarten students not only reached but exceeded the benchmark goals for the year, as the chart below shows. The school's averages steadily increased as they continued to implement Jolly Phonics and their average reading level for students at the end of kindergarten was typically around the middle of first grade level.

Maine

Windham Primary School is a large K-3 school in Southern Maine, with almost 800 students on roll and over 220 of those students in twelve kindergarten classes. Their end-of-year Kindergarten Developmental Reading Assessment (DRA) benchmark is a level 4. Before adopting Jolly Phonics, only a handful of students read beyond a DRA level 4. After implementing the program, students reached the DRA4 and continued to much higher levels, with many students reading a year or more above grade level. This new approach cut the below-grade-level numbers by one-third compared to 2017, and by over one-half compared to 2016 and 2018. The percentage of students who ended their kindergarten year above grade level more than doubled compared to 2017 and tripled compared to 2016 and 2018. On average, the number of students performing well below or below the benchmark dropped from 55 to 27 percent, while the number of students performing above the benchmark rose from 17 to 46 percent.

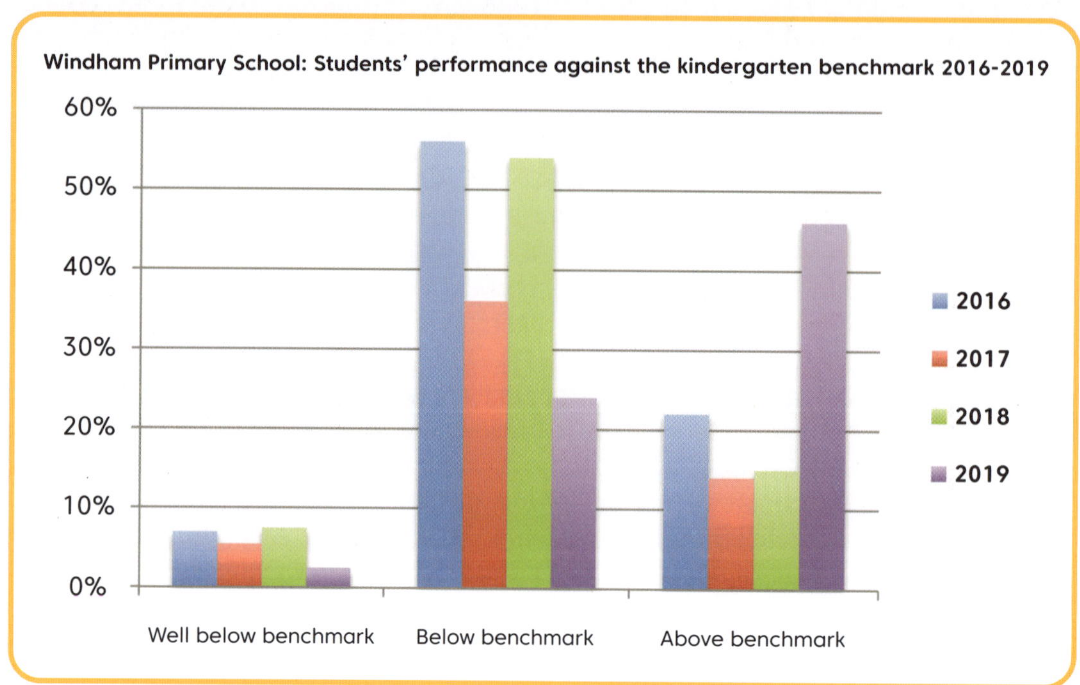

The above studies show that the Jolly Phonics approach is different from most traditional phonics programs as students are taught their letter sounds at the brisk pace of four to five per week in the first eight weeks of kindergarten. This means they will have learned one way to read and spell each of the main sounds of English by Thanksgiving. Students learn, from day one, how to blend sounds into words for reading and segment words into sounds for spelling, and phonemic awareness is embedded from the start. Full details of these case studies, as well as others in the U.S. and around the world, can be found in the Evidence section on the Jolly Learning website.

How to use the Jolly Phonics Teacher's Book

For ease of use, the Jolly Phonics Teacher's Book is divided into two distinct sections. The first part gives a comprehensive introduction to the Jolly Phonics program and explains the methodology. It is a good idea to read this before using the Student and Teacher's Books in the classroom. The second part provides structured lesson plans that give step-by-step guidance on all aspects of the lesson, including the Student Book activities. Step 1 has 39 daily lesson plans, and these are outlined on pages 38 to 76. Steps 2 and 3 each have 13 units, comprising a number of topics that can be taught over the week. The lesson plans for Step 2 are on pages 84 to 135 and those for Step 3 are on pages 142 to 180. The weekly units are not intended to take up all the time allocated for English lessons. This means that teachers are free to teach other aspects of literacy, such as comprehension and creative writing, in the remaining time.

Supplementary materials

Jolly Phonics has a wealth of supplementary materials to help teachers deliver the program in a fun and engaging way. These include the Jolly Phonics Cards, Jolly Phonics Word Bank, Finger Phonics Books (two sizes are available for either individual use or whole-class teaching), Jolly Songs, Jolly Phonics Wall Frieze, Tricky Word Wall Flowers, Jolly Phonics Little Word Books, Jolly Phonics Read and See books, Jolly Phonics Readers, Jolly Plays, and the Jolly Phonics Alternative Spelling and Alphabet Posters.

Parental support

Learning to read and write fluently is vital for students. All parents know this and want their children to master these skills. The majority of parents are keen to help, but they are often not sure how to go about it. It is a good idea to invite new parents to a meeting, where it is explained to them how reading and writing is taught in the school. These meetings provide an opportunity to introduce parents to the five key skills and to explain to them how they can support their children.

Assessment

The Jolly Phonics Student Checklist on page 33 provides teachers with an understanding of what the students should learn in the first year. It is also useful for tracking and recording the progress of any individual students who are struggling to keep up with the rest of the class (although it is also suitable for students of any age or stage of learning). More detailed beginning, middle, and end of year assessments can be found in the Resource Bank on the Jolly Learning website, along with progress monitoring sheets. These can be used to check how students are doing and to adjust support and intervention groups as necessary.

Support for struggling students

In every class there will be a few students who find it difficult to memorize the letter sounds and who struggle to blend and segment words. These students tend to have a weak visual memory and poor auditory skills. However, this does not mean that they need different teaching from the other students. In fact, they need the same teaching, but far more of it. For more information on how to support students who struggle to learn the basic skills, see pages 29 to 32.

1. Learning the Letter Sounds

It is generally accepted that there are approximately 44 sounds in English; however, only 26 letters are used to represent those sounds and many of them can be spelled in different ways. One, two, three, or even four letters can represent the sounds. In Step 1 of Jolly Phonics, the students are introduced to the 42 main sounds and taught one way to represent each of them, except for the sound /c k/, which is represented by the letters ‹c› and ‹k›:

1. s, a, t, i, p, n
2. c k, e, h, r, m, d
3. g, o, u, l, f, b
4. ai, j, oa, ie, ee, or
5. z, w, ng, v, little oo, long oo
6. y, x, ch, sh, voiced th, unvoiced th
7. qu, ou, oi, ue, er, ar

In Jolly Phonics, the letter sounds are arranged in seven groups. The letters in the first group can be used to make many simple words, such as *pin, tip, pan,* and *sat.* The letters ‹b› and ‹d›, which are often confused, appear in separate groups. The sound /c k/ is introduced early on because the letter ‹c› forms a template for writing the letters ‹a›, ‹d›, ‹o›, ‹g›, and ‹q›.

Rate of introduction

The first letter sound can be introduced on the first day of school. The students' enthusiasm for learning is high and this provides a meaningful start for them. Where possible, it is recommended that the letter sounds be introduced at the rate of one letter sound a day. Although this may seem a great deal at first, students are able to cope with it and look forward to their new letter sound every day. By learning all the letter sounds in nine weeks, the students become competent readers much sooner and, having so many letter sounds to use, produce more expressive independent writing at a much earlier stage than is usual. If the students are younger than four or five years old or there are other special factors, such as less frequent lessons, the rate of introduction is likely to be slower. The teacher will need to decide on the appropriate pace for his or her own class. If a slower pace is adopted, it is important to avoid asking the students to read books that contain letter sounds that they have not yet been taught. Students will not be able to decode words if they do not know the relevant letter sounds.

Introducing the letter sounds

Each letter sound is introduced through a story and action to help the students remember it. It is better if the suggested story is told in a personal way, using plenty of words with the target sound and making it as relevant as possible for the students. Stress the target sound when it appears and encourage the students to listen for it. Also, if the Finger Phonics Big Books are available, look for things in the story picture that have that sound in the word. Then show the students how to do the action for the letter sound. Young students learn particularly quickly when physical activity is involved, and here they are using movement, sight, hearing, and speech to help them remember the letter sound in a fun way. At the same time as learning the sound, the students are shown how the sound is represented in writing. The focus is on the lower-case letters at this stage, although the students do need to recognize the capitals for reading. In the first few lessons, the students can play "hunt the letter sound" by searching for the letter(s) in books, or around the classroom. This helps the students to understand the link between the letter sounds and the words in books.

Reinforcing the letter sounds

Reinforcement of the letter sounds is really important both at home and at school. While the students are learning the letter sounds, it is a good idea for them to have their own small sound book, which contains the letter sounds taught so far. The students take it home every day and practice the letter sounds for homework. It is also important to go through the book regularly with each student at school to see how well they are getting on. Visual rewards, such as stars stuck on the cover, provide much encouragement to parents and students alike and stimulate further interest and improvement.

Flashcards should be held up in class every day so that the students can call out the sounds and do the actions. This should be done quite quickly as a whole-class activity. Shuffle the flashcards beforehand so that the letter sounds come up in a different order each time. This way, related sounds, such as ‹ee› and ‹or›, do not follow each other. It is important that the students learn to recognize the sounds when they see them, rather than relying on a set order.

The faster the students become at recognizing the letters and saying the sounds, the easier it is for them to read and write. By watching the speed at which the students say the sounds and do the actions, it is easy to identify those who need more help. Slower learners tend to copy the other students and will need extra practice in small groups. Occasionally, the students should be encouraged to say the letter sounds without doing the action. On these occasions, they can be told to sit on their hands; this amuses the students and helps them to avoid doing the actions.

As well as using sound books and flashcards, there are lots of activities that will help the students to remember the letter sounds. Regularly dictating some of the letter sounds is one example; another is to place large letters in the corners of the room and tell the students to run to the correct corner when they see or hear one of the letter sounds. The Jolly Phonics Wall Frieze is also useful in the classroom. It makes a cheerful wall display and acts as a visual reminder of each letter sound. Young students also enjoy singing the Jolly Songs, which are linked to each letter sound.

Alternative spellings

Once the students have learned the 42 letter sounds taught in Step 1, they need to be aware of the alternative ways that some of the sounds, particularly the vowel sounds, can be written. These spellings are taught and then reviewed in Steps 2 and 3. The alternative spellings need to be reviewed regularly over the next few years to help the students with both their reading and spelling. For accurate spelling, the students need to make the right choice when deciding which alternative is needed to write a word like *snake:* should it be *snaik, snake,* or *snayk*? Being familiar with the alternatives will help them make the choice more easily. As the students become more widely read and familiar with words, the choice becomes easier still. Through their knowledge of sounds, and the letter patterns associated with them, the students' awareness of the details of spelling is heightened.

Jolly Phonics teaches the following alternative spellings for the vowel sounds:

Long ‹a›: ai, a_e, ay
Long ‹e›: ee, e_e, ea, y
Long ‹i›: ie, i_e, y, igh
Long ‹o›: oa, o_e, ow
Long ‹u›: ue, u_e, ew

/oo/: oo, ue, u_e, ew
/er/: er, ir, ur
/oi/: oi, oy
/ou/: ou, ow
/o/: o, aw, au, al

Step 3 also introduces the following phonic knowledge: the sound /air/ and its spellings ‹air›, ‹ear›, and ‹are›; the spelling ‹ph› for the sound /f/; and the soft ‹c› and soft ‹g› spellings, which say /s/ and /j/ respectively when they come before the letters ‹e›, ‹i›, or ‹y›.

Letter names and the alphabet

Jolly Phonics follows the convention of using different symbols to distinguish between letter names and letter sounds: the word *ship,* for example, starts with the letter ‹s› and its initial sound is /sh/. Initially, it is important to use the letter sounds when teaching the students how to read and write, not the letter names. If the students try to use the letter names when blending, they will not hear the word. Letter names are only needed when the students start to learn the alphabet in Step 2.

When introducing the alphabet, show the class the Jolly Phonics Alphabet Poster (as shown on the opposite page) or write the alphabet on the board. Point out that there are no digraphs (two letters representing one sound) and explain that this is because the alphabet is a way of ordering the single letters, not the sounds. This means that when we say the alphabet, we use the letter names. The alphabet can then be said or sung at the start of every Handwriting lesson. Gradually encourage the students to say the alphabet as quickly as possible without any visual prompts and ask them to identify which color group a letter belongs to, or which letters come before or after a given letter. In Jolly Phonics, the alphabet is taught in four color-coded sections, each one corresponding to roughly a quarter of the words in a dictionary: A–E (red), F–M (yellow), N–S (green), and T–Z (blue). Being able to navigate quickly around the alphabet, knowing that ‹w› is near the end, for example, will help students to find words in the dictionary more quickly. The extra attention is well worth the effort.

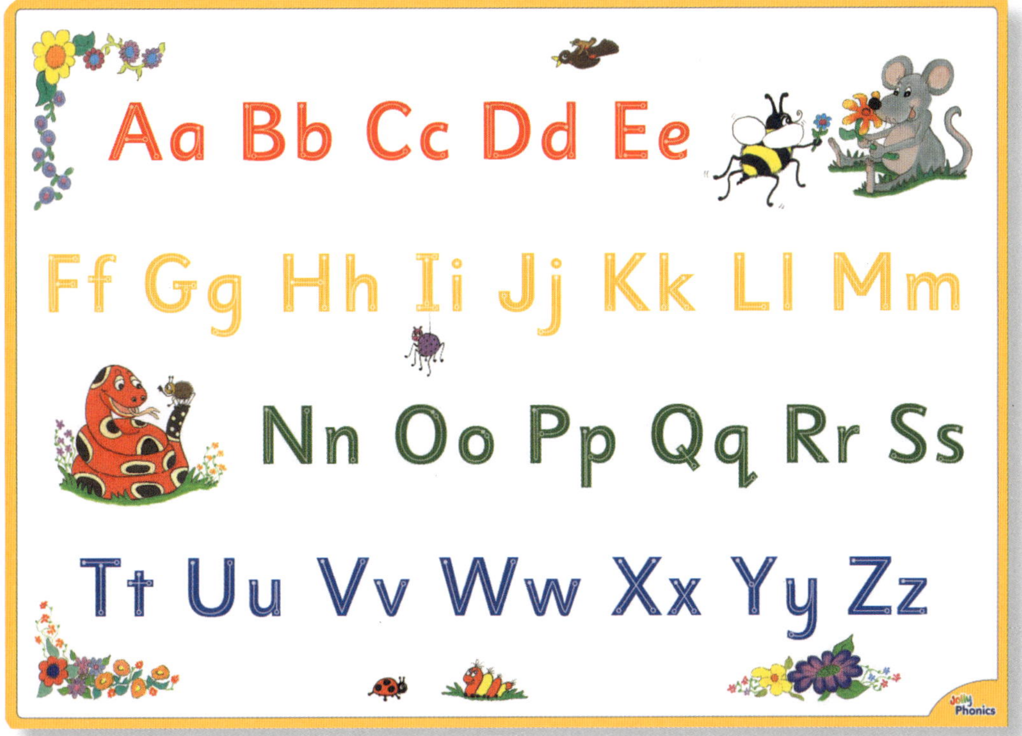

Conclusions

It is vital that the students know the letter sounds and are able to say the sound as soon as they see the letter(s). However, learning the letter sounds is not enough. The students need to know how to apply their letter knowledge. From the beginning, the students should be taught how to blend the sounds and listen for the word when reading. This is a technique that can be taught and is explained on pages 17 to 22. For writing, the students need to be taught how to listen for the sounds in a word and know which letter(s) represent those sounds; this is explained on pages 23 to 26.

2. Learning Letter Formation

To acquire fluent and neat handwriting, young students need to be taught how to hold their pencil and how to form letters correctly. It is much better to do this from the start and early mastery is well worth the effort. Trying to correct bad habits later on is extremely difficult, if not impossible. Regular letter-sound dictation and parental support can be invaluable here.

Pencil grip

The pencil rests between the thumb and the first finger. The next finger prevents the pencil falling down; the last two fingers are tucked away. The hand rests on the table and the movement of the pencil is through the thumb and first finger. It is important that the knuckles point outward. The movement of the pencil forward and backward with the knuckles pointing out can be likened to "froggy legs." The students always find this amusing and like to be reminded to use their froggy legs.

Teaching letter formation

A multisensory approach to teaching helps the students to learn more easily. The best approach is to introduce the formation of each letter to the students in the following ways:

1. Demonstrate how to write the letter(s) for the sound on the board.

2. Then show the formation in the air. Care should be taken when facing the class that letters are formed the correct way around for the students. (When the writing is formed "backward" from the teacher's own point of view, it is called mirror writing). The students hold up their fingers and follow the movement, saying the sound at the same time. They do this several times.

3. The students practice writing the letter(s) in their books. A line of dotted letters is provided on the lesson page. The first letter shows the formation as a

reminder. The dotted line helps the students to understand that the bodies of all the letters are the same size, except for the tall "sticks" (ascenders) and the "tails" (descenders). The students trace over the dotted letters and then try writing the letters for themselves, using the starting dots. As much as possible, watch the students write the letters and check that they are forming them correctly.

4. If the small Finger Phonics Books are available in the classroom, the students can feel the formation in the cut-out letter grooves.

Common letter shapes

When introducing and reviewing the formation of the lower-case letters, it is important to point out the following:

1. The bodies of all the letters should be the same size and sit on the line.

2. The tall letters ‹b›, ‹d›, ‹f›, ‹h›, ‹k›, ‹l›, and ‹t› have a "stick" that goes up above the body. Letter ‹t› is slightly shorter than the other tall letters.

3. The letters ‹g›, ‹j›, ‹p›, ‹q›, and ‹y› have tails that go down under the line.

4. Most letters either start at or near the top and go down to the line or start with a caterpillar /c/, as in ‹c›, ‹a›, ‹d›, ‹o›, ‹g›, and ‹q›. Before letter names are used, it helps to distinguish the letters ‹c› and ‹k› as caterpillar /c/ and kicking /k/.

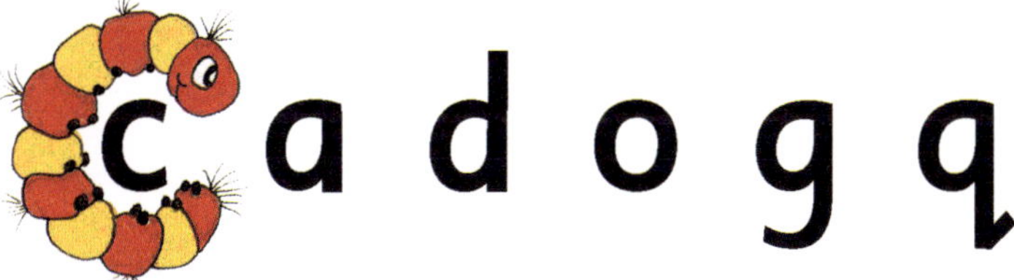

5. The exceptions are ‹e›, which starts halfway up the letter and goes toward the end of the page, and ‹z›, which starts at the top and goes toward the end of the page before coming across and down to the line.

The students should be reminded that the letters in a word are written close together, but without bumping. They also need to know that they should leave a space between each word.

Capital letters

Step 1 concentrates on the formation of the lower-case letters. Later, in Step 2, the formation of the capital letters is taught, along with alphabet work and a review of common letter shapes. The students need to know that capital letters are the same size as tall letters and that they all start at or near the top. The majority go down toward the line first, apart from the following: ‹C›, ‹G›, ‹O›, ‹Q›, and ‹S› go round counterclockwise, and ‹Z› starts by going toward the end of the page. The students also need to remember that capital letters are never joined.

Conclusions

By concentrating on correct letter formation and pencil grip from the beginning, bad habits can be prevented. It also makes it easier for the students to develop neat, fluent, joined handwriting later on and encourages them to take pride in their work.

3. Blending

Students need to understand the meaning of the words that they read but before they can do this, they have to be able to work out what the words say. In order to do this, the students look at the letters, say the sounds, run them together, and listen for the word. This process is called blending, which is also sometimes referred to as synthesizing. This is why Jolly Phonics is known as a synthetic phonics program.

Auditory blending

Auditory blending can begin on the students' first day of school. Show them the pictures on their lesson page or in the Finger Phonics story picture and ask if they can see a /s-u-n/. Any object can be used, but short words are preferable. At first, only a few students will hear the word after it has been split into its individual sounds but over time, with plenty of practice, the majority will succeed without the need for extra support.

Blending written words

After the first couple of lessons, the students know enough letter sounds to start blending written words. There are words for blending on each lesson page and word banks of suitable words in the Step 1 lesson plans. Words are also available in the Jolly Phonics Word Bank and Jolly Phonics Cards. In the early lessons, blend the words on the page with the students and encourage them to point to the dot underneath each sound as they say it. The actions should not be used when blending.

Once the students are able to hear the word when the letter sounds are said, they are ready to try saying the sounds and listening for the word by themselves. It helps to hear the word if the first sound is stressed and the following sounds are said quickly and softly, with as little schwa as possible. There are two types of sound in English. One type makes a pure, continuous sound, as in the following examples: /ssssss/, /ffffff/, /rrrrrr/, /mmmm/, /nnnnnn/, and /vvvvvv/. The other type includes sounds like /b/, /d/, and /h/, which have a schwa on the end. The schwa, which sounds like /uh/, is an unstressed vowel sound, and it can be heard on the end of many letter sounds.

Blending difficulties

Frequently, in a whole-class situation, the students who are good at blending call out the answer quickly and the less able copy them, as they do with letter sounds on flashcards. An extra blending session for the weaker students will help remedy this situation. There are two main reasons why some students find it difficult to hear the word when they have said the sounds. The first is that the students do not know the letter sounds well enough to say the sound automatically when they see the letter(s). By pausing to think, they lose track of the word. These students need to review the letter sounds regularly with flashcards, actions, and other letter-sound activities. The second reason is that the wrong sounds are emphasized. When blending the word *dog,* for example, the emphasis should be on the first letter sound: /**d**-o-g/. If the students put the emphasis on the last letter sound, they may try to start the word with that sound and fail to hear the word.

Word-blending boxes

The blending of regular words needs plenty of practice and should be done every day with the class, as well as in small groups, pairs, or individually, as necessary. Word-blending boxes are a useful resource when giving extra practice as each new letter sound is taught. Suitable words on small cards are organized in eight boxes, one for each letter-sound group, plus another for the early alternative spellings. The words in each box are color coded according to the target sound, so if /ai/ has just been taught, for example, the yellow cards from Box 4 can be easily identified and used. The words on these cards only use the target sound and any of the previously taught letter sounds, ensuring that the words are reliably decodable. The words for each box, as well as box labels and instructions can be downloaded from the Resource Bank on the Jolly Learning website or from Preventing Reading and Writing Problems, Parts 1 and 4 at www.tcrw.co.uk.

Silent blending

When the students become fluent, they should be encouraged to say and blend the sounds silently in their heads, only saying the word aloud. After a word has been blended a few times, it becomes known and then blending is only needed for reading unfamiliar words. The students should never be expected to read words that use letter sounds that have not yet been taught.

Ways to improve fluency in blending

There are several ways to help students become more fluent in blending words:

1. Regular blending of words with digraphs: When blending such words, the students must remember to look at the two letters and say one sound. This more complicated skill can be mastered with regular blending practice, and it is a good idea to make a set of flashcards for each digraph, with words like *pain, rain, train, Spain, hail,* and *snail* for the /ai/ sound, for example.

2. Regular practice of initial consonant blends: Being able to say blends fluently makes it easier to read words with initial consonant blends. This can be achieved by showing the students individual blends – such as /cr/, /fl/, and /str/ – and asking them to blend the sounds together. The students should only practice blends that contain the letter sounds they know, so they should not be given /sw/ to blend, for example, if the sound /w/ has not been introduced. When reading a word with an initial consonant blend, the students can then be encouraged to work it out by saying the blend, followed by the individual sounds: for example, saying /pl-a-n/, rather than /p-l-a-n/. In Step 1, words with initial consonant blends are introduced from the /r/ lesson onward. For more examples of initial consonant blends and words that use them, go to page 24.

3. Extra practice blending consonant-vowel combinations: Another way to develop speedy blending is to snap together initial consonant(s) and a short vowel. Some possible combinations include the following: *pa, pe, pi, po, pu; la,* *le, li, lo, lu; ra, re, ri, ro, ru; fra, fre, fri, fro, fru; sta, ste, sti, sto, stu; gra, gre, gri, gro, gru.* Writing a few consonant-vowel combinations on the board for the class to read on a regular basis will improve fluency, particularly for those students who are weaker at blending.

4. Activities to encourage silent blending: Initially, the students blend words by saying the sounds aloud, but gradually they should be encouraged to blend silently in their head to promote fluency for reading. One way to develop this skill is to do the actions for a word without saying the sounds and ask the students to work it out: for example, puff on your finger, wiggle your fingers on the end of your nose, and hold both arms out like the wings of a plane for the sounds /p/, /i/, and /n/ to make the word *pin.* Alternatively, a student could do the actions, or three students could do one action each. Another simple way to help students learn to blend sounds in their heads is to write letters randomly on the board and, without saying the sounds, point to one letter after another, spelling out a word. The students watch and blend the sounds silently to identify the word.

Helpful hints for blending more challenging words

In Steps 2 and 3, the students are given plenty of practice blending words with the main alternative spellings. The Further Practice sessions in every unit provide appropriate words and sentences for the students to read, and it is also a good idea to make sets of decodable words for each alternative for regular use. The Jolly Phonics Word Bank is a useful resource for finding suitable examples. The regular blending of words which use the main alternatives helps the students become familiar with the spellings and enables them to cope with a wider range of words when reading. Students deal with the alternative spellings more easily for reading than for spelling, so they are not expected to use them consistently in their writing at this stage.

The following hints enable the students to blend more words and the extra knowledge helps to develop their understanding and confidence. Eight of the main alternative vowel spellings cannot be worked out using these hints and will need to be learned: ‹igh›, ‹ow›, ‹ew›, ‹ir›, ‹ur›, ‹au›, ‹aw›, and ‹al›.

1. When two vowels go walking, the first does the talking: When two vowel letters appear together in a word, the sound made is often the long sound of the first vowel; the second vowel makes no sound. This amusing saying helps the students to remember how to say the main digraphs taught in Step 1, as well as the ‹ea› spelling of /ee/ and the hop-over ‹e› digraphs (also known as split digraphs or magic ‹e› digraphs) introduced in Step 2. When the students are older, they can learn that occasionally it is the second vowel that gives its short or long sound, as in the words *young* and *field*, and the students delight in finding the "naughty" second vowel.

2. If the short vowel does not work, try the long one: This is a good hint for blending and well worth teaching. It helps with words like *he, be, blind, mind, acorn, union, able, emu,* and *item.* It is also another useful reminder of how to cope with words that have a hop-over ‹e› digraph, such as *late, theme, pipe, home,* and *cube.*

3. The letter ‹i› is very shy, so toughy ‹y› takes its place: In Step 2, the students are told that English words like *day* and *boy* are not written "dai" or "boi" because ‹i› is too shy to go on the end of the word, so toughy ‹y› takes its place. The letter ‹i›, making either its short or long vowel sound, is also replaced by ‹y› in words like *funny, system,* and *sky.* (Although Jolly Phonics teaches ‹y› as /ee/, the sound made at the end of words like *funny* and *happy* is actually somewhere between an /i/ and an /ee/ sound.) For young students, it is enough for them to know that when ‹y› is not at the beginning of a word, it often takes the place of the letter ‹i› and becomes a vowel. Then the previous helpful hint also applies, so when blending unknown words where ‹y› is not the first letter, the students should try the short ‹i› vowel sound first and, if that does not work, try the long ‹i› vowel sound instead.

4. Soft ‹c› and soft ‹g›: If the letter ‹c› is followed by one of the vowels ‹e›, ‹i›, or ‹y›, the sound is usually softened to say /s/, as in the words *ice, race, city, circle,* and *cycle.* Similarly, when a letter ‹g› is followed by those vowels, the /g/ sound usually changes to /j/, as in *gently, magic,* and *apology.* This teaching is covered in Step 3.

Reading comprehension

For students to become fluent readers, they must be able to understand what they are reading. Comprehension is taught aurally in the early stages of teaching children to read. The students listen to stories, poems, and nursery rhymes, for example, and are encouraged to discuss what happens in them and also to give spoken answers to comprehension questions. This improves the students' understanding of language, develops a wider vocabulary, and increases their interest in learning to read.

At the end of Step 1, there are a number of activities that allow the students to put into practice the five skills they have been taught. Many of the activities require the students to demonstrate that they understand what they are reading: for example, they may have to match words and pictures, or draw pictures to illustrate the given words or sentences, or color pictures to match the descriptions. Similar activities are used in the Alternatives lessons throughout Step 2. Then, in Step 3, there is an even greater focus on reading comprehension in the Words and Sentences lessons. In a variety of activities, the students must respond to what they are reading by following instructions, drawing pictures, answering questions, and working out simple clues.

Introducing decodable books

Once the students are fluent in blending words, they can be given a reading book. Initially, it is important that only decodable books are used. This means books which only use the letter sounds and tricky words that have been taught. Students gain confidence and fluency when they can reliably work out the words for themselves and their letter-sound knowledge is reinforced. Jolly Phonics offers a range of decodable readers, organized in a number of progressively difficult levels, as outlined on the opposite page. The amount of text increases with each level, and light type is used for those letters that are not needed for blending words, such as the ‹b› in lamb. When the students have completed both Student Books and can read the Purple Level Readers fluently, they are able to read any material that is appropriate for their intellectual age and knowledge of vocabulary.

Jolly Phonics decodable readers

0. Orange Level

The Little Word Books and Read and See (Pack 1) provide a gradual and structured start for students who are just beginning to read. With two books for each letter-sound group, the students can apply their letter sound knowledge by blending simple decodable words that only use the letter sounds they have been taught so far. In Read and See (Pack 2), each book focuses on a different digraph or spelling pattern and the words selected use letter sounds from all seven groups. The Orange Readers are designed for students who have been taught the 42 letter sounds but who need extra practice to improve their confidence and fluency before starting the red level. The seven sets are aligned to the letter-sound groups, so that the decodable words only use the letter sounds for that group and below. A small number of tricky words are used in the last set.

1. Red Level

The words in these books can be read once the students know the 42 letter sounds and first 10 tricky words taught in Step 1. The students will also need to recognize the tricky word *of,* which is relatively straightforward to blend.

2. Yellow Level

These books can be read when the next ten tricky words have been learned, along with the letter ‹y› saying the sound /ee/ (found in words like *funny, happy,* and *floppy).* This teaching is covered by the end of Step 2 Unit 4.

3. Green Level

These books can be read when the next 20 tricky words have been learned, together with the hop-over ‹e› digraphs: ‹a_e›, ‹e_e›, ‹i_e›, ‹o_e›, and ‹u_e›. (These are the spellings used in words like *late, these, fine, hope,* and *cube).* This teaching is covered by the end of Step 2 Unit 13.

4. Blue Level

These books can be read when the next 20 tricky words and the alternative vowel spellings found in the following examples have been taught: *d**ay**, s**ea**t, sk**y**, l**igh**t, sn**ow**, br**ow**n, st**ew**, b**oy**, b**ir**d, t**ur**n, s**aw**, **Au**gust, and w**al**k.* This teaching is covered by the end of Step 3 Unit 9.

5. Purple Level

The Purple Readers can be read when the remaining tricky words and alternative spellings in Step 3 have been taught. The alternative spellings ‹ph›, soft ‹c›, soft ‹g›, and ‹air›, ‹ear›, ‹are› for /air/ are found in words such as *phone, nice, huge, chair, bear,* and *square.* This teaching is covered by the end of Student Book 2. The Jolly Phonics Plays are designed to help students become fluent and confident readers, with well-developed speaking and listening skills. There are six reproducible play scripts for students to perform or read aloud in group sessions, plus cross-curricular, story sequencing and reading comprehension activities. While the text is written to be decodable at the purple level, the scripts are color coded for differentiation, ensuring everyone can take part. They are ideal for Reader's Theater.

Some of the many decodable books in the Jolly Phonics range

Conclusions

Students who can blend words fluently have few problems with reading. Once the fluency is there, reading extension and comprehension become the more important aspects. A few students seem to have difficulty learning to blend and it is easy to think that they may never achieve this skill. However, with extra support and practice, they will succeed. Early phonic teaching with Jolly Phonics makes reading and writing easier for all students. For those students with a poor memory for words, it is absolutely essential.

4. Identifying the Sounds in Words

In order to write words, the students must be able to say a word, hear the sounds in that word, say the sounds in order, and then write the letters for those sounds. The ability to hear the sounds in words is called phonemic awareness.

From the beginning, the students are taught to hear the sounds in words. The first step is to ask the students to listen for the target sound. Every lesson in Step 1 has an activity based on this skill. For example, the first letter sound is /s/, so the students are asked to look at pictures of a sun, spider, snail, and tree and decide which word does not start with the sound /s/. Over time, these activities become more challenging: the students progress from identifying the initial sound in a word, to writing the letter(s) for that sound, to being able to hear and write a letter sound wherever it is heard in a word.

The next step is to ask the students to listen and identify all the sounds in a word (also known as segmenting). This skill is modeled for the students early on using short words from the word bank, but over time the students should try to do this for themselves. Some students will hear the sounds easily, while others will require more help. The later segmenting activities in Step 1 reflect this progression, requiring the students to identify the number of sounds in a word until, eventually, they have to listen and write all the sounds to make the word.

Initially, when practicing segmenting, the students can say the sounds and use magnetic letters or letter cards to spell short words. Then, when they can do this confidently, longer words can be tackled. Dictation is an excellent way of developing writing and, ideally, a little dictation every day is very effective. It can begin early on by calling out letter sounds for the students to write and then move on to words, phrases, and sentences. Regular dictation of letter sounds and words is provided in the Step 1 lesson plans and sentence dictation is practiced later in Step 3, once the students have had plenty of practice writing model sentences in Step 2. Again, it is important to only ask the students to write words that use the letter sounds they have been taught.

Ways to improve the students' ability to segment words fluently

There are several activities that can help students to improve their segmenting skills:

1. **Auditory segmenting:** From early on, the students should be encouraged to do some auditory segmenting every day. Call out a word and ask the students to listen carefully and say the sounds. The students do this, holding up a finger for each sound, starting with the thumb, then the index finger, and so on. In the beginning, it will be necessary to sound out the words with the students, but they should be encouraged to do it by themselves as soon as possible. This activity can be extended by writing the letters for the sounds on the board as the students say them. The word can then be blended and read. This allows the students to see the significance of encoding to write and decoding to read, and to see how these processes are linked. This process of segmenting and then blending words also allows plenty of practice of more challenging words.

2. Regular segmenting of consonant blends: If students fail to hear all the sounds in a consonant blend, it can lead to spelling mistakes, such as writing "fog" instead of *frog*, or "wet" instead of *went*. Regular segmenting of individual blends will help students avoid such errors. Call out a blend and ask the students to say the sounds, holding up a finger for each one. For example, say /cr/ and ask the students to respond with the sounds /c-r/. Make sure that the letter sounds in the blend have already been taught. Common examples of initial consonant blends include *bl-, br-, cl-, cr-, dr-, fl-, fr-, gl-, gr-, pl-, pr-, sc-, sk-, sl-, sm-, sn-, sp-, st-, sw-, tr-, tw-, scr-, shr-, spl-, spr-, str-, thr-*. Final consonant blends include *-ct, -ft, -lb, -ld, -lf, -lk, -lm, -ln, -lp, -lt, -mp, -nd, -nt, -pt, -sk, -sp, -st, -xt.*

3. Regular segmenting of words with consonant blends: The students also need plenty of practice identifying the sounds in blends when they are used in words. Any of the following examples are suitable for this activity. Words with initial consonant blends: *blot, bran, clap, clip, club, crab, crop, drag, drip, drop, drum, flag, flap, flat, frog, from, glad, grab, grip, plan, plot, plum, prod, scan, skip, slap, slim, slug, smog, snap, snug, spin, spot, stem, stop, swim, trip, twig, twin, scrub, shrug, splat, sprig, strum, throb.* Words with final consonant blends: *fact, gift, lift, soft, bulb, held, golf, milk, silk, film, kiln, gulp, help, belt, felt, melt, quilt, camp, damp, lamp, plump, ramp, bend, grand, mend, pond, wind, ant, bent, hunt, mint, pant, tent, went, kept, slept, desk, risk, crisp, best, frost, lost, must, nest, next.*

4. Word building: Regular word building using a letter board or magnetic letters is a practical way to show the students how to build up decodable words. A word board is a large piece of card with three smaller strips of card stapled across it. Letters for making words are slotted into the strips: the five vowels are placed on the top row and the selected consonants are put on the bottom row. Ask a student to make a word by putting the letters in the middle strip. The student listens to the word, picks out the letters, and places them in the correct order, from left to right. The rest of the class indicate whether they think the word is correct or not by holding their thumbs up for yes and down for no. All the students blend the word to check if it is correct and, if it is wrong, the student could try again. Then continue by asking, for example, *Who can change it from peg to pen?* followed by *Who can change pen to spend?*

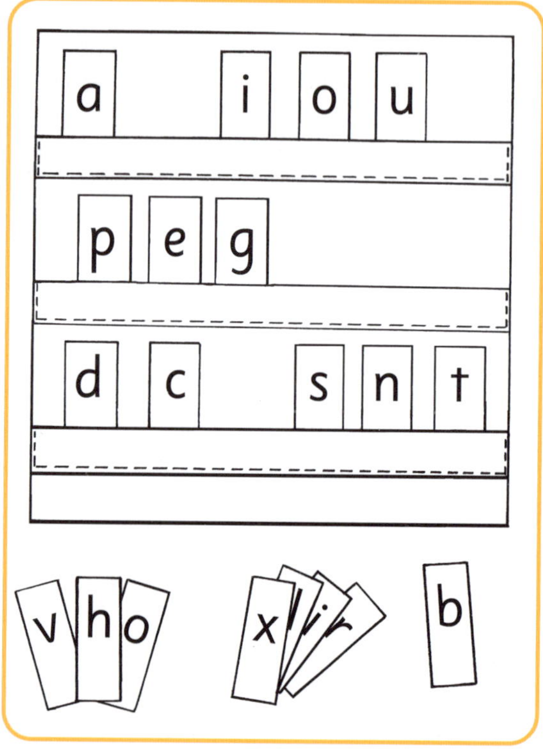

5. Regular dictation of letters, digraphs, words, capitals, and sentences: Dictation begins almost immediately in Step 1 with letter-sound dictation. In every lesson, call out some of the sounds that have been taught recently and ask the students to write the letter(s) for each one. Then write the letters on the board so that the students can see if they have written them correctly. In the beginning, the standard of achievement will probably range quite widely. Word dictation starts when the second letter-sound group is taught. Call out the words provided in the lesson plan and, for each one, ask the students to listen for the sounds and write the word. Afterward, sound out the words for the students, writing the letters on the board so that they can check their work. The students could be encouraged to put a little check mark next to the word if they are correct. Once the capital letters have been introduced in Step 2, dictation should be used to help the students write them quickly and accurately. Call out the sound, rather than the name of the capital letter, so that the students are able to read and write sentences and proper nouns correctly. Sentences with tricky words are provided for regular dictation in Step 3. These sentences do not use the alternative spellings, as the students are not expected to remember which ones to use in their writing at this stage.

Guided writing

Guided writing is an important step in preparing the students for independent writing. It gives them a basic understanding of what a sentence is and provides the initial support and guidance that most students need to write their first sentences. In Step 2, there is a model sentence in each Words and Sentences lesson. This sentence has a controlled vocabulary so that it uses only those tricky words that have been taught and regular words using the 42 letter sounds. Show the students the picture in their books and encourage them to talk about what is happening. Some of the students could also be invited to say a sentence about it. Then call out the words suggested in the lesson plan to segment and blend. Write the model sentence on the board and, at each stage, discuss what is happening with the students. For example, remind them that a sentence always starts with a capital letter and that capital letters are tall; that they need to leave a space between words; that the words *I, the, he, we, are,* and *to* are tricky; and that they must remember to put a period at the end. Encourage the students to call out the sounds before each word is written on the board and to blend the word afterward. Then read the sentence back with the class to check that it makes sense, before the students copy the sentence into their books.

Independent writing

When the students have learned the letter sounds, can identify the sounds in words, and have done some dictation, they are well on their way to writing independently. For instance, on the following page is an example of a student's writing (reduced to one half of its original size) around halfway through the Jolly Phonics program. The spelling is not accurate at this stage, but the work is still readable. As the students' knowledge increases and they read more widely, their spelling will improve. Independent writing is introduced in Step 2, where the students are encouraged to write a few sentences of their own about each picture in the guided writing sessions. Later, in Step 3, the students have the opportunity to write something based on the activity topic in each

Words and Sentences lesson. This could be a story, or a description, or even clues that the students read to each other and then try to answer. Although ideas are suggested in the lesson plan, it is best to choose a writing topic that is most relevant to the class.

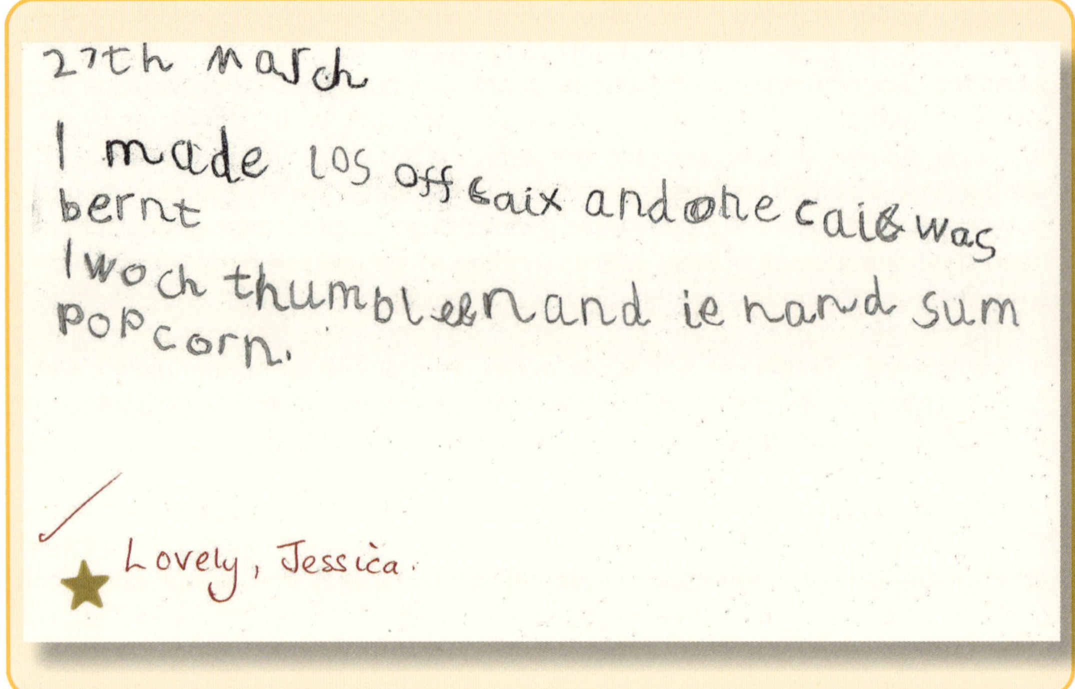

Marking policy

The students' earliest efforts at independent writing do not need rigorous marking. Missing sounds can be pointed out and any tricky words that have already been taught can be corrected, but it is important not to mark everything and risk discouraging the students from writing freely. It is best to restrict the marking to about four words that the students should have written correctly. These words can then be practiced by the students. If a mistake is made writing a more advanced word and the error is not due to carelessness, a dot can be placed underneath it. This tells the students that the word is spelled wrongly, but that their attempt was a good one and the correct spelling will be taught later.

Conclusions

The aim of this teaching is to enable the students to hear the sounds in regular words and to write the letters that relate to those sounds. A different technique is needed for those frequently used words that are not totally decodable. Advice on how to teach the tricky words is covered in the next section.

5. Tricky Words

When students start to write sentences, there are some frequently used words that they need to be able to use, such as *I, the, he, she, me, we, be, was, to, do, are,* and *all.* However, these words are tricky because the students cannot read or write them simply by using the sounds they have been taught so far. There are tricky parts that have to be learned, such as the alternative spellings for /ie/ in *my* and *like* or the irregular spellings in words like *said* and *two.* These words need to be taught in a systematic way with plenty of practice.

When teaching a tricky word to the students, say the word and then blend the sounds, working out together which parts are regular and which are tricky. For example, when reading the word *said,* the /s/ and /d/ can be sounded out reliably, but the students will need to remember that the ‹ai› says the sound /e/. Working out these tricky parts and being made aware of any spelling patterns that the tricky words share – such as the letter ‹o› saying the sound /oa/ in *go, no,* and *so* – will help the students to remember the word.

A total of 72 tricky words is taught in Jolly Phonics, with two or three words usually taught together. The first tricky word, *I,* is introduced in the lesson for /sh/, so that the second word *the* can be taught in the next lesson, alongside the voiced sound /th/. By this stage, the students are able to apply their phonic knowledge to help them work out which part is tricky and this extra attention to detail helps to store the word in the students' memories. The students need lots of practice reading and writing tricky words. For reading, it is important to review the tricky words regularly with flashcards. The Jolly Phonics Cards include a set of tricky word flashcards, or the Tricky Word Wall Flowers could be used instead. Smaller cards can be made and used for games like Snap or Pairs. There are also sentences for reading in the later word banks, the Further Practice sessions, and the Step 3 Tricky Word lessons. For spelling, the students practice writing the tricky words using the tricky word spelling routine (see below). Once they have done this several times, the students are able to try writing the words from dictation. Later, once the students are familiar with writing sentences in the guided writing sessions, they are ready to write sentences from dictation that use the known tricky words.

Techniques for remembering the tricky part

The students find it easier to remember the tricky part of the spelling if the following techniques are used:

1. Say it as it sounds: Say the word as it should be pronounced according to its spelling. For example, when teaching the words *was* and *mother,* point out that the spellings say /w-a-s/ to rhyme with *mass* and /m-o-th-er/ to rhyme with *bother*. This technique is useful for learning any word with one element that makes it difficult to spell, such as *Wednesday* (Wed-**nes**-day) or *doctor* (doct**or**).

2. Word families or patterns: Point out any words that share the same, or similar, spelling pattern. The following are all good examples: the tricky words *he, she, me, we,* and *be* all have a single ‹e› making the /ee/ sound; similarly, *to* and *do* have a single ‹o› making the long /oo/ sound; the tricky word *you* is at the beginning of *your,* and *any* is at the end of *many;* in the words *could, should,* and *would,* the ‹oul› makes the little /oo/ sound.

3. Tricky word spelling routine: First, the students look at the word and identify the tricky part. Then they write the word by copying it. Next, they cover the word and try writing it again by themselves. Finally, they uncover the word and check whether it is correct, before covering it again and having another go.

4. Tricky word wall flowers: The tricky words are presented on six sets of flowers, with a different color for each set (blue, yellow, red, green, pink, brown). Build up the display as the tricky words are taught and use them regularly to review the tricky words. If the Tricky Word Wall Flowers are not available, the class could make their own display.

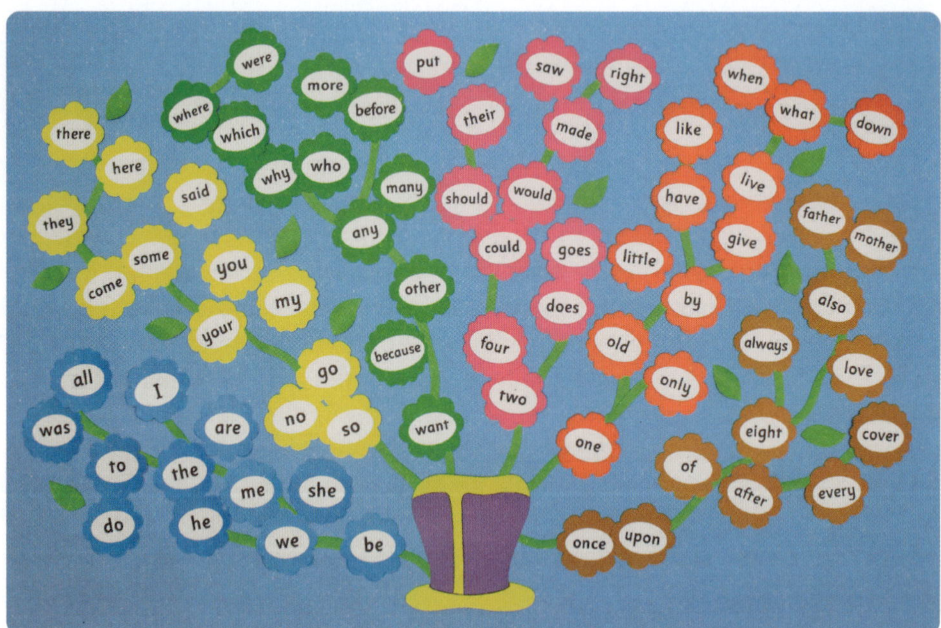

5. Mnemonics: A few words are so irregular that it is difficult to remember how to spell them. Using mnemonics can be useful in these cases. Mnemonics are phrases in which the first letter of every word gives the spelling. A good example is "**b**ig **e**lephants **c**atch **a**nts **u**nder **s**mall **e**lephants" for the tricky word *because.* Another one is "**o u l**ucky **d**uck" for the common spelling pattern shared by *could, should,* and *would.*

Conclusions

The tricky words in English always cause problems. However, learning to read these words is easier than learning to spell them. By teaching the students how to identify the tricky parts and by using certain techniques to reinforce the spelling, the students are able to be more accurate in their writing. A certain amount of rigor is needed when teaching the tricky words, particularly when teaching students who do not have a good visual memory.

Support for Struggling Students

Even with good phonics teaching, there will be some students who struggle to master the basic skills and who need intervention support to catch up and keep up with the rest of the class. These students tend to have a weak visual memory and/or poor auditory skills, and a poor ability to remember the letter sounds is often one of the first indications that difficulties are developing for a student. Early intervention is needed to develop fluency and automatic recall, as well as to establish the letter sounds in the student's long-term memory.

Intervention should focus on practicing the skills that the students most need to improve, whether it be their letter-sound knowledge, their ability to blend and/or segment, or learning tricky words. It can be done one-to-one or with a group of students who have similar learning difficulties. There are lots of activities suitable for intervention sessions, which are outlined below, but all are based on the same teaching as the students receive in their lessons; it is simply more targeted and provides more practice to ensure that the students master the five skills.

Early intervention with letter-sound boxes is the ideal way to practice letter sounds one-to-one. Letter-sound flashcards can be used in group sessions to see how quickly students can call out the letter sounds or how long it takes them to choose the correct letter sound when it is said. Dictation is an excellent way to review target letter sounds and also to help students struggling to form letters correctly. Auditory blending practice is important for students who struggle to hear a word when its sounds are said, and word-blending boxes and modeling using the *I say it, we say it, you say it* approach help to improve blending skills. Extra practice, word building, and dictation are the best ways to improve segmenting skills, while flashcards and dictation will help with the tricky words. More information on letter-sound and word-blending boxes can be found in the Resource Bank on the Jolly Learning website and further practical advice is given in Preventing Reading and Writing Problems, Parts 1 and 4, at www.tcrw.co.uk.

Activities for intervention support

The following ideas are merely suggestions. Teachers and teaching assistants will have further ideas of their own. The important thing is to choose activities that focus on practicing the skills that the students most need to improve. It is always important to keep in mind the aim of the intervention session: to catch up and keep up with the rest of the class by learning the letter sounds, blending, segmenting, learning tricky words, and improving spelling.

1. Learning the letter sounds

In most classes, there will be a few students who are not learning the sounds fast enough to keep up with the other students. This could be for any number of the following reasons:

- The student may have a poor memory for letter sounds and words.
- The student's attendance is, for some reason, limited.
- The student's concentration is poor.
- There is little individual help given at home.

Whatever the reason, the problem must be overcome. Intervention can be done one-to-one or as a group. Ideally, when organizing an intervention group, select students of similar learning difficulties and aim to concentrate the teaching on two or more letter-sound correspondences that are not known well enough. It helps to keep in mind the "catch up and keep up" aim when preparing for each session.

One-to-one practice with a letter-sound box

Once the students who are having difficulty learning the letter sounds have been identified, they can be given their own letter-sound box. Identify the letter sounds that each student knows reasonably well and place them in his or her box (or envelope) for practice at home or at school. Ideally, someone should listen to the student saying these letter sounds every day. If an adult is not available, it could be another student who knows the letter sounds well. Then, as soon as possible after some intervention support, remove any really well known letter sounds and add others that need extra practice.

Small group activities for learning the letter sounds

There are several flashcard activities that the teacher or teaching assistant can do with a group of three or four students to practice the letter sounds. The simplest activity involves holding up the letter-sound cards, one by one. The students call out the sounds as quickly as possibly as the letters are shown. This can be turned into a race by seeing who can say the sound first. This not only adds a sense of fun but encourages greater fluency and works well with evenly matched students. Whoever says the sound first gets the card; if two students say the sound at the same time, it goes back in the pile. The student with the most cards at the end of the game is the winner.

Another activity involves laying out a few letter-sound cards on the table. Call out the letter sounds one at a time, and ask a different student to touch the correct card each time. Alternatively, call out each sound and see who is the first to touch the correct card. This is good, competitive fun as long as it does not disturb the rest of the students or other classes. Another option is to deal out a few cards to each student and ask them to point to the letters and say the sounds as fast as possible. From this it is possible to see which students know their letter sounds and how well they know them.

2. Letter formation

Learning to form the letters for the sounds correctly and neatly is an important skill. Writing a few from dictation in each intervention session gives students who are struggling with formation the extra practice they need and allows the teacher to assess their progress. It is also an opportunity for reviewing the letter sounds themselves.

Each session should focus on two particular letter sounds that need extra practice. Show the letter-sound cards to the students and ask if anyone remembers them. Then practice the formation in two stages: firstly, while the students can see the letter sound and then from dictation. The students either write the letter or form it on the table with their finger. Watch carefully to see whether the students form the letters correctly.

Some students struggle with formation because they have poor motor control. Coloring the story pictures in the Student Books and tracing the letters on the lesson page can help these students to develop this skill. In addition, using lined paper for extra formation and writing practice encourages the students to limit the size of their letters and allows for greater accuracy when it comes to their letter formation.

3. Blending

Students who struggle to hear a word after they have said the sounds need more auditory blending practice. This is where the teacher says the sounds and the students listens for the word. Some teachers tap their arm to model auditory blending of CVC words: on the shoulder for the first sound, then on the elbow, and then on the wrist. Then, as they blend the sounds together and say the word, they run their hand down their arm. The blending process can also be modeled with a few words in each session, using the *I say it, we say it and you say it* approach. This prepares the students for the ultimate skill of blending unknown words.

The simplest auditory blending activity is to say, for example, *I hear, with my little ear, a word. What is it? /f-o-x/.* The students respond, giving the answer *fox*. Alternatively, picture cards or a bag of objects can be used to help the students hear a word when the sounds are said. For example, show two pictures of a cow and a car and ask *Which one is the /c-ar/?* Repeat with other cards and, as the students improve, increase the number of pictures to three or four to make the activity that little bit harder. Another activity involves holding a picture card so that it cannot be seen and saying, for example, *In my hand is a /m-oo-n/. What do I have in my hand?* Whoever says *moon* gets the picture. This can be varied by putting several objects in a bag, such as a book, fork, and comb, and sounding out the object you are holding. As always, it is better to stick to short words.

There are many activities that are suitable for students who need extra support in improving their blending fluency. These include word-blending boxes, targeted practice of initial consonant blends, and targeted practice of blending a consonant and a short vowel (see pages 18 and 19 for further detail). In these sessions it is important to include words that focus on two particular letter sounds that need extra practice.

4. Segmenting

Students who struggle to hear the sounds in words benefit from extra practice. They listen to a word as it is called out and then, with support, say the sounds, holding up a finger for each one. Alternatively, they could tap the back of their hand or tap their head. Hearing the sounds in a word with a consonant blend is more difficult, so encourage the students to say the word slowly: for example, /sss-lll-u-g/. Having identified the sounds, the students could then do some word building, using plastic letters or letter-sound cards to make the words. Make sure that two letter sounds that need extra practice are used in some of them. Not only do these activities develop the students' ability to hear the sounds in words, they also show the students why they need to be able to do so: namely, to work words out in preparation for writing. Dictation is the best way to develop the skill of writing. Make sure the dictation includes the two target letter sounds, as well as some words that use those letter sounds. Keep it snappy, ensuring a fast pace.

5. Tricky words

If the whole class is learning the tricky words, start with the first two: *I* and *the*. Teach these words using flashcards and dictation. In addition, use suitable methods to help the students remember how to spell the tricky parts (see pages 27 and 28). If there is time, encourage the students to read a few short sentences: for example, *I am hot, The dog is black, The dress has a bad stain.* The sentences should use regular words that can be worked out, as well as the target tricky words. The Jolly Phonics Word Bank is a useful resource for making up sentences. Having blended the words in the sentence once, encourage the students to read them again, this time without the blending.

Conclusions

Early intervention is extremely important, so It is necessary to regularly assess and identify any students who are struggling to remember the letter sounds, blend words, write letters, or identify the sounds in words. The student checklist on the opposite page can be used to track and record the progress of any individual students who are struggling to keep up with the rest of the class.

Some students develop the skills of blending and segmenting naturally, while others do not. However, the structured teaching in Jolly Phonics, along with early intervention for those who need it, helps the students develop these skills and smooths their way to becoming fluent, independent readers and writers. This also applies to students who are showing signs of dyslexia or other learning difficulties.

Jolly Phonics: Student Checklist

Name: .... Date: ....

	Says sound in response to letter(s)	Writes letter(s) in response to sound	Blends regular words with these sounds	Writes regular words with these sounds
s a t i p n				
ck e h r m d				
g o u l f b				
ai j oa ie ee or				
z w ng v oo oo				
y x ch sh th th				
qu ou oi ue er ar				
y[1] a_e e_e i_e o_e u_e				
ay oy ea y igh ow[2]				
ir ur ew aw au al				
ph soft c soft g ue[3] u_e[3] ew[3]				
air ear are				

[1]‹y› as /ee/ [2]‹ow› as /oa/ and /ou/

[3]‹ue›, ‹u_e›, ‹ew› as long /oo/

	Knows letter sound	Knows letter name	Forms letter correctly
Alphabet: lower-case letters			
Alphabet: capital letters			

	Can sing/recite	Knows the four alphabet quarters
Alphabet order		

	1-12	13-24	25-36	37-48	49-60	61-72
Able to read tricky words						
Able to write tricky words						

	Slowly	Steadily	Fluently
Able to read regular words, phrases, and sentences			

	With consonant blends	With digraphs	In phrases	In sentences using known tricky words
Able to write from dictation regular words				

English Alphabetic Code Chart

This chart aims to give an overall understanding of the English alphabetic code. It is not exhaustive and some letter-sound correspondences have hardly any words that use them. Nevertheless it is helpful to see how the code works. Care should be taken with ‹qu› and ‹x› as technically they both have two sounds blended together: ‹qu› is /kw/ and ‹x› is /ks/. Initially, it is easier for young students to think of them as one sound. Also, it is not necessary to teach the /ier/ sound early on. Young students can blend words like *beer, fear*, and *here* as /b-ee-r/, /f-ea-r/, and /h-ee-r/ and hear the word, without needing to know that technically each has an /ier/ sound.

/s/	/a/	/t/	/i/	/p/	/n/
sun fu**ss** **c**ent **c**inema **c**ycle boun**ce** hou**se** ca**st**le **ps**alm an**sw**er **sc**ience	**a**nt	**t**en mi**tt**en hopp**ed** de**bt** was**te** casse**tte** **th**yme **pt**erodactyl **tw**o	**i**nk p**y**ramid bisc**ui**t min**u**te saus**a**ge wom**e**n barg**ai**n s**ei**ve	**p**et ha**pp**y she**ph**erd	**n**et fu**nn**y **kn**ow **gn**at go**ne** **pn**eumonia **mn**emonic
/c k/	**/e/**	**/h/**	**/r/**	**/m/**	**/d/**
cat **k**itten du**ck** **ch**emist con**qu**er uni**que** o**cc**ur Ira**q** **kh**aki	**e**dge h**ea**d h**ei**fer l**eo**pard s**ai**d s**ay**s fri**e**nd **a**ny b**u**ry	**h**at **wh**o	**r**at ca**rr**ot **wr**ite **rh**ino	**m**an ha**mm**er la**mb** hy**mn** co**me**	**d**og te**dd**y clean**ed** jo**dh**purs
/g/	**/o/**	**/u/**	**/l/**	**/f/**	**/b/**
gap fo**gg**y **gh**ost **gu**ide va**gue**	**o**dd w**a**s h**au**l t**a**lk s**aw** c**ou**gh b**ough**t c**augh**t kn**ow**ledge	**u**nder l**o**ve c**ou**ntry bl**oo**d d**oe**s	**l**eg be**ll** gaze**lle**	**f**un o**ff** **ph**oto tou**gh** gira**ffe**	**b**at ra**bb**it
/ai/	**/j/**	**/oa/**	**/ie/**	**/ee/**	**/or/**
aim l**a**k**e** pl**ay** v**ei**n w**eigh** th**ey** **a**pron ball**et** gr**ea**t sund**ae** str**aigh**t	**j**am **g**entle **g**iant **g**ym lar**ge** a**dj**ust bri**dge**	**oa**k h**o**p**e** sl**ow** g**o** t**oe** d**ough** plat**eau** s**ou**l s**ew** **oh** m**au**ve	p**ie** t**i**m**e** n**igh**t sk**y** f**i**nd **ei**der **ai**sl**e** b**ye** b**uy** h**eigh**t **eye**	b**ee** sunn**y** th**e**m**e** dr**ea**m ch**ie**f k**ey** w**e** rec**ei**v**e** rad**i**o larv**ae** p**eo**ple	**or**der sh**ore** w**ar**m s**oar** f**our** d**oor** dinos**aur**

/z/	/w/	/ng/	/v/	/oo/	/oo/
zoo bu**zz** i**s** rou**se** snoo**ze** sci**ss**ors Wedn**es**day **x**ylophone	**w**eb **wh**istle pen**gu**in	si**ng** wi**n**k	**v**an slee**ve** o**f** sa**vv**y	b**oo**k p**u**sh c**oul**d w**o**man	m**oo**n bl**ue** r**u**de dr**ew** fl**u** d**o** fr**ui**t s**ou**p thr**ough** sl**eu**th sh**oe** **oeu**vre l**ieu**

/y/	/x/	/ch/	/sh/	/th/	/th/
yes on**i**on	fo**x** hoo**ks** la**kes** du**cks** e**xc**ellent a**cc**ept	**ch**op ha**tch** na**t**ure	**sh**ip ma**ch**ine musi**ci**an sta**ti**on ten**si**on ti**ss**ue **s**ugar crè**che** appre**ci**ate permi**ssi**on fa**sh**ion **sch**wa	**th**is soo**the**	**th**in

/qu/	/ou/	/oi/	/ue/	/er/	/ar/
queen	**ou**t **ow**l b**ough**	**oi**l b**oy**	res**cue** **cu**be **few** **u**nicorn **feu**d **beau**tiful	h**er**b b**ir**d h**ur**t l**ear**n w**or**d w**ere** gramm**ar** press**ure** zeph**yr** p**urr** chauff**eur**	**ar**m h**ear**t s**er**geant **are**

/air/	/zh/	/ool/	/ier/	schwa /uh/	
ch**air** st**are** p**ear** wh**ere** **aer**obic th**eir** pr**ayer** p**ar**ent	vi**s**ion trea**s**ure cour**g**ette sei**z**ure colla**ge**	app**le** loc**al** lab**el** penc**il** symb**ol** tear**ful**	f**ier**ce n**ear** ch**eer** h**er**o	th**e** **A**meric**a** poss**i**bly t**o**day	min**u**s anxi**ou**s mart**y**r Micha**e**l

Teaching Step 1

Jolly Phonics Step 1 provides daily lessons that introduce students to the main sounds of English. The students learn to recognize the letter sounds and are taught one way to write each one. At the same time, they learn how to use this knowledge to read and write simple regular words. The teaching is cumulative, so the more letter sounds the students learn, the more words they can read and write. Each lesson teaches

1. Lesson objective
The target letter sound for this lesson.

2. Flashcards
Quickly review the letter sounds already taught before introducing the new sound.

3. Story
Introduces the new sound in an engaging way. It is also an opportunity for vocabulary development and comprehension. Use the Jolly Phonics Big Books to look for words with the target sound.

4. Action
Helps students remember the new letter sound in a fun, multisensory way.

5. Letter formation
Show the students how to form the letter(s) correctly and encourage them to write the letter(s) in the air before practicing in their books.

6. Blending and segmenting
From the start, Jolly Phonics teaches grapheme-phoneme correspondences to enable decoding for reading and encoding for writing.

7. Word bank
A list of words and phrases for regular blending and auditory segmenting practice to promote fluency.

8. Answer sheet
Demonstrates how the lesson page should be completed correctly.

9. Dictation
Dictate letters and words every day to practice segmenting skills.

10. Developing accuracy and fluency
Sending the students home with a sound book every day is an excellent way to reinforce the letter sounds. Later on, introduce the Jolly Phonics Little Word Books to students who can independently blend simple regular words.

Teacher's Book

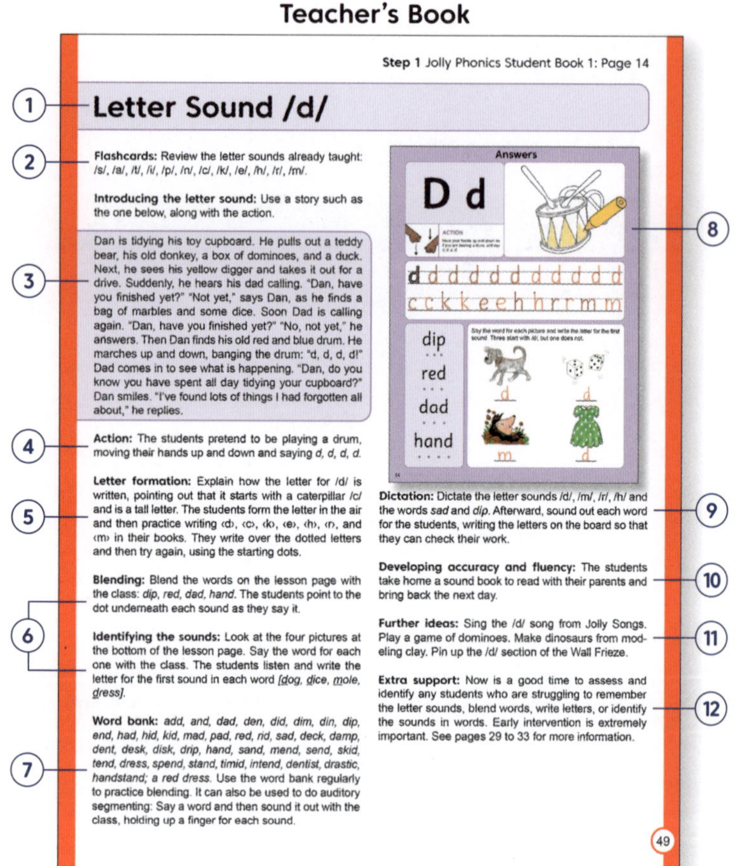
Step 1 Jolly Phonics Student Book 1: Page 14

Letter Sound /d/

Flashcards: Review the letter sounds already taught: /s/, /a/, /t/, /i/, /p/, /n/, /c/, /k/, /e/, /h/, /r/, /m/.

Introducing the letter sound: Use a story such as the one below, along with the action.

Dan is tidying his toy cupboard. He pulls out a teddy bear, his old donkey, a box of dominoes, and a duck. Next, he sees his yellow digger and takes it out for a drive. Suddenly, he hears his dad calling. "Dan, have you finished yet?" "Not yet," says Dan, as he finds a bag of marbles and some dice. Soon Dad is calling again. "Dan, have you finished yet?" "No, not yet," he answers. Then Dan finds his old red and blue drum. He marches up and down, banging the drum: "d, d, d, d!" Dad comes in to see what is happening. "Dan, do you know you have spent all day tidying your cupboard?" Dan smiles. "I've found lots of things I had forgotten all about," he replies.

Action: The students pretend to be playing a drum, moving their hands up and down and saying *d, d, d, d.*

Letter formation: Explain how the letter for /d/ is written, pointing out that it starts with a caterpillar /c/ and is a tall letter. The students form the letter in the air and then practice writing ‹d›, ‹c›, ‹k›, ‹e›, ‹h›, ‹r›, and ‹m› in their books. They write over the dotted letters and then try again, using the starting dots.

Blending: Blend the words on the lesson page with the class: *dip, red, dad, hand.* The students point to the dot underneath each sound as they say it.

Identifying the sounds: Look at the four pictures at the bottom of the lesson page. Say the word for each one with the class. The students listen and write the letter for the first sound in each word *[dog, dice, mole, dress].*

Word bank: *add, and, dad, den, did, dim, din, dip, end, had, hid, kid, mad, pad, red, rid, sad, deck, damp, dent, desk, disk, drip, hand, sand, mend, send, skid, tend, dress, spend, stand, timid, intend, dentist, drastic, handstand; a red dress.* Use the word bank regularly to practice blending. It can also be used to do auditory segmenting: Say a word and then sound it out with the class, holding up a finger for each sound.

Answers

D d

dip
red
dad
hand

Say the word for each picture and write the letter for the first sound. Three start with /d/, but one does not.

Dictation: Dictate the letter sounds /d/, /m/, /r/, /h/ and the words *sad* and *dip.* Afterward, sound out each word for the students, writing the letters on the board so that they can check their work.

Developing accuracy and fluency: The students take home a sound book to read with their parents and bring back the next day.

Further ideas: Sing the /d/ song from Jolly Songs. Play a game of dominoes. Make dinosaurs from modeling clay. Pin up the /d/ section of the Wall Frieze.

Extra support: Now is a good time to assess and identify any students who are struggling to remember the letter sounds, blend words, write letters, or identify the sounds in words. Early intervention is extremely important. See pages 29 to 33 for more information.

49

11. Further ideas
The Jolly Songs, Wall Frieze, and craft activities are all fun ways to reinforce the letter sound. More ideas can be found in the Jolly Phonics Bumper Book.

12. Extra support
Early intervention is extremely important, so regularly assess and identify any students who are struggling to keep up with the rest of the class. A good time to do this is at the end of each letter-sound group.

one letter sound, or two related sounds, and is structured to give the students a solid grounding in the key skills of Jolly Phonics. As well as the activities found on the lesson page, there are regular activities in the lesson plans, which are designed to consolidate and reinforce the learning. Regular practice is important because in order to become fluent readers and writers, students must become proficient in all five skills.

Student Book

1. The letter(s) that represent the sound: Although lower-case letters are the focus for Step 1, students need to recognize the capitals in order to read names and sentences correctly.

2. Story picture: Coloring this in helps students improve their pencil grip and fine motor controls.

3. Action: Uses movement, sight, hearing, and speech to help remember the letter sound.

4. Letter formation practice: An opportunity to reinforce correct pencil grip, letter formation, and spacing.

5. Words for blending: Carefully selected words use only the letter sounds taught so far. Encourage the students to point to the dot underneath each sound as they say it.

6. Segmenting: There is a different activity for each letter-sound group. These activities develop phonemic awareness, enabling the students to identify all the sounds in words.

7. Tricky words: The first set of tricky words are introduced toward the end of Step 1. Encourage the students to listen to the word, blend the letter sounds, and identify the tricky parts.

The segmenting activities in Step 1 gradually become more challenging. Initially, the students progress from identifying the initial sound in a word to being able to hear and write a letter sound wherever it is heard in a word. Eventually, they have to listen and write all the sounds to make the word.

Letter Sound /s/

Introducing the letter sound: Use a story such as the one below, along with the action.

Sam has a dog called Samson. One sunny morning, Sam takes Samson for a walk down by the stream. While Samson snuffles about in the grass, Sam looks around. He sees a swan swimming past a snail on a stone. He also spots a toadstool, some spiders, a small mouse, and a bird on her nest. Sam picks up a stick and throws it for Samson to fetch. Samson chases after it and sniffs around for the stick in the grass. Suddenly, he starts barking, "Woof, woof, woof!" Sam skips over to see what Samson has found. In front of Samson is a large, spotty snake. It is sitting up and hissing, "Ssssss!" Sam grabs hold of Samson and the snake slithers slowly away.

Action: The students weave their hand like a snake, while making a continuous /ssssss/ sound.

Letter formation: Explain how the letter for /s/ is written. The students form the letter in the air and then practice writing it in their books. They write over the dotted letters and then try again, using the starting dots.

Blending: Say the sound /s/ with the students and encourage them to point to the dot under the ‹s› in their books as they do so. Then do some auditory blending. Call out the sounds in a word and ask the class to blend them together and say the word. For example, say the sounds in *sun* – /s-u-n/ – and encourage the students to call out "sun."

Identifying the sounds: Look at the four pictures at the bottom of the lesson page. Say the word for each one with the class: *sun, spider, snail, tree.* The students listen for the word that does not start with the sound /s/ and cross out its picture *[tree]*.

Developing accuracy and fluency: The students take home a sound book to read with their parents and bring back the next day.

Further ideas: Sing the /s/ song from Jolly Songs. Make snake shapes from dough or modeling clay. Paint ‹s› snakes cut out of paper or card and make mobiles or a collage. Pin up the /s/ section of the Wall Frieze.

Letter Sound /a/

Flashcards: Review the letter sound /s/. The students look at the letter, say the sound, and do the action.

Introducing the letter sound: Use a story such as the one below, along with the action.

The Smith family is having a picnic. They spread out a big picnic blanket and lay all their food on it. Adam unpacks the apples and Annie helps to make the jam sandwiches. As they start eating, Annie rubs her arm. "Something is tickling me," she says. "Something is tickling me, too," says Adam, eating his apple. All of a sudden, Annie shouts, "A…a…a...a!" They all look at Annie and see some ants crawling up her arm. Everyone jumps up quickly. There are ants everywhere! "Oh dear," says Dad. "We must have put the blanket over an ants' nest." They pack up their things and move to a nicer spot.

Action: The students pretend that ants are crawling up their arm and say *a, a, a, a*.

Letter formation: Explain how the letter for /a/ is written. The students form the letter in the air and then practice writing ‹a› and ‹s› in their books. They write over the dotted letters and then try again, using the starting dots.

Blending: Say the sounds /s/ and /a/ with the students and encourage them to point to the dot under each sound in their books as they do so. Then do some auditory blending. Call out the sounds in a word and ask the class to blend them together and say the word. For example, say the sounds in *ant* – /a-n-t/ – and encourage the students to call out "ant."

Identifying the sounds: Look at the four pictures at the bottom of the lesson page. Say the word for each one with the class: *ant, arrow, sock, apple*. The students listen for the word that does not start with the sound /a/ and cross out its picture *[sock]*.

Dictation: Call out the sounds /a/ and /s/ and ask the students to write the letter for each one.

Developing accuracy and fluency: The students take home a sound book to read with their parents and bring back the next day.

Further ideas: Sing the /a/ song from Jolly Songs. Cut some apples in half and use them to print colorful shapes. Paint large letter ‹a›s cut out of paper or card and make mobiles or a collage. Pin up the /a/ section of the Wall Frieze.

Letter Sound /t/

Flashcards: Review the letter sounds /s/ and /a/. The students look at each letter, say the sound, and do the action.

Introducing the letter sound: Use a story such as the one below, along with the action.

It is a sunny day, and Tom and Tamiko are playing outside with their toys. At first, they sit in the tent and play with a toy train, a spinning top, and a teddy bear. Then they think about what to do next. "I know," says Tamiko, "let's play a game of tennis!" The two children grab their rackets and start to play over by the tulips. Each time the ball hits the racket, it makes a noise. They have a great time, taking turns to hit the ball to each other: "t, t, t, t." A cat, a toad, and a turtle are watching them play. The animals turn their heads from side to side as they watch the ball go back and forth, just like people at a tennis match: "t, t, t, t."

Action: The students pretend to watch a game of tennis, turning their heads from side to side as they say *t, t, t, t.*

Letter formation: Explain how the letter for /t/ is written, pointing out that it is a tall letter and starts slightly higher up than the letters ‹s› and ‹a›. The students form the letter in the air and then practice writing ‹t›, ‹s›, and ‹a› in their books. They write over the dotted letters and then try again, using the starting dots.

Blending: Ask the students to look at the words *at* and *sat* in their books. Say the sounds with the class, and then blend the sounds together to read the word. The students point to the dot underneath each sound as they say it.

Identifying the sounds: Look at the four pictures at the bottom of the lesson page. Say the word for each one with the class: *tent, squirrel, teddy (bear), turtle.* The students listen for the word that does not start with the sound /t/ and cross out its picture *[squirrel].*

Dictation: Call out the sounds /t/, /a/, /s/ and ask the students to write the letter for each one.

Developing accuracy and fluency: The students take home a sound book to read with their parents and bring back the next day.

Further ideas: Sing the /t/ song from Jolly Songs. Make model turtles from modeling clay. Ask the students to bring in their teddies and have a teddy bear day. Pin up the /t/ section of the Wall Frieze.

Letter Sound /i/

Flashcards: Review the letter sounds /s/, /a/, and /t/. The students look at each letter, say the sound, and do the action.

Introducing the letter sound: Use a story such as the one below, along with the action.

Zack has a white pet mouse, who lives in a cage on his bedroom desk. One day, Zack forgets to close the cage door properly and the little mouse escapes. She runs along the desk and knocks over a bottle of ink. Crash! The lid comes off and the ink spills everywhere! It even splashes the little mouse; "i, i, i, i," she squeaks and scampers off to a mouse hole close by. Zack follows the inky paw prints across the carpet, but he cannot find the little mouse. Safe in her hiding place, she sits and scrubs her fur, but the ink will not come off. She decides that from now on she will make the mouse hole her home and call herself Inky Mouse.

Action: The students pretend to be a mouse stroking its whiskers and say *i, i, i, i.*

Letter formation: Explain how the letter for /i/ is written. The students form the letter in the air and then practice writing ‹i›, ‹s›, ‹a›, and ‹t› in their books. They write over the dotted letters and then try again, using the starting dots.

Blending: Ask the students to look at the words *it* and *sit* in their books. Say the sounds with the class, and then blend the sounds together to read the word. The students point to the dot underneath each sound as they say it.

Identifying the sounds: Look at the four pictures at the bottom of the lesson page. Say the word for each one with the class: *insects, ink, octopus, igloo.* The students listen for the word that does not start with the sound /i/ and cross out its picture *[octopus].*

Dictation: Call out the sounds /i/, /t/, /a/, /s/ and ask the students to write the letter for each one.

Developing accuracy and fluency: The students take home a sound book to read with their parents and bring back the next day.

Further ideas: Sing the /i/ song from Jolly Songs.

Make pictures from inky fingerprints. Look for the letter ‹i› in books or on posters in the classroom. Pin up the /i/ section of the Wall Frieze.

Letter Sound /p/

Flashcards: Review the letter sounds /s/, /a/, /t/, /i/. The students look at each letter, say the sound, and do the action.

Introducing the letter sound: Use a story such as the one below, along with the action.

It is Paul's birthday and his friends Ping, Pavlo, and Pat have come to his party. They play Musical Chairs and Pass the Parcel and then Paul opens some of his presents. "Perfect!" says Paul, as he unwraps a toy polar bear, "That is my favorite animal!" Then they sit down to drink fizzy pop and eat some party food: peanut butter sandwiches, popcorn, apple pie, and cupcakes. While they are eating, Paul's mother produces a big pink cake with five candles on it. Paul tries to blow out the candles, but every time he puffs one out, it lights up again. They are trick candles! Everyone laughs and tries to puff out the candles: "p, p, p, p."

Action: The students hold up their finger as if it is a candle and pretend to puff it out, saying *p, p, p, p*.

Letter formation: Explain how the letter for /p/ is written, pointing out that it has a tail that goes down under the line. The students form the letter in the air and then practice writing ‹p›, ‹s›, ‹a›, ‹t›, and ‹i› in their books. They write over the dotted letters and then try again, using the starting dots.

Blending: Blend the words on the lesson page with the class: *pit, pat, tip, tap.* The students point to the dot underneath each sound as they say it.

Identifying the sounds: Look at the four pictures at the bottom of the lesson page. Say the word for each one with the class: *panda, yogurt, pen, parrot.* The students listen for the word that does not start with the sound /p/ and cross out its picture *[yogurt]*.

Word bank: *pat, pip, pit, sap, sip, tap, tip, spat, spit.* Use the word bank regularly to practice blending. It can also be used to do auditory segmenting: Say a word and then sound it out with the class, holding up a finger for each sound.

Dictation: Call out the sounds /p/, /i/, /t/, /a/, /s/ and ask the students to write the letter for each one.

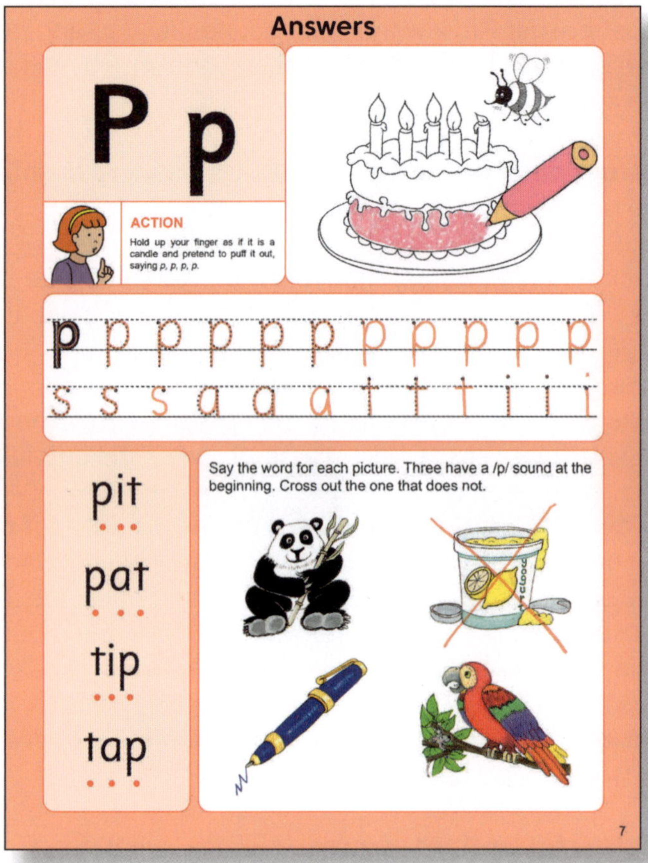

Developing accuracy and fluency: The students take home a sound book to read with their parents and bring back the next day.

Further ideas: Sing the /p/ song from Jolly Songs. Use feathers to make a parrots collage. Paint pictures of porcupines or pink poodles. Pin up the /p/ section of the Wall Frieze.

Letter Sound /n/

Flashcards: Review the letter sounds /s/, /a/, /t/, /i/, /p/. The students look at each letter, say the sound, and do the action.

Introducing the letter sound: Use a story such as the one below, along with the action.

It is Sunday afternoon and Nicola has gone fishing with her grandfather. While Grandpa sets up his fishing rod, Nicola puts her net in the pond and places a big bucket on the ground. "Now remember, Nicola," says Grandpa, "don't make any noise, or you will scare the fish away." Nicola sits very still and watches the birds and insects. She sees a line of little ants, a big white swan, and a brown and green newt. It is very peaceful; all she can hear are the robins singing. Suddenly, a plane flies over the pond, doing a noisy loop-the-loop. "What a nasty noise!" says Grandpa, but Nicola laughs. She holds out her arms and pretends to fly like the plane: "nnnnnn!"

Action: The students put their arms out and pretend to be a nasty noisy plane, making a continuous /nnnnnn/ sound.

Letter formation: Explain how the letter for /n/ is written. The students form the letter in the air and then practice writing ‹n›, ‹a›, ‹t›, ‹i›, and ‹p› in their books. They write over the dotted letters and then try again, using the starting dots.

Blending: Blend the words on the lesson page with the class: *tin, ant, nip, pan.* The students point to the dot underneath each sound as they say it.

Identifying the sounds: Look at the four pictures at the bottom of the lesson page. Say the word for each one with the class: *box, net, nest, neck.* The students listen for the word that does not start with the sound /n/ and cross out its picture *[box].*

Word bank: *an, in, ant, nap, nip, nit, pan, pin, tan, tin, pant, snap, snip, span, spin, tint, insist; a pin.* Use the word bank regularly to practice blending. It can also be used to do auditory segmenting: Say a word and then sound it out with the class, holding up a finger for each sound.

Dictation: Call out the sounds n/, /p/, /i/, /t/, /a/, /s/ and ask the students to write the letter for each one.

Developing accuracy and fluency: The students take home a sound book to read with their parents and bring back the next day.

Further ideas: Sing the /n/ song from Jolly Songs. Make nests from twigs and moss. Draw pictures of some nasty noisy things. Pin up the /n/ section of the Wall Frieze.

Letter Sound /c k/

Flashcards: Review the letter sounds already taught: /s/, /a/, /t/, /i/, /p/, /n/.

Introducing the letter sound: Use a story such as the one below, along with the action.

The Khan family is on a trip to Spain. In the morning, they hire a car and visit a castle, high on a cliff. On the way back, they pass a cow grazing, some people having a picnic, and a donkey drinking from a bucket of water. "I think it's time for a snack," says Mrs. Khan, "Let's go to the courtyard café by the beach." They sit outside to eat and watch a cat and her kittens play nearby. As the clock strikes four, some Spanish dancers appear, clicking their castanets: "c, k, ck, ck." They start to dance and clap to the music, swirling their bright crimson dresses. The children spot a crab clicking its claws on the sand: "c, k, ck, ck." "Look, the crab is joining in too," they laugh.

Action: The students pretend to play Spanish castanets and snap their fingers in the air, saying *c, k, ck, ck*.

Letter formation: Explain how a caterpillar /c/ and a kicking /k/ are written. Point out that kicking /k/ is a tall letter. The students form the letters in the air and then practice writing them in their books. They write over the dotted letters and then try again, using the starting dots.

Blending: Blend the words on the lesson page with the class: *kit, cap, pick, sack.* The students point to the dot underneath each sound as they say it. Explain that when two letters making the same sound are next to each other, you only say the sound once: /p-i-ck/ and /s-a-ck/, not /p-i-c-k/ and /s-a-c-k/.

Identifying the sounds: Look at the four pictures at the bottom of the lesson page. Say the word for each one with the class. The students listen and write the letter for the first sound in each word *[cat, crab, kangaroo, penguin].*

Word bank: *act, can, cap, cat, kin, kit, kick, kiss, pack, pick, sack, sick, tack, tick, scan, skip, skin, tact, snack, stack, stick, attic, panic, napkin, picnic; a sick cat.* Use the word bank regularly to practice blending. It can also be used to do auditory segmenting: Say a word and then sound it out with the class, holding up a finger for each sound.

Dictation: Ask the students to write a caterpillar /c/ and a kicking /k/. Then say the words *it* and *at*. For each one, ask the students to listen for the sounds and write the word. Afterward, sound out the words for the students, writing the letters on the board so that they can check their work.

Developing accuracy and fluency: The students take home a sound book to read with their parents and bring back the next day.

Further ideas: Sing the /c k/ song from Jolly Songs. Create a cats and kittens collage. Make castanets from folded paper plates (decorate plain plates or use patterned ones). Pin up the /c k/ section of the Wall Frieze.

Letter Sound /e/

Flashcards: Review the letter sounds already taught: /s/, /a/, /t/, /i/, /p/, /n/, /c/, /k/.

Introducing the letter sound: Use a story such as the one below, along with the action.

Every summer, Eric and his family spend seven days at Ten Acre Farm. In the morning, everyone gets up early to watch the cows being milked. Then Eric likes to help with the chores. He fetches water from the well and gives it to the cows to drink. Then he feeds the hens and collects the eggs for breakfast. Back in the kitchen, he gives the eggs to Ellie, the farmer's wife. "How would you like your eggs today? asks Ellie. "I'd like fried eggs," Eric replies. Ellie takes an egg and taps it gently on the side of the pan: "e, e, e." Then she cracks it open: "e!" Eric watches Ellie and pretends to crack open the eggs too, saying, "E...e...e...e...eggs!"

Action: The students pretend to crack open an egg. They tap with one hand saying *e, e, e,* and then mime opening the eggshell, saying *e*.

Letter formation: Explain how the letter for /e/ is written, pointing out that it is unusual because it does not start at or near the top of the letter, but halfway up. The students form the letter in the air and then practice writing ‹e›, ‹t›, ‹t›, ‹i›, ‹p›, ‹n›, ‹c›, and ‹k› in their books. They write over the dotted letters and then try again, using the starting dots.

Blending: Blend the words on the lesson page with the class: *ten, pet, tent, neck.* The students point to the dot underneath each sound as they say it. Remind them that when two letters making the same sound are next to each other, you only say the sound once: /n-e-ck/, not /n-e-c-k/.

Identifying the sounds: Look at the four pictures at the bottom of the lesson page. Say the word for each one with the class. The students listen and write the letter for the first sound in each word *[egg, statue, elbow, elephant].*

Word bank: *net, pen, pet, set, ten, neck, peck, kept, nest, pest, sent, step, tent, test, speck, spent, tennis, insect, inspect; a pet cat.* Use the word bank regularly to practice blending. It can also be used to do auditory

segmenting: Say a word and then sound it out with the class, holding up a finger for each sound.

Dictation: Dictate the letter sounds /e/, /c k/, /n/, /p/ and the words *net* and *pen*. Remind the students that the sound /c k/ can be written as a caterpillar /c/ or a kicking /k/. Afterward, sound out each word for the students, writing the letters on the board so that they can check their work.

Developing accuracy and fluency: The students take home a sound book to read with their parents and bring back the next day.

Further ideas: Sing the /e/ song from Jolly Songs. Draw pictures of animals that hatch from eggs. Plant cress or mustard seeds in empty eggshells. Pin up the /e/ section of the Wall Frieze.

Letter Sound /h/

Flashcards: Review the letter sounds already taught: /s/, /a/, /t/, /i/, /p/, /n/, /c/, /k/, /e/.

Introducing the letter sound: Use a story such as the one below, along with the action.

It is the school's summer fun day, and the children are outside, having lots of races. There are running races, jumping races, and hopping races. Helen, Harry, Hanif, and Harriet are in the hopping race. They line up in a row, ready for Mr. Heath to start the race. "One, two, three, GO!" he shouts, waving his hat high in the air. Helen, Harry, Hanif, and Harriet hop, hop, hop as fast as they can, but hopping is hard work on a hot day. By the time the children get to the finishing line, they are huffing and puffing: "h, h, h, h!" They sit down on the grass to cool down and Miss Hopkins gives them a nice cold drink. "Well done, everyone," she says, "That was very hard!"

Action: The students pretend to pant, holding their hand up to their mouth and saying *h, h, h, h*.

Letter formation: Explain how the letter for /h/ is written, pointing out that it is a tall letter. The students form the letter in the air and then practice writing ‹h›, ‹i›, ‹p›, ‹n›, ‹c›, ‹k›, and ‹e› in their books. They write over the dotted letters and then try again, using the starting dots.

Blending: Blend the words on the lesson page with the class: *hip, hat, hen, hiss.* The students point to the dot underneath each sound as they say it. Remind them that when two letters making the same sound are next to each other, you only say the sound once: /h-i-ss/, not /h-i-s-s/.

Identifying the sounds: Look at the four pictures at the bottom of the lesson page. Say the word for each one with the class. The students listen and write the letter for the first sound in each word *[hedgehog, hill, hand, tennis].*

Word bank: *hat, hen, hip, hit, hiss, hint, hectic; a hen in a pen.* Use the word bank regularly to practice blending. It can also be used to do auditory segmenting: Say a word and then sound it out with the class, holding up a finger for each sound.

Dictation: Dictate the letter sounds /h/ /e/, /c k/, /n/ and the words *hat* and *hen*. Remind the students that the sound /c k/ can be written as a caterpillar /c/ or a kicking /k/. Afterward, sound out each word for the students, writing the letters on the board so that they can check their work.

Developing accuracy and fluency: The students take home a sound book to read with their parents and bring back the next day.

Further ideas: Sing the /h/ song from Jolly Songs. Have a hopping race. Make pictures of hedgehogs with handprint prickles. Pin up the /h/ section of the Wall Frieze.

Letter Sound /r/

Flashcards: Review the letter sounds already taught: /s/, /a/, /t/, /i/, /p/, /n/, /c/, /k/, /e/, /h/.

Introducing the letter sound: Use a story such as the one below, along with the action.

Robert's family has a playful new puppy, but they cannot decide what to call him: Rocky, Rebel, or Rover. It is raining, so the puppy follows Robert up to his bedroom to play. The puppy sniffs around the room and finds a racing car, a rocket, some roller skates, a toy rabbit, and a rocking horse. Then he goes under the bed and pulls out an old blanket. He grips the blanket in his teeth and shakes it from side to side: "Rrrrrr!" "Rrrrrr!" Robert tries to take it away, but the puppy hangs on tightly until the blanket rips into rags. "Oh no!" says Robert, holding the blanket up. "Well, I know what to call you now." And from that day on, the puppy is known as Rags.

Action: The students shake their heads, like a puppy with a rag, making a continuous /rrrrrr/ sound.

Letter formation: Explain how the letter for /r/ is written. The students form the letter in the air and then practice writing ‹r›, ‹p›, ‹n›, ‹c›, ‹k›, ‹e›, and ‹h› in their books. They write over the dotted letters and then try again, using the starting dots.

Blending: Blend the words on the lesson page with the class: *rip, rat, rest, trap.* The students point to the dot underneath each sound as they say it.

Identifying the sounds: Look at the four pictures at the bottom of the lesson page. Say the word for each one with the class. The students listen and write the letter for the first sound in each word *[rain, rabbit, hen, rocket].*

Word bank: *ran, rap, rat, rip, rack, rent, rest, risk, trap, trek, trip, crack, press, prick, track, trick, crept, crisp, print, scrap, strap, strip, stress, spirit, strict; cracks in a pan.* Use the word bank regularly to practice blending. It can also be used to do auditory segmenting: Say a word and then sound it out with the class, holding up a finger for each sound.

Dictation: Dictate the letter sounds /r/, /h/ /e/, /c k/ and the words *rip* and *rat*. Remind the students that the sound /c k/ can be written as a caterpillar /c/ or a kicking /k/. Afterward, sound out each word for the students, writing the letters on the board so that they can check their work.

Developing accuracy and fluency: The students take home a sound book to read with their parents and bring back the next day.

Further ideas: Sing the /r/ song from Jolly Songs. Paint pictures of rockets. Use pieces of rag to make a dog collage. Pin up the /r/ section of the Wall Frieze.

Letter Sound /m/

Flashcards: Review the letter sounds already taught: /s/, /a/, /t/, /i/, /p/, /n/, /c/, /k/, /e/, /h/, /r/.

Introducing the letter sound: Use a story such as the one below, along with the action.

Milly and Molly have come over for dinner with Mrs. Morris and her son, Marvin. When Mrs. Morris calls "Dinnertime!" the children wash their hands and sit down at the table, ready to eat their meal. "Mmmm, I'm really hungry!" says Marvin, rubbing his tummy. "I hope it's spaghetti and meatballs." "Mmmm, I'm hungry, too," says Molly. "I hope it's tomato soup." "Well, I hope it's chicken and mushroom pie," says Milly, and they all rub their tummies, hungrily. In a few minutes, Mrs. Morris brings in a large dish, heaped full of tasty food. "Lamb and peas," say the children. "We like that meal most of all. Mmmmmmm!"

Action: The students rub their tummies and make a continuous /mmmmmm/ sound.

Letter formation: Explain how the letter for /m/ is written. The students form the letter in the air and then practice writing ‹m›, ‹n›, ‹c›, ‹k›, ‹e›, ‹h›, and ‹r› in their books. They write over the dotted letters and then try again, using the starting dots.

Blending: Blend the words on the lesson page with the class: *men, him, miss, man.* The students point to the dot underneath each sound as they say it. Remind them that when two letters making the same sound are next to each other, you only say the sound once: /m-i-ss/, not /m-i-s-s/.

Identifying the sounds: Look at the four pictures at the bottom of the lesson page. Say the word for each one with the class. The students listen and write the letter for the first sound in each word *[mug, robot, milk, moon].*

Word bank: *hem, him, imp, man, map, mat, men, met, ram, rim, mass, mess, miss, camp, mint, mist, ramp, stem, trim, smack, mimic, stamp, tempt, tramp; a man in a hat.* Use the word bank regularly to practice blending. It can also be used to do auditory segmenting: Say a word and then sound it out with the class, holding up a finger for each sound.

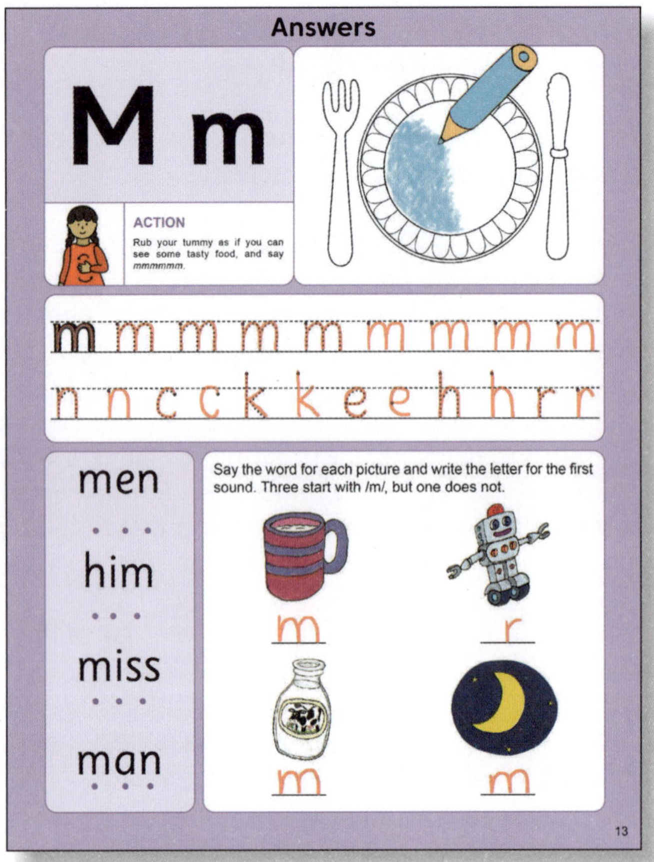

Dictation: Dictate the letter sounds /m/, /r/, /h/, /e/ and the words *map* and *rim*. Afterward, sound out each word for the students, writing the letters on the board so that they can check their work.

Developing accuracy and fluency: The students take home a sound book to read with their parents and bring back the next day.

Further ideas: Sing the /m/ song from Jolly Songs. Make masks out of different materials. Stick magazine pictures onto paper plates to make a collage of many meals. Pin up the /m/ section of the Wall Frieze.

Letter Sound /d/

Flashcards: Review the letter sounds already taught: /s/, /a/, /t/, /i/, /p/, /n/, /c/, /k/, /e/, /h/, /r/, /m/.

Introducing the letter sound: Use a story such as the one below, along with the action.

Dan is tidying his toy cupboard. He pulls out a teddy bear, his old donkey, a box of dominoes, and a duck. Next, he sees his yellow digger and takes it out for a drive. Suddenly, he hears his dad calling. "Dan, have you finished yet?" "Not yet," says Dan, as he finds a bag of marbles and some dice. Soon Dad is calling again. "Dan, have you finished yet?" "No, not yet," he answers. Then Dan finds his old red and blue drum. He marches up and down, banging the drum: "d, d, d, d!" Dad comes in to see what is happening. "Dan, do you know you have spent all day tidying your cupboard?" Dan smiles. "I've found lots of things I had forgotten all about," he replies.

Action: The students pretend to be playing a drum, moving their hands up and down and saying *d, d, d, d.*

Letter formation: Explain how the letter for /d/ is written, pointing out that it starts with a caterpillar /c/ and is a tall letter. The students form the letter in the air and then practice writing ‹d›, ‹c›, ‹k›, ‹e›, ‹h›, ‹r›, and ‹m› in their books. They write over the dotted letters and then try again, using the starting dots.

Blending: Blend the words on the lesson page with the class: *dip, red, dad, hand.* The students point to the dot underneath each sound as they say it.

Identifying the sounds: Look at the four pictures at the bottom of the lesson page. Say the word for each one with the class. The students listen and write the letter for the first sound in each word *[dog, dice, mole, dress].*

Word bank: *add, and, dad, den, did, dim, din, dip, end, had, hid, kid, mad, pad, red, rid, sad, deck, damp, dent, desk, disk, drip, hand, sand, mend, send, skid, tend, dress, spend, stand, timid, intend, dentist, drastic, handstand; a red dress.* Use the word bank regularly to practice blending. It can also be used to do auditory segmenting: Say a word and then sound it out with the class, holding up a finger for each sound.

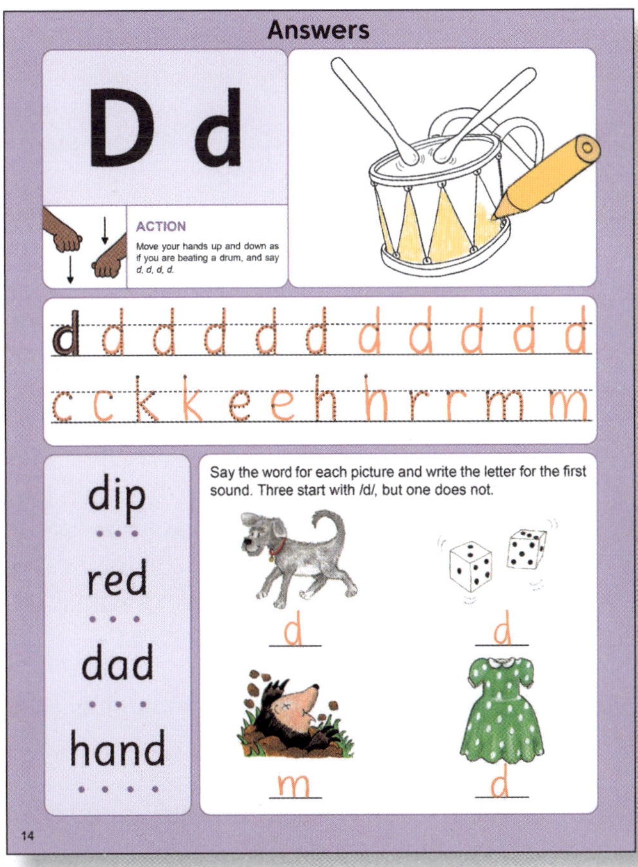

Dictation: Dictate the letter sounds /d/, /m/, /r/, /h/ and the words *sad* and *dip*. Afterward, sound out each word for the students, writing the letters on the board so that they can check their work.

Developing accuracy and fluency: The students take home a sound book to read with their parents and bring back the next day.

Further ideas: Sing the /d/ song from Jolly Songs. Play a game of dominoes. Make dinosaurs from modeling clay. Pin up the /d/ section of the Wall Frieze.

Extra support: Now is a good time to assess and identify any students who are struggling to remember the letter sounds, blend words, write letters, or identify the sounds in words. Early intervention is extremely important. See pages 29 to 33 for more information.

Letter Sound /g/

Flashcards: Review the letter sounds already taught: /s/, /a/, /t/, /i/, /p/, /n/, /c/, /k/, /e/, /h/, /r/, /m/, /d/.

Introducing the letter sound: Use a story such as the one below, along with the action.

Gail is staying with her grandmother. One morning, Gail and Granny go into the garden to check on the goat and the geese. Gail finds a frog and watches it hop off under the gate. Back inside, Granny sends Gail to the bathroom to wash her hands. When she is finished, Gail pulls out the plug, but nothing happens. "Granny," she cries, "the sink is blocked and full of water." Her grandmother comes to have a look. "Oh dear," says Granny, "I'll have to call the plumber. He'll come and fix it." When he arrives, the plumber puts on his gloves and checks the pipes under the sink. Gail watches and when the sink is unblocked, the water gurgles down the drain: "g, g, g, g."

Action: The students pretend their hand is water spiraling down a drain and say *g, g, g, g.*

Letter formation: Explain how the letter for /g/ is written, pointing out that it starts with a caterpillar /c/ and has a tail that goes down under the line. The students form the letter in the air and then practice writing ‹g›, ‹e›, ‹h›, ‹r›, ‹m›, and ‹d› in their books. They write over the dotted letters and then try again, using the starting dots.

Blending: Blend the words on the lesson page with the class: *egg, dig, peg, grin.* The students point to the dot underneath each sound as they say it.

Identifying the sounds: Look at the four pictures at the bottom of the lesson page. Say the word for each one with the class: *grapes, log, lamp, frog.* The students listen for the word without the sound /g/ and cross out its picture *[lamp].*

Word bank: *egg, dig, gap, gas, get, nag, peg, rag, rig, sag, tag, crag, drag, gram, grid, grim, grin, grip, snag, stag, grand, granddad; granddad is sad.* Use the word bank regularly to practice blending. It can also be used to do auditory segmenting: Say a word and then sound it out with the class, holding up a finger for each sound.

Dictation: Dictate the letter sounds /g/, /d/, /m/, /r/ and the words *sag, peg, dig, get.* Afterward, sound out each word for the students, writing the letters on the board so that they can check their work.

Developing accuracy and fluency: The students take home a sound book to read with their parents and bring back the next day.

Further ideas: Sing the /g/ song from Jolly Songs. Paint pictures of green frogs. Read the story of The Three Billy Goats Gruff. Pin up the /g/ section of the Wall Frieze.

Letter Sound /o/

Flashcards: Review the letter sounds already taught: /s/, /a/, /t/, /i/, /p/, /n/, /c/, /k/, /e/, /h/, /r/, /m/, /d/, /g/.

Introducing the letter sound: Use a story such as the one below, along with the action.

Oliver and Holly have bunk beds in their new bedroom. Holly has the top bunk and Oliver has the bottom bunk. That night, Holly goes to sleep, and Oliver reads his comic. “Turn the light off when you’ve finished,” calls Dad. Oliver finishes the comic, but he is not sleepy yet. He plays with Oscar, his toy octopus, before turning off the light. “Off it goes,” he says, flicking the switch. Then he turns it back on again: “O…o…o…o…on it goes,” he laughs. Oliver turns the light on and off, on and off until, suddenly, he hears his father’s voice. “Stop turning the light on and off, Oliver! You will break it.” Oliver turns the light off and goes to sleep.

Action: The students point their finger as if pushing a wall switch on and off and say *o-o, o-o*.

Letter formation: Explain how the letter for /o/ is written, pointing out that it starts with a caterpillar /c/. The students form the letter in the air and then practice writing ‹o›, ‹h›, ‹r›, ‹m›, ‹d›, and ‹g› in their books. They write over the dotted letters and then try again, using the starting dots.

Blending: Blend the words on the lesson page with the class: *hot, dog, hop, socks.* The students point to the dot underneath each sound as they say it.

Identifying the sounds: Look at the four pictures at the bottom of the lesson page. Say the word for each one with the class: *doll, pond, otter, cow.* The students listen for the word without the sound /o/ and cross out its picture *[cow]*.

Word bank: *on, odd, cod, cog, cot, dog, dot, got, hop, hot, mop, nod, not, pod, pop, pot, rod, rot, top, dock, mock, rock, sock, crop, drop, pond, spot, stop, trod, trot, cross, comic, topic, cannot, tick-tock, desktop; a rock in a pond.* Use the word bank regularly to practice blending. It can also be used to do auditory segmenting: Say a word and then sound it out with the class, holding up a finger for each sound.

Dictation: Dictate the letter sounds /o/, /g/, /d/, /m/

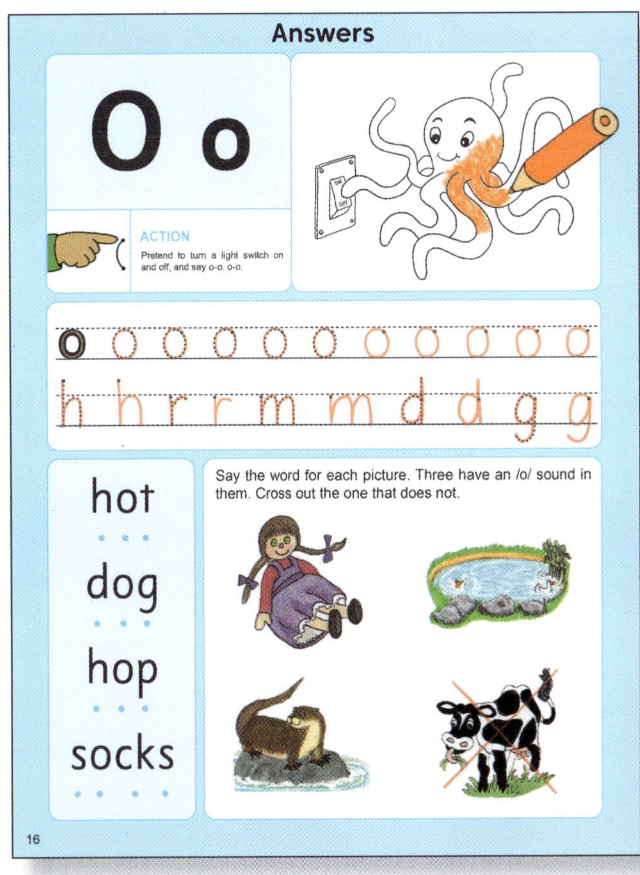

and the words *hop, dot, nod, cog*. Afterward, sound out each word for the students, writing the letters on the board so that they can check their work.

Developing accuracy and fluency: The students take home a sound book to read with their parents and bring back the next day.

Further ideas: Sing the /o/ song from Jolly Songs. Make an octopus with paper-chain tentacles. Print ‹o› patterns, using the ends of cardboard tubes. Pin up the /o/ section of the Wall Frieze.

Letter Sound /u/

Flashcards: Review the letter sounds already taught: /s/, /a/, /t/, /i/, /p/, /n/, /c/, /k/, /e/, /h/, /r/, /m/, /d/, /g/, /o/.

Introducing the letter sound: Use a story such as the one below, along with the action.

Uncle Bud is visiting Anna and Ulric. He has brought them each a big umbrella. Anna's umbrella is blue and spotty, while Ulric's umbrella has red and white stripes. In the afternoon, the family decides to go for a walk. It is a sunny day, but Anna and Ulric insist on taking their umbrellas. Everyone laughs, except Uncle Bud. "I'll take my umbrella, too," he says. It is not long before some big black clouds appear on the horizon. A little while later, they feel the first raindrops starting to fall. Soon it is pouring with rain! Uncle Bud, Anna, and Ulric put up their umbrellas, shouting, "U...u...u...up umbrellas!" They jump around in the muddy puddles, having a lovely time.

Action: The students pretend to hold an umbrella and put it up, saying *u, u, u, u*.

Letter formation: Explain how the letter for /u/ is written. The students form the letter in the air and then practice writing ‹u›, ‹r›, ‹m›, ‹d›, ‹g›, and ‹o› in their books. They write over the dotted letters and then try again, using the starting dots.

Blending: Blend the words on the lesson page with the class: *up, sun, mud, truck.* The students point to the dot underneath each sound as they say it.

Identifying the sounds: Look at the four pictures at the bottom of the lesson page. Say the word for each one with the class: *spoon, duck, nuts, umbrella.* The students listen for the word without the sound /u/ and cross out its picture *[spoon]*.

Word bank: *up, us, cup, cut, dug, gum, hug, hum, hut, mud, mug, nun, nut, pun, pup, rug, run, rut, sum, sun, tug, duck, muck, putt, suck, tuck, drug, drum, dump, dusk, dust, gust, hump, hunt, must, pump, rump, rust, snug, spun, tusk, stuck, truck, crust, grunt, mumps, stump, trust, undid, upset, eggcup, hiccup, sunset, suntan, discuss, rucksack, undress, product, pumpkin, instruct; a red sunset.* Use the word bank regularly to practice blending. It can also be used to do auditory segmenting: Say a word and then sound it out with the class, holding up a finger for each sound.

Dictation: Dictate the letter sounds /u/, /o/, /g/, /d/ and the words *run, sum, cut, hug*. Afterward, sound out each word for the students, writing the letters on the board so that they can check their work.

Developing accuracy and fluency: The students take home a sound book to read with their parents and bring back the next day.

Further ideas: Sing the /u/ song from Jolly Songs. Make umbrella mobiles with cut-out raindrops. Paint patterned umbrellas and make a collage. Pin up the /u/ section of the Wall Frieze.

Letter Sound /l/

Flashcards: Review the letter sounds already taught: /s/, /a/, /t/, /i/, /p/, /n/, /c/, /k/, /e/, /h/, /r/, /m/, /d/, /g/, /o/, /u/.

Introducing the letter sound: Use a story such as the one below, along with the action.

It is Luca's birthday, and he is having a party with all his friends. The house is decorated with lots of balloons and the table is laid out with some lovely food. There are lettuce and tomato sandwiches, little cupcakes, licorice laces, and lots of lemonade to drink. Most importantly, there is a large birthday cake decorated with a lion. Luca's friends give him his presents, and then they play some party games. They lie down on the floor for Sleeping Lions, and then they have a game of Blind Man's Buff and Pin the Tail on the Donkey. Lucy wins Pin the Tail on the Donkey and gets a lime lollipop as a prize. "It's very tasty," says Lucy and she licks her lollipop: "llllll."

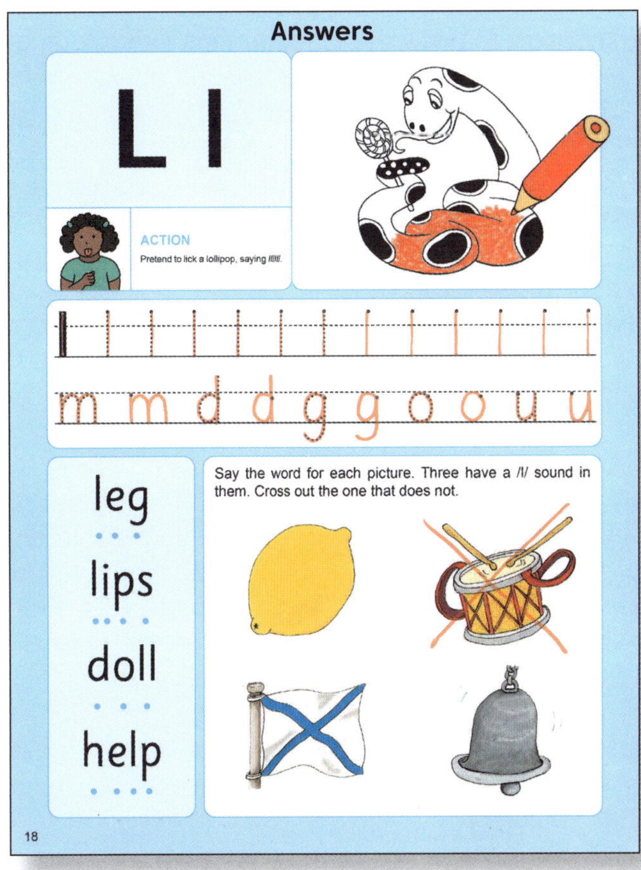

Action: The students pretend to lick a lollipop, sticking out their tongues and making a continuous /llllll/ sound.

Letter formation: Explain how the letter for /l/ is written, pointing out that it is a tall letter. The students form the letter in the air and then practice writing ‹l›, ‹m›, ‹d›, ‹g›, ‹o›, and ‹u› in their books. They write over the dotted letters and then try again, using the starting dots.

Blending: Blend the words on the lesson page with the class: *leg, lips, doll, help.* The students point to the dot underneath each sound as they say it.

Identifying the sounds: Look at the four pictures at the bottom of the lesson page. Say the word for each one with the class: *lemon, drum, flag, bell.* The students listen for the word without the sound /l/ and cross out its picture *[drum].*

Word bank: *ill, elk, lad, lap, led, leg, let, lid, lip, lit, log, lot, pal, dill, doll, dull, gill, gull, hill, kill, lass, less, lick, lock, loss, luck, mill, pill, sell, sill, tell, till, clap, clip, clog, glad, glum, gulp, held, help, kilt, lamp, land, lend, lent, limp, list, lost, lump, melt, milk, plan, plop, plot, plug, plum, plus, silk, slam, slap, slid, slim, slip, slit, slot, slug, sulk, tilt, click, clock, skill, skull, smell, spell, spill, still, adult, clamp, clump, halal, limit, plump, slept, spelt, spilt, split, solid, until, unless, unlock, insult, stilts, laptop, unplug, plastic, lipstick, clarinet, splendid; a lost dog.* Use the word bank regularly to practice blending. It can also be used to do auditory segmenting: Say a word and then sound it out with the class, holding up a finger for each sound.

Dictation: Dictate the letter sounds /l/, /u/, /o/, /g/ and the words *lap, lot, leg, lid.* Afterward, sound out each word for the students, writing the letters on the board so that they can check their work.

Developing accuracy and fluency: The students take home a sound book to read with their parents and bring back the next day.

Further ideas: Sing the /l/ song from Jolly Songs. Make some lemonade. Paint pictures of lollipops. Pin up the /l/ section of the Wall Frieze.

Letter Sound /f/

Flashcards: Review the letter sounds already taught: /s/, /a/, /t/, /i/, /p/, /n/, /c/, /k/, /e/, /h/, /r/, /m/, /d/, /g/, /o/, /u/, /l/.

Introducing the letter sound: Use a story such as the one below, along with the action.

Freda, Fred, and their friend Felix are at the beach. Fred has a large, floating, inflatable fish. Freda has a new flowery sun hat and a bucket and spade. First, the children go into the water to play with the inflatable fish. Then Freda and Felix build sandcastles, while Fred puts on his flippers and goes for a swim. Freda and Felix have fun decorating their castles. Freda puts flags on the four towers of hers, and Felix goes off to finds some shells and seaweed for his. Suddenly, the children hear a strange sound. They look around to see Fred's inflatable fish getting smaller and smaller and smaller. Its plug has come out and all the air is escaping: "ffffff!"

Action: The students slowly bring their hands together to mime an inflatable fish deflating, making a continuous /ffffffff/ sound.

Letter formation: Explain how the letter for /f/ is written, pointing out that it is a tall letter. The students form the letter in the air and then practice writing ‹f›, ‹d›, ‹g›, ‹o›, ‹u›, and ‹l› in their books. They write over the dotted letters and then try again, using the starting dots.

Blending: Blend the words on the lesson page with the class: *fit, fun, puff, soft.* The students point to the dot underneath each sound as they say it.

Identifying the sounds: Look at the four pictures at the bottom of the lesson page. Say the word for each one with the class: *flower, golf, leaf, bed.* The students listen for the word without the sound /f/ and cross out its picture *[bed].*

Word bank: *if, off, elf, fan, fat, fed, fig, fin, fit, fog, fun, cuff, fell, fill, fuss, huff, puff, tiff, fact, felt, film, fist, flag, flan, flap, flat, flip, flop, fond, font, frog, from, fund, gift, golf, left, lift, loft, self, sift, soft, tuft, cliff, flick, flock, fluff, frock, gruff, sniff, stiff, drift, frost, muffin, puffin, infect, traffic, frantic, himself, fantastic; a fat frog on a log.* Use the word bank regularly to practice blending. It can also be used to do auditory segmenting: Say a word and then sound it out with the class, holding up a finger for each sound.

Dictation: Dictate the letter sounds /f/, /l/, /u/, /o/ and the words *fan, fit, fog, elf.* Afterward, sound out each word for the students, writing the letters on the board so that they can check their work.

Developing accuracy and fluency: The students take home a sound book to read with their parents and bring back the next day.

Further ideas: Sing the /f/ song from Jolly Songs. Find out about different types of fish. Make a model aquarium with foil fish. Pin up the /f/ section of the Wall Frieze.

Letter Sound /b/

Flashcards: Review the letter sounds already taught: /s/, /a/, /t/, /i/, /p/, /n/, /c/, /k/, /e/, /h/, /r/, /m/, /d/, /g/, /o/, /u/, /l/, /f/.

Introducing the letter sound: Use a story such as the one below, along with the action.

Granny is taking Bill and his baby brother Ben for a walk in the park. They stop to watch the boats on the lake and listen to the brass band. Then Granny finds a bench and sits down. Soon she and baby Ben are dozing in the sun. Bill sees his friends Rob and Betty with a box of bats and balls. “Would you like to play baseball with us?” asks Betty. The children take turns to throw the ball to each other and hit it with the bat: “b, b, b, b.” When it is Betty’s turn, she bashes the ball as hard as she can. It bounces and hits the bench, just missing Granny! Granny and baby Ben wake up. “I think Ben and I better move to a safer spot,” laughs Granny.

Action: The students pretend to hold a bat and hit a ball, saying *b, b, b, b*.

Letter formation: Explain how the letter for /b/ is written, pointing out that it is a tall letter that goes down the “bat” and bounces up and around the “ball.” The students form the letter in the air and then practice writing ‹b›, ‹d›, ‹g›, ‹o›, ‹u›, ‹l›, and ‹f› in their books. They write over the dotted letters and then try again, using the starting dots.

Blending: Blend the words on the lesson page with the class: *big, bag, bell, crab.* The students point to the dot underneath each sound as they say it.

Identifying the sounds: Look at the four pictures at the bottom of the lesson page. Say the word for each one with the class: *car, butterfly, web, zebra.* The students listen for the word without the sound /b/ and cross out its picture *[car]*.

Word bank: *bad, bag, ban, bat, bed, beg, bet, bib, big, bin, bit, bud, bug, bun, bus, but, cab, cub, pub, rob, rub, back, bell, bill, boss, buck, belt, bend, bent, best, bulb, bump, club, crab, crib, grab, grub, scab, black, block, brick, blend, blond, habit, robin, rabbit; a big red bus.* Use the word bank regularly to practice blending. It can also be used to do auditory segmenting: Say a word and then sound it out with the class, holding up a finger for each sound.

Dictation: Dictate the letter sounds /b/, /f/, /l/, /u/ and the words *bed, bus, bat, bib.* Afterward, sound out each word for the students, writing the letters on the board so that they can check their work.

Developing accuracy and fluency: The students take home a sound book to read with their parents and bring back the next day.

Further ideas: Sing the /b/ song from Jolly Songs. Go on a bug hunt. Play games with a bat and ball. Pin up the /b/ section of the Wall Frieze.

Extra support: Remember to assess and identify any students who are struggling, and provide them with the extra support they need. See pages 29 to 33 for more information.

Letter Sound /ai/

Flashcards: Review the letter sounds already taught: /s/, /a/, /t/, /i/, /p/, /n/, /c/, /k/, /e/, /h/, /r/, /m/, /d/, /g/, /o/, /u/, /l/, /f/, /b/.

Introducing the letter sound: Use a story such as the one below, along with the action.

Ainsley is having trouble with his hearing. Whenever his mother speaks to him, he puts his hand to his ear and says, "ai?" "I'm taking you to see the doctor today," his mother tells him, "And say *pardon,* not *ai.*" While they are waiting for the doctor, Ainsley looks around the room. It is a rainy day and Ainsley sees a snail on the windowpane. Then he finds a box of toys and plays with a whale, a sailboat, and a train. Just then, Dr. Ail appears and calls his name. The doctor looks in Ainsley's ears. "You have a lot of wax in your ears, Ainsley. That's why you're having trouble with your hearing." Dr. Ail gives him some ear drops to take home. "Not another *ai* now, Ainsley," says his mother.

Action: The students cup one hand over their ear, as if they are trying to hear something, and say *ai?*

Letter formation: The sound /ai/ is written with two letters. When two letters make one sound it is called a digraph. Remind the class how both letters are formed. The students form the letters for the digraph in the air and then practice writing ‹ai›, ‹g›, ‹o›, ‹u›, ‹l›, ‹f›, and ‹b› in their books.

Blending: Blend the words on the lesson page with the class: *rain, tail, snail, paint.* The students point to the dot underneath each sound as they say it.

Identifying the sounds: Look at the three pictures at the bottom of the lesson page and say the word for each one. The students listen and call out the sounds in each word. Then they write ‹ai› in the correct sound dot *[ch-**ai**-n; n-**ai**-l; t-r-**ai**-n].*

Word bank: *aid, ail, aim, bait, fail, gain, hail, laid, maid, mail, main, nail, paid, pail, pain, raid, rail, rain, sail, tail, brain, claim, drain, faint, grain, paint, plain, saint, snail, stain, trail, train, sprain, strain, raindrop; a snail trail.* Use the word bank regularly to practice blending. It can also be used to do auditory segmenting: Say a word and sound it out with the class, holding up a finger for each sound.

Dictation: Dictate the letter sounds /ai/, /b/, /f/, /l/ and the words *aim, rail, pain, bait.* Afterward, sound out each word for the students, writing the letters on the board so that they can check their work.

Developing accuracy and fluency: The students take home a sound book to read with their parents and bring back the next day.

Further ideas: Sing the /ai/ song from Jolly Songs. Make snails from modeling clay. Paint rainy-day pictures on large paper raindrops. Pin up the /ai/ section of the Wall Frieze.

Letter Sound /j/

Flashcards: Review the letter sounds already taught: /s/, /a/, /t/, /i/, /p/, /n/, /c/, /k/, /e/, /h/, /r/, /m/, /d/, /g/, /o/, /u/, /l/, /f/, /b/, /ai/.

Introducing the letter sound: Use a story such as the one below, along with the action.

Jane loves jello, so her mom has promised to make some for Jane this afternoon. When Jane gets home from school, she has a slice of bread and jam and a glass of orange juice. Then she tells her mom about the jigsaw puzzle of a juggler that she made at school with her friend Javinda. Jane's mom shows her the giant jello she has made. "Wow," says Jane. The jello is tall and red and has four layers. When it is ready, Jane helps her mom to tip it carefully onto a plate. As Jane's mom carries it to the table, the jello jiggles and joggles. Jane laughs and wobbles just like the jello, saying, "Jello on a plate, jello on a plate, j...j...j...j... jello on a plate."

Action: The students wobble like jello, saying *j, j, j, j*.

Letter formation: Explain how the letter for /j/ is written, pointing out that it has a tail that goes down under the line. The students form the letter in the air and then practice writing ‹j›, ‹o›, ‹u›, ‹l›, ‹f›, ‹b›, and ‹ai› in their books. They write over the dotted letters and then try again, using the starting dots.

Blending: Blend the words on the lesson page with the class: *jet, jog, just, jump.* The students point to the dot underneath each sound as they say it.

Identifying the sounds: Look at the three pictures at the bottom of the lesson page and say the word for each one. The students listen and call out the sounds in each word. Then they write ‹j› in the correct sound dot *[**j**-ar; **j**-a-m; **j**-i-g-s-aw].*

Word bank: *jab, jam, jet, jig, job, jog, jot, jug, jut, jack, jail, jump, just, object, project, subject; a traffic jam.* Use the word bank regularly to practice blending. It can also be used to do auditory segmenting: Say a word and then sound it out with the class, holding up a finger for each sound.

Dictation: Dictate the letter sounds /j/, /ai/, /b/, /f/ and

the words *jet, job, jam, jug*. Afterward, sound out each word for the students, writing the letters on the board so that they can check their work.

Developing accuracy and fluency: The students take home a sound book to read with their parents and bring back the next day.

Further ideas: Sing the /j/ song from Jolly Songs. Make a multicolored jello. Make a jellyfish with a paper-cup body and crêpe-paper tentacles. Pin up the /j/ section of the Wall Frieze.

Letter Sound /oa/

Flashcards: Review the letter sounds already taught: /s/, /a/, /t/, /i/, /p/, /n/, /c/, /k/, /e/, /h/, /r/, /m/, /d/, /g/, /o/, /u/, /l/, /f/, /b/, /ai/, /j/.

Introducing the letter sound: Use a story such as the one below, along with the action.

A bad-tempered goat lives in a field. The field is close to a stream at the side of the road. Mona and Jonah often walk past and stroke the goat on their way home. One windy day, Mona and Jonah put on their coats. They want to see if their new model boat will float in the stream. When they arrive, the goat is stamping his hooves and snorting at two cheeky robins in the old oak tree. The robins have been flying down and stealing oats from the goat. The goat charges at the tree and butts the trunk as hard as he can. CRASH! The tree falls on the goat. "Oh, no! You poor thing!" cry Mona and Jonah. "Don't worry, we'll get the farmer. He will rescue you."

Action: The students cover their mouth with one hand as if something is wrong and say *oa!*

Letter formation: The sound /oa/ is written with two letters. When two letters make one sound it is called a digraph. Remind the class how both letters are formed. The students form the letters for the digraph in the air and then practice writing ‹oa›, ‹u›, ‹l›, ‹f›, ‹b›, ‹ai›, and ‹j› in their books.

Blending: Blend the words on the lesson page with the class: *goat, road, soap, toast.* The students point to the dot underneath each sound as they say it.

Identifying the sounds: Look at the three pictures at the bottom of the lesson page and say the word for each one. The students listen and call out the sounds in each word. Then they write ‹oa› in the correct sound dot *[c-**oa**-t; b-**oa**-t; t-**oa**-d].*

Word bank: *oak, boat, coal, coat, foal, foam, goal, goat, load, loaf, moan, moat, oats, road, roam, soak, soap, toad, boast, cloak, coast, croak, float, groan, roast, toast, unload, raincoat; A toad croaks.* Use the word bank regularly to practice blending. It can also be used to do auditory segmenting: Say a word and then sound it out with the class, holding up a finger for each sound.

Dictation: Dictate the letter sounds /oa/, /j/, /ai/, /b/ and the words *coat, loaf, moan, soap*. Afterward, sound out each word for the students, writing the letters on the board so that they can check their work.

Developing accuracy and fluency: The students take home a sound book to read with their parents and bring back the next day.

Further ideas: Sing the /oa/ song from Jolly Songs. Read about different types of toads. Make paper boats and see if they float. Pin up the /oa/ section of the Wall Frieze.

Letter Sound /ie/

Flashcards: Review the letter sounds already taught: /s/, /a/, /t/, /i/, /p/, /n/, /c/, /k/, /e/, /h/, /r/, /m/, /d/, /g/, /o/, /u/, /l/, /f/, /b/, /ai/, /j/, /oa/.

Introducing the letter sound: Use a story such as the one below, along with the action.

Clive has been invited to a party. He needs to find a costume to wear, and he decides to go as a sailor. Clive's dad is in the navy, so he gives Clive a hat from his ship. His mother makes the rest of the outfit herself. Clive tries it on, and it is not too tight. It is just the right size. Just before the party, Clive's dad comes home on leave. Clive quite likes the idea of wearing his new outfit to meet him. He smiles and waves and gives his dad a big hug. His dad admires Clive's outfit and salutes him, saying, "ie-ie!" "Now you need to learn how to do that too," says Dad. When they get home, Clive practices his salute in front of the mirror. He stands to attention and says, "ie-ie!"

Action: The students pretend to be sailors and salute, saying *ie-ie*.

Letter formation: The sound /ie/ is written with two letters. When two letters make one sound it is called a digraph. Remind the class how both letters are formed. The students form the letters for the digraph in the air and then practice writing ‹ie›, ‹f›, ‹b›, ‹ai›, ‹j›, and ‹oa› in their books.

Blending: Blend the words on the lesson page with the class: *lie, tied, untie, magpie.* The students point to the dot underneath each sound as they say it.

Identifying the sounds: Look at the three pictures at the bottom of the lesson page and say the word for each one. The students listen and call out the sounds in each word. Then they write ‹ie› in the correct sound dot *[p-**ie**; t-**ie**; f-l-**ie**-s]*.

Word bank: *die, lie, pie, tie, died, lied, tied, cried, dried, fried, spied, tried, untie, magpie, untied, terrified; a fried egg.* Use the word bank regularly to practice blending. It can also be used to do auditory segmenting: Say a word and then sound it out with the class, holding up a finger for each sound.

Dictation: Dictate the letter sounds /ie/, /oa/, /j/, /ai/

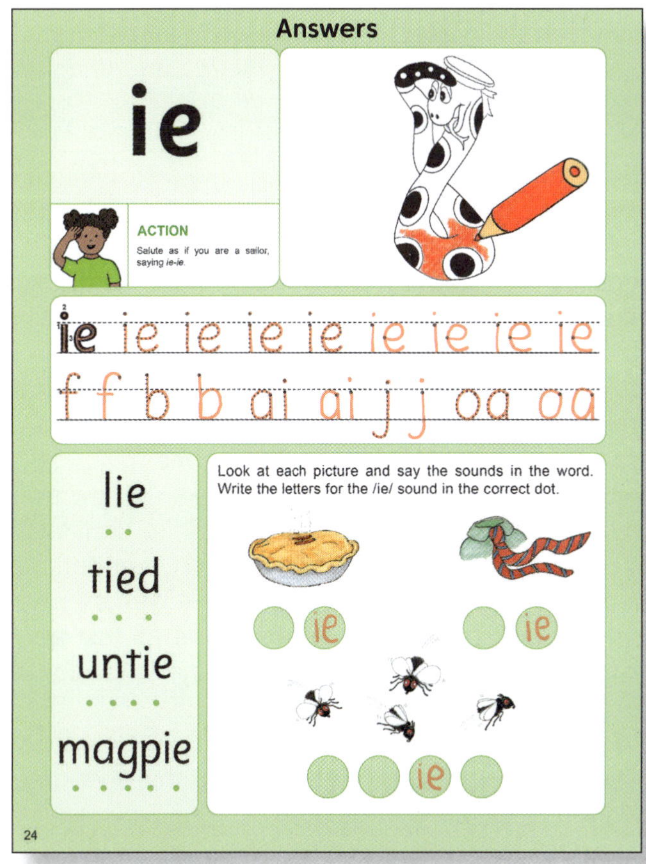

and the words *pie, tie, lie, die*. Afterward, sound out each word for the students, writing the letters on the board so that they can check their work.

Developing accuracy and fluency: The students take home a sound book to read with their parents and bring back the next day.

Further ideas: Sing the /ie/ song from Jolly Songs. Decorate cut-out paper ties. Create symmetrical butterflies (paint half the body and one wing, fold the paper over, rub, and unfold.) Pin up the /ie/ section of the Wall Frieze.

Letter Sounds /ee/ and /or/

Flashcards: Review the letter sounds already taught: /s/, /a/, /t/, /i/, /p/, /n/, /c/, /k/, /e/, /h/, /r/, /m/, /d/, /g/, /o/, /u/, /l/, /f/, /b/, /ai/, /j/, /oa/, /ie/.

Introducing the letter sounds: Use a story such as the one below, along with the action.

A donkey lives with a horse and some sheep next to a small cornfield. Nora, Jaycee, and Jakeem like to talk to the donkey, who is always pleased to see them. One August morning, the children go for a walk in the cornfield. The donkey brays, "ee-or!" and waggles his ears up and down in greeting. Nora gives him a carrot. "This comes from my garden," she says. "I grow sweet corn there too." As the children talk to the donkey, big raindrops begin to fall. Behind them is an enormous rain cloud. "We should get home quickly," says Jaycee. "A storm is coming. We'd better run home as fast as we can." The children run off, waving goodbye to the donkey.

Action: The students put their hands on their head like a donkey's ears and say *ee,* pointing their hands up, and then *or,* pointing them down.

Letter formation: The sounds /ee/ and /or/ are both written with two letters. When two letters make one sound it is called a digraph. Remind the class how the letters in each digraph are formed. The students form the letters for each digraph in the air and then practice writing them in their books.

Blending: Blend the words on the lesson page with the class: *bee, tree, sleep; corn, fork, storm.* The students point to the dot underneath each sound as they say it.

Identifying the sounds: Look at the four pictures at the bottom of the lesson page and say the word for each one. The students listen and call out the sounds in each word. Then they write ‹ee› or ‹or› in the correct sound dot *[th-r-**ee**; sh-**ee**-p; h-**or**-se; h-**or**-n].*

Word bank: ***/ee/*** *bee, eel, see, beef, been, deep, feed, feel, feet, free, heel, jeep, keen, keep, leek, meet, need, peek, peel, peep, reef, reel, seed, seek, seem, seen, tree, bleed, creek, creep, greed, green, greet, sleep, speed, steel, steep, coffee, settee, toffee, screen, street, indeed, canteen: a deep sleep;* ***/or/*** *or, for, born, cord, cork, corn, fork, form, fort, horn, lord, port, sort, torn, snort, sport, stork, storm, inform, foghorn, popcorn, portrait, landlord, platform; a fork in a road.* Use the word bank regularly to practice blending. It can also be used to do auditory segmenting: Say a word and then sound it out with the class, holding up a finger for each sound.

Dictation: Dictate the letter sounds /or/, /ee/, /ie/, /oa/ and the words *eel, bee, for, sort.* Afterward, sound out each word for the students, writing the letters on the board so that they can check their work.

Developing accuracy and fluency: The students take home a sound book to read with their parents and bring back the next day.

Further ideas: Sing the /ee or/ song from Jolly Songs. Create a collage of trees in a storm. Make seesaws from modeling clay. Pin up the /ee or/ section of the Wall Frieze.

Extra support: Remember to assess and identify any students who are struggling, and provide them with the extra support they need. See pages 29 to 33 for more information.

Letter Sound /z/

Flashcards: Review the letter sounds already taught: /s/, /a/, /t/, /i/, /p/, /n/, /c/, /k/, /e/, /h/, /r/, /m/, /d/, /g/, /o/, /u/, /l/, /f/, /b/, /ai/, /j/, /oa/, /ie/, /ee/, /or/.

Introducing the letter sound: Use a story such as the one below, along with the action.

Zara is playing outside with Zebedee, the zebra from her toy zoo. Suddenly, Zara hears a loud buzzing sound: "Zzzzzzz." She looks around and sees a big honeybee, buzzing around the flowers. The bee is collecting pollen to be made into honey back at the hive. Zara watches the bee as it buzzes from flower to flower, landing on each one and collecting the pollen. Then Zara stands up and runs around. She flaps her arms like the wings of the bee, saying, "Zzzzzz!" She stops by a gazania and bends down, pretending to collect the pollen from the flower. Then, "Zzzzzz," she buzzes, and off she goes to collect more pollen from the zinnias and daisies.

Action: The students put their arms out at their sides and flap them like a bee, making a continuous /zzzzzz/ sound.

Letter formation: Explain how the letter for /z/ is written. The students form the letter in the air and then practice writing ‹z›, ‹oa›, ‹ie›, ‹ee›, and ‹or› in their books. They write over the dotted letters and then try again, using the starting dots.

Blending: Blend the words on the lesson page with the class: *zap, buzz, fizz, unzip.* The students point to the dot underneath each sound as they say it.

Identifying the sounds: Show the students the four pictures at the bottom of the lesson page. Ask them to listen carefully, and say the word for each one. The students count the sounds in each word and color in the correct number of dots *[**2** z-oo; **6** z-i-g-z-a-g; **3** k-i-te; **3** m-a-ze]*. Then they listen for the word without the sound /z/ and cross out its picture *[kite]*.

Word bank: *zap, zip, zit, buzz, fizz, jazz, zest, unzip, zigzag; A bee buzzes.* Use the word bank regularly to practice blending. It can also be used to do auditory segmenting: Say a word and then sound it out with the class, holding up a finger for each sound.

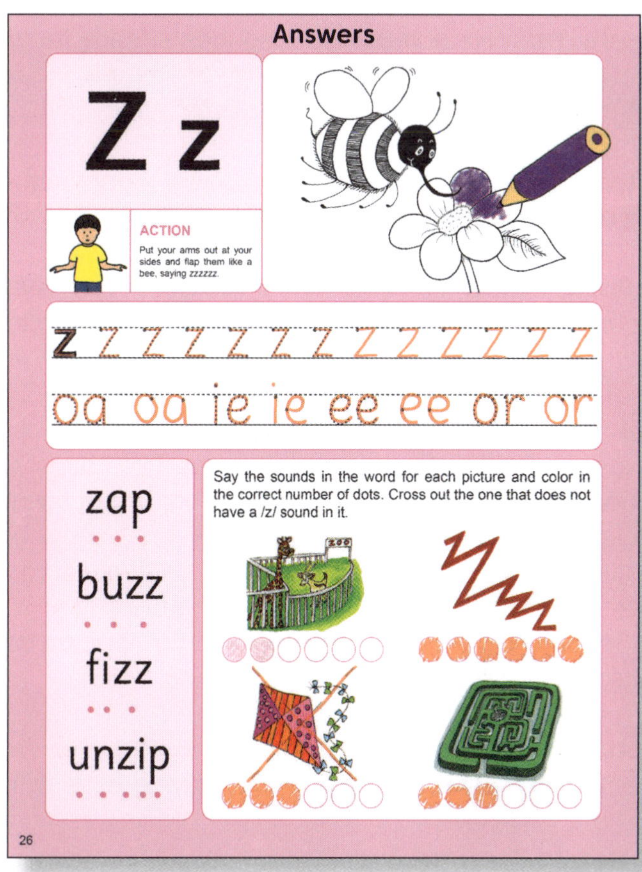

Dictation: Dictate the letter sounds /z/, /or/, /ee/, /ie/ and the words *zip, zest, zap, zit.* Afterward, sound out each word for the students, writing the letters on the board so that they can check their work.

Developing accuracy and fluency: The students take home a sound book to read with their parents and bring back the next day.

Further ideas:
Sing the /z/ song from Jolly Songs. Make a zoo with toy zebras and other animals. Paint yellow and black stripes on paper plates and add doily wings to make some bees. Pin up the /z/ section of the Wall Frieze.

Letter Sound /w/

Flashcards: Review the letter sounds already taught: /s/, /a/, /t/, /i/, /p/, /n/, /c/, /k/, /e/, /h/, /r/, /m/, /d/, /g/, /o/, /u/, /l/, /f/, /b/, /ai/, /j/, /oa/, /ie/, /ee/, /or/, /z/.

Introducing the letter sound: Use a story such as the one below, along with the action.

In Aesop's fable, the west wind and the sun are having an argument about who is the strongest. "You see that man down there?" the west wind says to the sun. "Well, I bet I can blow so hard that his coat comes off." The west wind blows and blows – "w, w, w, w," – but the man holds on tightly to his warm winter coat. The harder the wind blows, the tighter the man holds on. The sun waits patiently while the wind blows. "Now I will show you what I can do." As the sun starts to shine, the man gets warmer and unbuttons his collar. Then the sun shines so brightly that the man gets too hot in his coat and takes it off. "I win," says the sun, smiling sweetly.

Action: The students cup their hands and blow on them, as if they are being the wind, saying *w, w, w, w*.

Letter formation: Explain how the letter for /w/ is written. The students form the letter in the air and then practice writing ‹w›, ‹ie›, ‹ee›, ‹or›, and ‹z› in their books. They write over the dotted letters and then try again, using the starting dots.

Blending: Blend the words on the lesson page with the class: *web, twig, week, wind.* The students point to the dot underneath each sound as they say it.

Identifying the sounds: Show the students the four pictures at the bottom of the lesson page. Ask them to listen carefully, and say the word for each one. The students count the sounds in each word and color in the correct number of dots *[**3** w-e-ll; **4** s-w-a-n; **5** w-i-n-d-ow; **3** g-oa-t]*. Then they listen for the word without the sound /w/ and cross out its picture *[goat]*.

Word bank: *wag, web, wet, wig, win, well, wick, will, wail, wait, weed, week, weep, worn, swam, swim, swum, twig, twin, went, wept, west, wilt, wind, swell, sweep, sweet, tweet, waist, swept, swift, twist, unwell, cobweb, wigwam, wombat, weekend, windmill, sweetcorn; flies in a web.* Use the word bank regularly to practice blending. It can also be used to do auditory segmenting: Say a word and then sound it out with the class, holding up a finger for each sound.

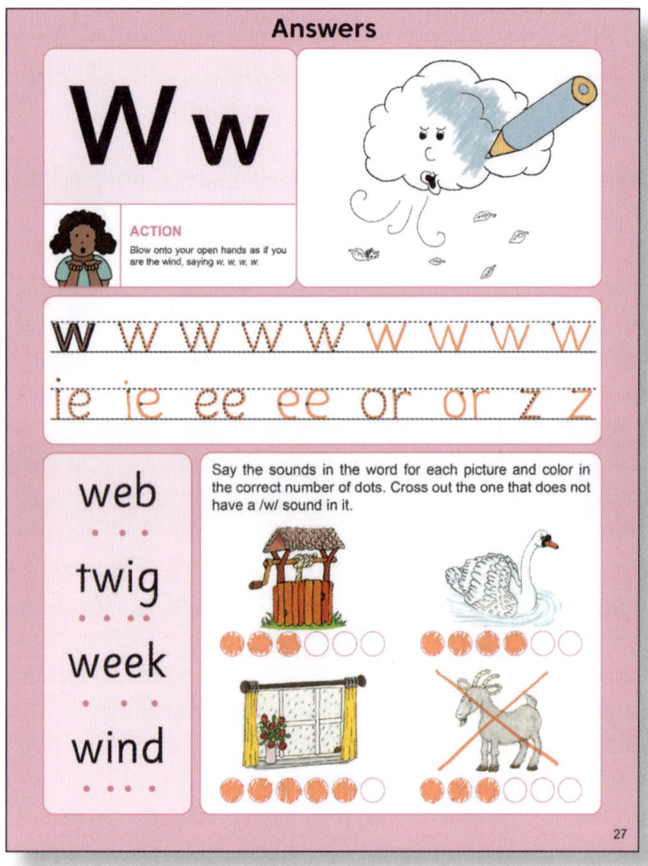

Dictation: Dictate the letter sounds /w/, /z/, /or/, /ee/ and the words *wag, win, wet, weep*. Afterward, sound out each word for the students, writing the letters on the board so that they can check their work.

Developing accuracy and fluency: The students take home a sound book to read with their parents and bring back the next day.

Further ideas: Sing the /w/ song from Jolly Songs. Make spiderwebs with wool. Draw pictures of a window and the view beyond. Pin up the /w/ section of the Wall Frieze.

Letter Sound /ng/

Flashcards: Review the letter sounds already taught: /s/, /a/, /t/, /i/, /p/, /n/, /c/, /k/, /e/, /h/, /r/, /m/, /d/, /g/, /o/, /u/, /l/, /f/, /b/, /ai/, /j/, /oa/, /ie/, /ee/, /or/, /z/, /w/.

Introducing the letter sound: Use a story such as the one below, along with the action.

It is Saturday morning, and Bing has come to play at Mark's house. They spend a long time playing ping-pong, hitting the ball to each other with their bats. Then they play with their racing cars. "Let's see what's on TV," says Mark. "There might be some motor racing." They turn on the television and see a big man, lifting some huge weights. "Look at him!" says Bing. "He must be a weightlifter." The man grunts as he lifts the heavy weights: "ngngng!" "I wish I was that strong," says Bing. "I know," says Mark, "let's be weightlifters." Using a broom and a mop, they pretend to lift some heavy weights; "ngngng," they grunt, just like the weightlifter.

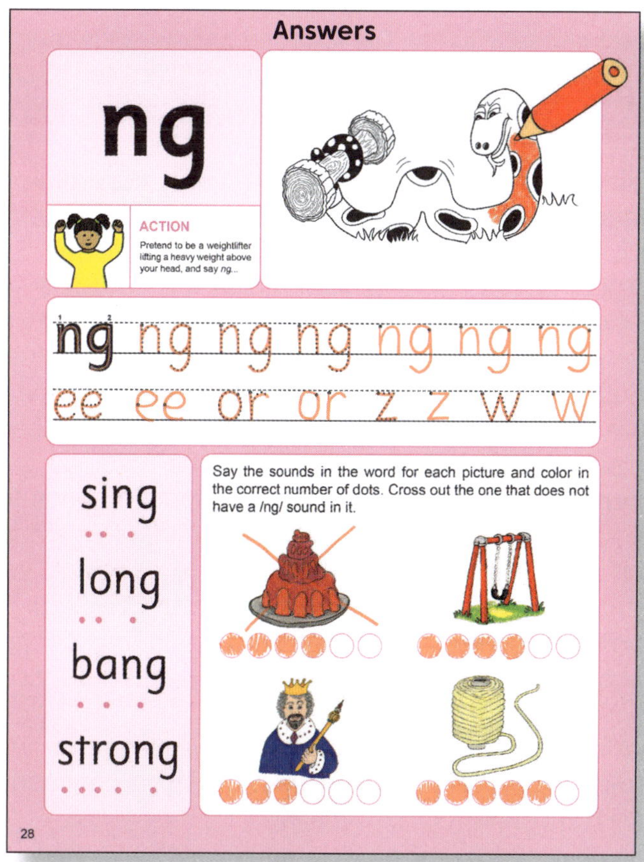

Action: The students pretend to lift a heavy weight above their head and say *ng...*

Letter formation: The sound /ng/ is written with two letters. When two letters make one sound it is called a digraph. Remind the class how both letters are formed. The students form the letters for the digraph in the air and then practice writing ‹ng›, ‹ee›, ‹or›, ‹z›, and ‹w› in their books.

Blending: Blend the words on the lesson page with the class: *sing, long, bang, strong.* The students point to the dot underneath each sound as they say it.

Identifying the sounds: Show the students the four pictures at the bottom of the lesson page. Ask them to listen carefully, and say the word for each one. The students count the sounds in each word and color in the correct number of dots *[**4** j-e-ll-o; **4** s-w-i-ng; **3** k-i-ng; **5** s-t-r-i-ng]*. Then they listen for the word without the sound /ng/ and cross out its picture *[jello]*.

Word bank: *bang, gang, gong, hang, hung, king, long, lung, rang, ring, rung, sang, sing, song, sung, wing, zing, bring, clang, cling, clung, fling, flung, sling, sting, stung, swing, swung, seeing, oblong, sprang, spring, string, strong, buzzing, running, sitting, wedding, willing, feeling, meeting, morning, railing, soaking, weeping, jumping, landing, spelling, swelling, ding-dong, freezing, painting, ping-pong, sleeping, speeding, training, smuggling; a freezing morning.* Use the word bank regularly to practice blending. It can also be used to do auditory segmenting: Say a word and then sound it out with the class, holding up a finger for each sound.

Dictation: Dictate the letter sounds /ng/, /w/, /z/, /or/ and the words *hang, wing, song, lung.* Afterward, sound out each word for the students, writing the letters on the board so that they can check their work.

Developing accuracy and fluency: The students take home a sound book to read with their parents and bring back the next day.

Further ideas: Sing the /ng/ song from Jolly Songs. Play a game of ping-pong. Make pictures of things using string. Pin up the /ng/ section of the Wall Frieze.

Letter Sound /v/

Flashcards: Review the letter sounds already taught: /s/, /a/, /t/, /i/, /p/, /n/, /c/, /k/, /e/, /h/, /r/, /m/, /d/, /g/, /o/, /u/, /l/, /f/, /b/, /ai/, /j/, /oa/, /ie/, /ee/, /or/, /z/, /w/, /ng/.

Introducing the letter sound: Use a story such as the one below, along with the action.

Zack and Jess are helping Uncle Vic to make his deliveries. They sit in the back of the van as Vic drives through the village, waving to his friends. "We have a lot to do today," says Uncle Vic. "First, we need to collect an order from Val's Fruit and Veg. He stops outside the door and loads the boxes onto the van. Then they are off again. "Vvvvvv...VROOM," goes the van as they zoom along. Next, Uncle Vic delivers the fruit and vegetables to old Mrs. Vernon. They are busy with the deliveries all day, but eventually it is time for Zack and Jess to go home. "Come and visit us very soon!" they call, as they wave goodbye to Uncle Vic.

Action: The students pretend to be driving a van, turning the steering wheel and making a continuous /vvvvvv/ sound.

Letter formation: Explain how the letter for /v/ is written. The students form the letter in the air and then practice writing ‹v›, ‹or›, ‹z›, ‹w›, and ‹ng› in their books. They write over the dotted letters and then try again, using the starting dots.

Blending: Blend the words on the lesson page with the class: *vet, van, vest, seven.* The students point to the dot underneath each sound as they say it.

Identifying the sounds: Show the students the four pictures at the bottom of the lesson page. Ask them to listen carefully, and say the word for each one. The students count the sounds in each word and color in the correct number of dots *[**3** v-a-se; **2** b-ee; **4** g-l-o-ve; **3** f-i-ve]*. Then they listen for the word without the sound /v/ and cross out its picture *[bee]*.

Word bank: *van, vat, vet, vain, vent, vest, seven, livid, vivid, vomit, advent, invent, invest, victim; a man in a van.* Use the word bank regularly to practice blending. It can also be used to do auditory segmenting: Say a word and then sound it out with the class, holding up a finger for each sound.

Dictation: Dictate the letter sounds /v/, /ng/, /w/, /z/ and the words *vat, vet, van, vain.* Afterward, sound out each word for the students, writing the letters on the board so that they can check their work.

Developing accuracy and fluency: The students take home a sound book to read with their parents and bring back the next day.

Further ideas: Sing the /v/ song from Jolly Songs. Set up a vet's surgery for toy animals. Wrap up parcels for Uncle Vic to deliver. Pin up the /v/ section of the Wall Frieze.

Letter Sounds /oo/ and /oo/

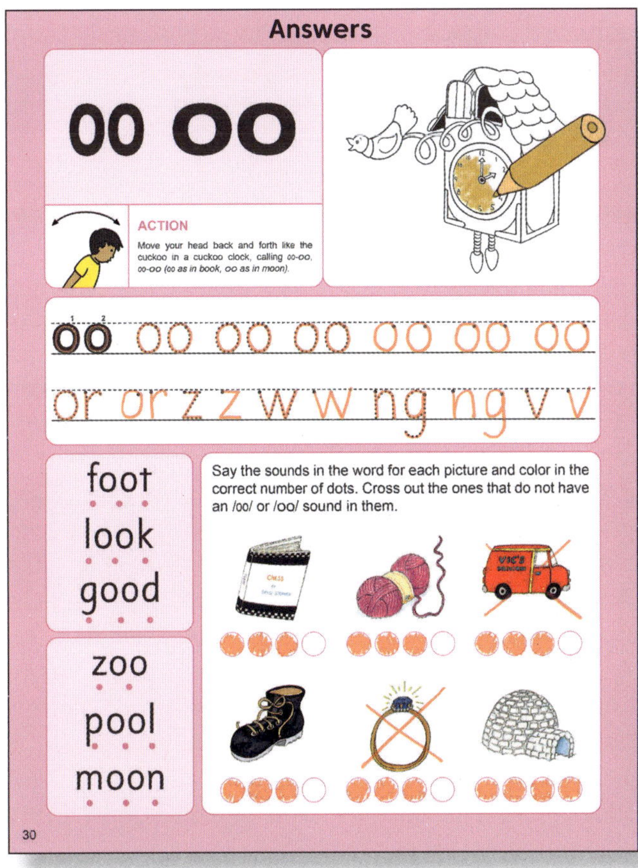

Flashcards: Review the letter sounds already taught: /s/, /a/, /t/, /i/, /p/, /n/, /c/, /k/, /e/, /h/, /r/, /m/, /d/, /g/, /o/, /u/, /l/, /f/, /b/, /ai/, /j/, /oa/, /ie/, /ee/, /or/, /z/, /w/, /ng/, /v/.

Introducing the letter sounds: Use a story such as the one below, along with the action.

Oona is visiting Great Aunt Ivy in her big house in the woods. Oona likes visiting Great Aunt Ivy because she has lots of interesting things and a large friendly cat called Noodle. The thing Oona likes best is Great Aunt Ivy's cuckoo clock. It hangs on the wall and has a little wooden door in the roof. On the hour, the door opens, and a red, blue, and yellow cuckoo pops out, calling, "oo-oo, oo-oo." Noodle and Oona like to wait by the clock at the foot of the stairs, knowing that the cuckoo will come out soon. As the little bird goes in and out, Oona pretends to be the cuckoo. She moves her head back and forth, calling out, "oo-oo, oo-oo!"

Action: The students pretend to be the cuckoo in the clock, moving their heads back and forth, saying *oo-oo, oo-oo*.

Letter formation: Remind the students how the letter ‹o› is formed and explain how to write the digraph ‹oo›. Point out that one size of writing is used for both sounds. The students form the letters for the digraph in the air and then practice writing ‹oo›, ‹or›, ‹z›, ‹w›, ‹ng›, and ‹v› in their books.

Blending: Blend the words on the lesson page with the class: */oo/ foot, look, good; /oo/ zoo, pool, moon.* The students point to the dot underneath each sound as they say it.

Identifying the sounds: Show the students the six pictures at the bottom of the lesson page. Ask them to listen carefully, and say the word for each one. The students count the sounds in each word and color in the correct number of dots *[**3** b-oo-k; **3** w-oo-l; **3** v-a-n; **3** b-oo-t; **3** r-i-ng; **4** i-g-l-oo]*. Then they listen for the words without /oo/ or /oo/ and cross out the pictures *[van/ring]*.

Word bank: ***/oo/*** *book, cook, foot, good, hood, hook, look, rook, soot, took, wood, woof, wool, brook, crook, stood, scrapbook, footsteps; a good cook;* ***/oo/*** *boo, moo, too, zoo, boom, boot, cool, food, hoof, hoop, hoot, loop, mood, moon, noon, pool, roof, room, root, soon, tool, toot, zoom, bloom, broom, droop, gloom, igloo, proof, roost, scoop, spook, spoon, stool, stoop, swoop, tattoo, bedroom, cloakroom, broomstick; Sit on a stool.* Use the word bank regularly to practice blending. It can also be used to do auditory segmenting: Say a word and then sound it out with the class, holding up a finger for each sound.

Dictation: Dictate the letter sounds /oo/, /oo/, /v/, /ng/ and the words *wood, foot, zoom, hoop*. Afterward, sound out each word for the students, writing the letters on the board so that they can check their work.

Developing accuracy and fluency: The students take home a sound book to read with their parents and bring back the next day.

Further ideas: Sing the /oo oo/ song from Jolly Songs. Make a model cuckoo clock. Look at books about the moon. Pin up the /oo oo/ section of the Wall Frieze.

Extra support: Remember to assess and identify any students who are struggling, and provide them with the extra support they need. See pages 29 to 33.

Letter Sound /y/

Flashcards: Review the letter sounds already taught: /s/, /a/, /t/, /i/, /p/, /n/, /c/, /k/, /e/, /h/, /r/, /m/, /d/, /g/, /o/, /u/, /l/, /f/, /b/, /ai/, /j/, /oa/, /ie/, /ee/, /or/, /z/, /w/, /ng/, /v/, /oo/, /oo/.

Introducing the letter sound: Use a story such as the one below, along with the action.

It is lunchtime at school and Yasmin, Ron, and Yamal are having something to eat. Yamal eats his food quickly, so that he can play with his yo-yo. Yasmin and Ron sit at the table and look in their lunch boxes. Yasmin has a cheese and tomato sandwich, a red apple, and a pot of yogurt. Ron has some fried yam, a hard-boiled egg, and a carton of fruit juice. "That yogurt looks good," says Ron. "Yes, it is," says Yasmin. "It's a yellow banana yogurt. I chose it yesterday when I went shopping with my younger sister. I love yellow." "May I try some, please?" asks Ron. "Yes," says Yasmin. "Mmmm, it's nice," says Ron. "A y...y...y...yummy, yellow yogurt!"

Action: The students pretend to eat yogurt from a spoon and say *y, y, y, y*.

Letter formation: Explain how the letter for /y/ is written, pointing out that it has a tail that goes down under the line. The students form the letter in the air and then practice writing ‹y›, ‹z›, ‹w›, ‹ng›, ‹v›, and ‹oo› in their books. They write over the dotted letters and then try again, using the starting dots.

Blending: Blend the words on the lesson page with the class: *yes, yak, yell, yelp.* The students point to the dot underneath each sound as they say it.

Identifying the sounds: Show the students the four pictures at the bottom of the lesson page. Ask them to listen carefully, and say the word for each one. The students count the sounds in each word, color in the correct number of dots, and write ‹y› in the correct sound dot(s) *[**3 y**-ol-k; **4 y**-o-**y**-o; **3 y**-a-k; **4 y**-e-ll-ow].*

Word bank: *yak, yam, yap, yen, yes, yet, yum, yell, yuck, yelp; a big yelp.* Use the word bank regularly to practice blending. It can also be used to do auditory segmenting: Say a word and then sound it out with the class, holding up a finger for each sound.

Dictation: Dictate the letter sounds /y/, /oo/, /oo/, /v/ and the words *yam, yet, yum, yen*. Afterward, sound out each word for the students, writing the letters on the board so that they can check their work.

Developing accuracy and fluency: The students take home a sound book to read with their parents and bring back the next day. If available, start using the Jolly Phonics Little Word Books with students who can independently blend simple regular words.

Further ideas: Sing the /y/ song from Jolly Songs. Paint pictures of something yellow. Make a yak collage using wool. Pin up the /y/ section of the Wall Frieze.

Letter Sound /x/

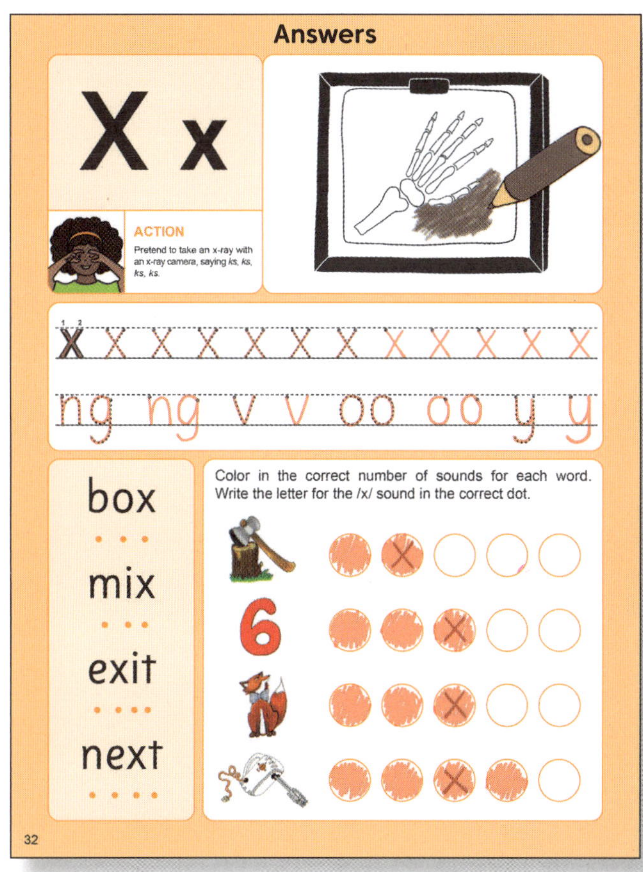

Flashcards: Review the letter sounds already taught: /s/, /a/, /t/, /i/, /p/, /n/, /c/, /k/, /e/, /h/, /r/, /m/, /d/, /g/, /o/, /u/, /l/, /f/, /b/, /ai/, /j/, /oa/, /ie/, /ee/, /or/, /z/, /w/, /ng/, /v/, /oo/, /oo/, /y/.

Introducing the letter sound: (Which is really two sounds blended together: /ks/.) Use a story such as the one below, along with the action.

Max and Ti are at the hospital. They were playing astronauts and aliens when Ti fell out of a tree and hurt his arm. Ti has to keep the arm very still while some x-rays are taken: "ks, ks, ks, ks." The x-rays show that Ti's arm is broken. Ti sits down, while the nurse puts a plaster cast on his arm. "Try to relax," she says. "It won't take long." "Can you fix my arm?" he asks. "Don't worry, this will keep the broken bone in place," the nurse explains. "That means it will mend properly. I expect it to be as good as new, very soon." Ti smiles and looks relieved. Max is watching from the doorway. He pretends to take an x-ray with his camera: "ks, ks, ks, ks."

Action: The students pretend to take an x-ray with an x-ray camera and say *x, x, x, x*.

Letter formation: Explain how the letter for /x/ is written. The students form the letter in the air and then practice writing ‹x›, ‹ng›, ‹v›, ‹oo›, and ‹y› in their books. They write over the dotted letters and then try again, using the starting dots.

Blending: Blend the words on the lesson page with the class: *box, mix, exit, next.* The students point to the dot underneath each sound as they say it.

Identifying the sounds: Show the students the four pictures at the bottom of the lesson page. Ask them to listen carefully, and say the word for each one. The students count the sounds in each word, color in the correct number of dots, and write ‹x› in the correct sound dot *[**2** a-**x**e; **3** s-i-**x**; **3** f-o-**x**; **4** m-i-**x**-er].*

Word bank: *ox, box, fax, fix, fox, mix, sax, six, tax, wax, coax, hoax, exit, flex, next, text, index, boxing, sixteen, toolbox, paintbox, textbook; A red fox sits in a box.* Use the word bank regularly to practice blending. It can also be used to do auditory segmenting: Say a word and then sound it out with the class, holding up a finger for each sound.

Dictation: Dictate the letter sounds /x/, /y/, /oo/, /oo/ and the words *fox, six, wax, next.* Afterward, sound out each word for the students, writing the letters on the board so that they can check their work.

Developing accuracy and fluency: The students take home a sound book to read with their parents and bring back the next day. If available, start using the Jolly Phonics Little Word Books with students who can independently blend simple regular words.

Further ideas: Sing the /x/ song from Jolly Songs. Look at pictures of skeletons and x-rays. Make x-ray pictures with white straws and black paper. Pin up the /x/ section of the Wall Frieze.

Letter Sound /ch/

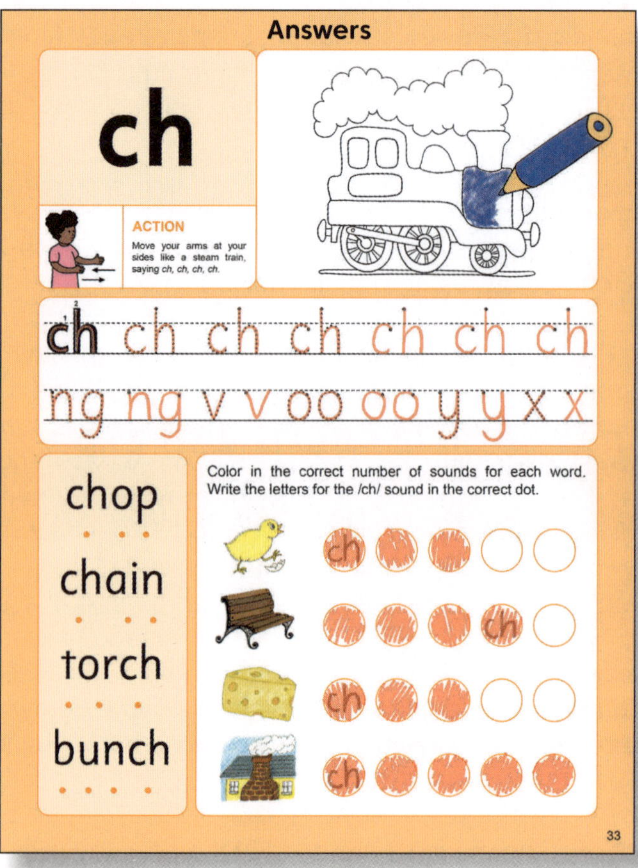

Flashcards: Review the letter sounds already taught: /s/, /a/, /t/, /i/, /p/, /n/, /c/, /k/, /e/, /h/, /r/, /m/, /d/, /g/, /o/, /u/, /l/, /f/, /b/, /ai/, /j/, /oa/, /ie/, /ee/, /or/, /z/, /w/, /ng/, /v/, /oo/, /oo/, /y/, /x/.

Introducing the letter sound: Use a story such as the one below, along with the action.

The students in Charlie's class are visiting a transport museum. They have cheese or chicken sandwiches for lunch. Then their teacher tells them that they will be having a ride in an old steam train. They are very excited. They wait on the platform, chatting to each other about how much fun they are going to have. Then it is time to climb aboard. The train starts chugging slowly: "ch, ch, ch, ch." Then it starts to go faster, chuffing loudly: "ch, ch, ch, ch!" It gets faster and faster until steam comes out of the funnel and the whistle blows, "Choo-choo!" At school the next day, the students pretend to be trains. They chuff around saying, "Ch…ch…ch…choo-choo!"

Action: The students move their arms at their sides like a steam train and say *ch, ch, ch, ch*.

Letter formation: The sound /ch/ is written with two letters. When two letters make one sound it is called a digraph. Remind the class how both letters are formed. The students form the letters for the digraph in the air and then practice writing ‹ch›, ‹ng›, ‹v›, ‹oo›, ‹y›, and ‹x› in their books.

Blending: Blend the words on the lesson page with the class: *chop, chain, torch, bunch.* The students point to the dot underneath each sound as they say it.

Identifying the sounds: Show the students the four pictures at the bottom of the lesson page. Ask them to listen carefully, and say the word for each one. The students count the sounds in each word, color in the correct number of dots, and write ‹ch› in the correct sound dot *[**3 ch**-i-ck; **4** b-e-n-**ch**; **3 ch**-ee-se; **5 ch**-i-m-n-ey].*

Word bank: *chat, chin, chip, chop, chug, inch, much, rich, such, check, chess, chick, chill, chain, cheek, coach, poach, porch, torch, bench, bunch, chest, chimp, chomp, finch, hunch, lunch, munch, pinch, punch, speech, crunch, drench, trench, screech, ostrich, cockroach, chopsticks, chimpanzee; an ostrich in a zoo.* Use the word bank regularly to practice blending. It can also be used to do auditory segmenting: Say a word and then sound it out with the class, holding up a finger for each sound.

Dictation: Dictate the letter sounds /ch/, /x/, /y/, /oo/ and the words *chin, chat, much, coach*. Afterward, sound out each word for the students, writing the letters on the board so that they can check their work.

Developing accuracy and fluency: The students take home a sound book to read with their parents and bring back the next day. If available, start using the Jolly Phonics Little Word Books with students who can independently blend simple regular words.

Further ideas: Sing the /ch/ song from Jolly Songs. Make paper-chain decorations. Form a line and chuff around like a steam train, saying, *Ch, ch, ch! Choo, choo!* Pin up the /ch/ section of the Wall Frieze.

Letter Sound /sh/

Flashcards: Review the letter sounds already taught: /s/, /a/, /t/, /i/, /p/, /n/, /c/, /k/, /e/, /h/, /r/, /m/, /d/, /g/, /o/, /u/, /l/, /f/, /b/, /ai/, /j/, /oa/, /ie/, /ee/, /or/, /z/, /w/, /ng/, /v/, /oo/, /oo/, /y/, /x/, /ch/.

Introducing the letter sound: Use a story such as the one below, along with the action.

Mrs. Shaw has just had a baby. The baby's name is Shannon. Shannon has an older brother, Sam. Sam loves his baby sister, but he wishes she would stop crying. While his mother tries to get Shannon to sleep, Sam wonders what to do. He thinks about tidying away his shoes and shorts or playing with his toy ship. Instead, he sits down and plays with his cash register. He opens and shuts the drawer, putting money in and then taking it out. Every time it opens, the drawer goes TING! "Shshshsh," whispers Mrs. Shaw, putting her finger to her lips. "Shannon is nearly asleep. Let's go downstairs for a while." Sam agrees, saying, "Shshshsh," as they tiptoe quietly away.

Action: The students place their index finger against their lips and make a continuous /shshshsh/ sound.

Letter formation: The sound /sh/ is written with two letters. When two letters make one sound it is called a digraph. Remind the class how both letters are formed. The students form the letters for the digraph in the air and then practice writing ‹sh›, ‹v›, ‹oo›, ‹y›, ‹x›, and ‹ch› in their books.

Blending: Blend the words on the lesson page with the class: *dish, shop, sheep, brush.* The students point to the dot underneath each sound as they say it.

Identifying the sounds: Show the students the four pictures at the bottom of the lesson page. Ask them to listen carefully, and say the word for each one. The students count the sounds in each word, color in the correct number of dots, and write ‹sh› in the correct sound dot *[**2 sh**-oe; **3 sh**-e-ll; **3** f-i-**sh**; **6** m-u-**sh**-r-oo-m].*

Word bank: *ash, bash, cash, dash, dish, fish, hush, mash, posh, rash, rush, shed, shin, ship, shop, shot, shut, wish, shall, shell, shock, sheep, sheet, shook, shoot, short, blush, brush, crash, crush, flash, flush, fresh, shelf, shift, shred, shrug, slush, smash, shrill, finish, polish, punish, shrimp, splash, vanish, eggshell, shampoo, shopping, selfish, shellfish, mushroom, paintbrush; sixteen books on a shelf.* Use the word bank regularly to practice blending and auditory segmenting.

Dictation: Dictate the letter sounds /sh/, /ch/, /x/, /y/ and the words *rash, shed, wish, sheet.* Afterward, sound out each word for the students, writing the letters on the board so that they can check their work.

Tricky word "I": Explain that this is tricky because instead of being written as it sounds, it uses its letter name and, being very shy, it puffs itself up into its capital letter. Ask the students to underline the word in purple to show the tricky part. Pin up the Tricky Word Wall Flower.

Developing accuracy and fluency: The students take home a sound book to read with their parents and bring back the next day. If available, start using the Jolly Phonics Little Word Books with students who can independently blend simple regular words.

Further ideas: Use the Jolly Song and Wall Frieze section for /sh/. Make sheep with cotton ball fleeces or a shaker with two yogurt pots and some uncooked rice.

Letter Sounds /th/ and /th/

Flashcards: Review the tricky word *I* and the letter sounds already taught: /s/, /a/, /t/, /i/, /p/, /n/, /c/, /k/, /e/, /h/, /r/, /m/, /d/, /g/, /o/, /u/, /l/, /f/, /b/, /ai/, /j/, /oa/, /ie/, /ee/, /or/, /z/, /w/, /ng/, /v/, /oo/, /oo/, /y/, /x/, /ch/, /sh/.

Introducing the letter sounds: Use a story such as the one below, along with the action.

Matthew and Nathan are having a great time at the circus. It opens with the ringmaster, who thanks everyone for coming and introduces the acts. Then a juggler entertains the crowd, throwing three rings high into the air. Now, two naughty clowns are running around the ring. First, they throw water at the ringmaster, who tells them both off. Then they chase one another back and forth, tickling each other with feathers. The crowd thinks this is very funny. The thin clown is rather rude. He sticks the tip of his tongue out and says, "th!" The other clown is very rude. He sticks his tongue out much further, saying "thththth!" Everyone laughs and claps.

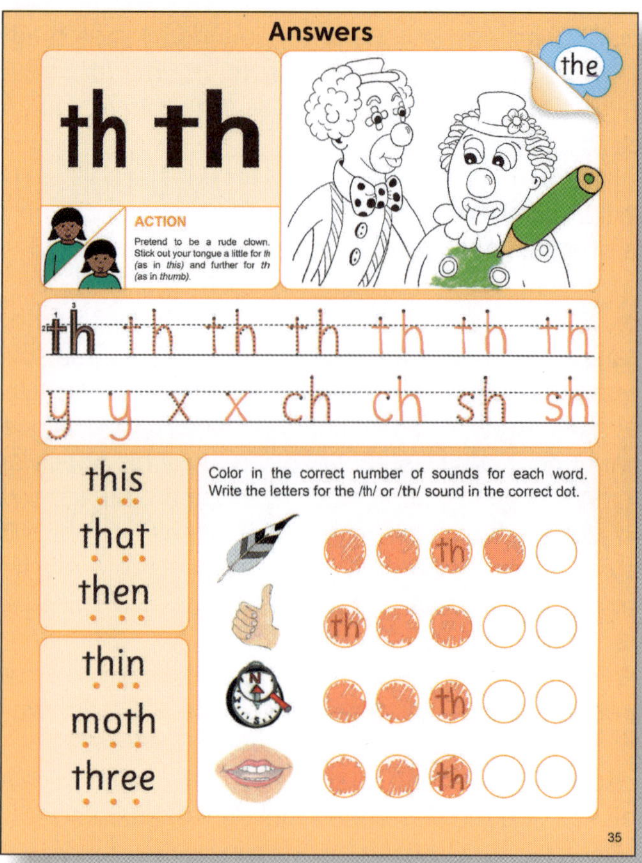

Action: The students act like rude clowns, sticking out their tongues a little for /th/ and further for /th/.

Letter formation: Explain how to write the digraph ‹th›, pointing out that one size of writing is used for both sounds. Remind the class how both letters are formed. The students form the letters for the digraph in the air and then practice writing them in their books.

Blending: Blend the words on the lesson page with the class: */th/ this, that, then; /th/ thin, moth, three.* The students point to the dot underneath each sound as they say it.

Identifying the sounds: Show the students the four pictures at the bottom of the lesson page. Ask them to listen carefully, and say the word for each one. The students count the sounds in each word, color in the correct number of dots, and write ‹th› in the correct sound dot *[4 f-ea-**th**-er; 3 **th**-u-mb; 3 n-or-**th**; 3 m-ou-**th**].*

Word bank: */th/ than, that, them, then, this, with, smooth, within; a goat with big horns; /**th**/ moth, thin, thud, thick, faith, north, teeth, thing, thorn, three, tooth, broth, cloth, froth, sixth, tenth, theft, throb, thump, thrill, length, throat, thrush, strength, toothbrush; thick socks for boots.*

Dictation: Dictate the letter sounds /th/, /th/, /sh/, /ch/ and the words *than, with, tooth, thud.* Afterward, sound out each word for the students, writing the letters on the board so that they can check their work.

Tricky word "the": This is tricky because although the ‹th› is written as it sounds, the class must remember to write an ‹e› on the end. Work this out with the students and ask them to underline the tricky part in purple. Pin up the Tricky Word Wall Flower.

Developing accuracy and fluency: The students take home a sound book to read with their parents and bring back the next day. If available, start using the Jolly Phonics Little Word Books with students who can independently blend simple regular words.

Further ideas: Use the Jolly Song and Wall Frieze section for /th/ and /th/. Make pictures decorated with feathers. Find out about different types of moths.

Extra support: Remember to assess and identify any students who are struggling, and provide them with the extra support they need. See pages 29 to 33.

Letter Sound /qu/

Flashcards: Review the tricky words *I, the* and the letter sounds already taught: /s/, /a/, /t/, /i/, /p/, /n/, /c/, /k/, /e/, /h/, /r/, /m/, /d/, /g/, /o/, /u/, /l/, /f/, /b/, /ai/, /j/, /oa/, /ie/, /ee/, /or/, /z/, /w/, /ng/, /v/, /oo/, /oo/, /y/, /x/, /ch/, /sh/, /th/, /th/.

Introducing the letter sound: (Which is really two sounds blended together: /kw/.) Use a story such as the one below, along with the action.

Quentin goes to the park with his family quite a lot. They like to take a quilt and have a picnic down by the pond. They always bring some stale bread for the ducks and squirrels. When the squirrels see Quentin with the bread, they scamper over quickly and quietly. Two squirrels grab the same slice. They begin to quarrel, squeaking at each other and tugging at the bread. Quentin laughs and throws some pieces of bread into the pond for the ducks. The ducks see the bread and rush to the side of the pond, quacking loudly, "qu, qu, qu, qu!" Quentin greets the ducks, pretending that he is a duck too. He opens and shuts his hands like a beak, going, "qu, qu, qu, qu."

Action: The students open and close their hands like a duck's beak and say *qu, qu, qu, qu*.

Letter formation: The sound /qu/ is written with two letters. When two letters make one sound it is called a digraph. Remind the class how both letters are formed. The students form the letters for the digraph in the air and then practice writing ‹qu›, ‹x›, ‹ch›, ‹sh›, and ‹th› in their books.

Blending: Blend the words on the lesson page with the class: *quiz, squid, quack, squirrel.* The students point to the dot underneath each sound as they say it.

Identifying the sounds: The students look at the three pictures at the bottom of the lesson page and say the sounds in each word. Then they write ‹qu› in the correct sound dot for the first two words and write all the sounds for the third *[s-**qu**-i-d; **qu**-i-l-t; **qu-ee-n**]*.

Word bank: *quin, quit, quiz, quack, quick, quill, quail queen, quench, quest, quilt, squid, liquid, squint, quacking, quicksand; three quacking ducks; She will win the quiz.* Use the word bank regularly to practice blending and auditory segmenting.

Dictation: Dictate the letter sounds /qu/, /th/, /th/, /sh/ and the words *quit, quail, quin, quest*. Afterward, sound out each word for the students, writing the letters on the board so that they can check their work.

Tricky words "he" and "she": These are tricky because although the ‹h› in *he* and ‹sh› in *she* are written as they sound, the sound /ee/ in both words is written with only one ‹e›. Work this out with the students and ask them to underline the tricky parts in purple. Pin up the Tricky Word Wall Flowers.

Developing accuracy and fluency: The students take home a sound book to read with their parents and bring back the next day. If available, start using the Jolly Phonics Little Word Books with students who can independently blend simple regular words.

Further ideas: Use the Jolly Song and Wall Frieze section for /qu/. Draw ducks quacking or squirrels quarreling. Make a squirrel collage, using wool for the tails.

Letter Sound /ou/

Flashcards: Review the tricky words *I, the, he, she* and the letter sounds already taught: /s/, /a/, /t/, /i/, /p/, /n/, /c/, /k/, /e/, /h/, /r/, /m/, /d/, /g/, /o/, /u/, /l/, /f/, /b/, /ai/, /j/, /oa/, /ie/, /ee/, /or/, /z/, /w/, /ng/, /v/, /oo/, /oo/, /y/, /x/, /ch/, /sh/, /th/, /th/, /qu/.

Introducing the letter sound: Use a story such as the one below, along with the action.

Emily is staying at Granny's house. Her granny likes to sew and is very proud of the things she has made. Now Granny has promised to show Emily how to sew too. Emily wants to make a present for her parents. On the wall is a picture of a brown owl. Emily thinks she could sew something like that. "That sounds like a good idea," says Granny. "You could make a little round mat." They sit down on the couch and get out the sewing basket. Granny gives Emily a piece of cloth and threads two needles, one with brown thread and the other with black. Emily does a few stitches. Suddenly, she frowns and shouts, "ou!" She has pricked her thumb with the needle!

Action: The students pretend that their finger is a needle and use it to prick their thumb, saying *ou!*

Letter formation: The sound /ou/ is written with two letters. When two letters make one sound it is called a digraph. Remind the class how both letters are formed. The students form the letters for the digraph in the air and then practice writing ‹ou›, ‹ch›, ‹sh›, ‹th›, and ‹qu› in their books.

Blending: Blend the words on the lesson page with the class: *out, loud, shout, mouth.* The students point to the dot underneath each sound as they say it.

Identifying the sounds: The students look at the three pictures at the bottom of the lesson page and say the sounds in each word. Then they write ‹ou› in the correct sound dot for the first two words and write all the sounds for the third *[h-**ou**-se; m-**ou**-se; **c-l-ou-d**].*

Word bank: *out, ouch, loud, noun, couch, mouth, pouch, shout, south, cloud, count, found, hound, joust, pound, proud, round, scout, snout, sound, spout, stout, trout, wound, crouch, outing, slouch, ground, outfit, sprout, without, background; big black rain clouds; We found the missing ring.* Use the word bank regularly to practice blending and auditory segmenting.

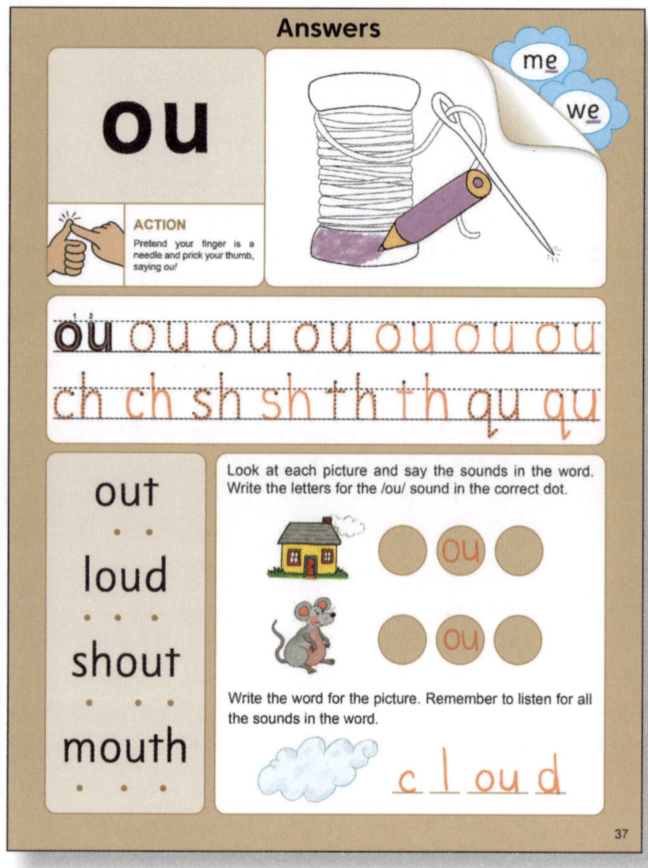

Dictation: Dictate the letter sounds /ou/, /qu/, /th/, /th/ and the words *south, couch, found, joust*. Afterward, sound out each word for the students, writing the letters on the board so that they can check their work.

Tricky words "me" and "we": These are tricky because although the ‹m› in *me* and ‹w› in *we* are written as they sound, the /ee/ in both words is written with only one ‹e›. Work this out with the students and ask them to underline the tricky parts in purple. Pin up the Tricky Word Wall Flowers.

Developing accuracy and fluency: The students take home a sound book to read with their parents and bring back the next day. If available, start using the Jolly Phonics Little Word Books with students who can independently blend simple regular words.

Further ideas: Use the Jolly Song and Wall Frieze section for /ou/. Make pictures of houses, using card and colored laces. Create mobiles of cut-out clouds decorated with cotton balls or black paint.

Letter Sound /oi/

Flashcards: Review the tricky words *I, the, he, she, me, we* and the letter sounds already taught: /s/, /a/, /t/, /i/, /p/, /n/, /c/, /k/, /e/, /h/, /r/, /m/, /d/, /g/, /o/, /u/, /l/, /f/, /b/, /ai/, /j/, /oa/, /ie/, /ee/, /or/, /z/, /w/, /ng/, /v/, /oo/, /oo/, /y/, /x/, /ch/, /sh/, /th/, /th/, /qu/, /ou/.

Introducing the letter sound: Use a story such as the one below, along with the action.

Roy's dad has a little boat called Sailor Boy. Early one morning, Roy joins his dad and Uncle Martin for a trip out to sea. They pack their things, climb aboard, and set off. Dad says, "I hope you haven't brought too many toys, Roy." They sail up the coast and are really enjoying themselves when, BANG! There is a loud noise as they hit something in the water. "Look!" says Dad, pointing. "We've hit an oil drum and it's made a hole. We won't get back to shore without some help." Just then, they see a much bigger boat nearby: "Oi! Ship ahoy!" they cry. The sailors hear their voices and come to the rescue. Roy, Dad, and Uncle Martin make it safely back to shore.

Action: The students cup their hands around their mouth, as if they are hailing a passing boat, and say *oi, ship ahoy!*

Letter formation: The sound /oi/ is written with two letters. When two letters make one sound it is called a digraph. Remind the class how both letters are formed. The students form the letters for the digraph in the air and then practice writing ‹oi›, ‹sh›, ‹th›, ‹qu›, and ‹ou› in their books.

Blending: Blend the words on the lesson page with the class: *oil, join, soil, point.* The students point to the dot underneath each sound as they say it.

Identifying the sounds: The students look at the three pictures at the bottom of the lesson page and say the sounds in each word. Then they write ‹oi› in the correct sound dot for the first two words and write all the sounds for the third *[b-**oi**-l; t-**oi**-l-e-t; **c-oi-n**]*.

Word bank: *oil, boil, coil, coin, foil, join, soil, toil, void, joint, moist, point, spoil, oilcan, tinfoil, topsoil, boiling, spoilsport; boiling oil; He will be joining us.* Use the word bank regularly to practice blending. It can also be used to do auditory segmenting: Say a word and then sound it out with the class, holding up a finger for each sound.

Dictation: Dictate the letter sounds /oi/, /ou/, /qu/, /th/ and the words *toil, moist, foil, joint*. Afterward, sound out each word for the students, writing the letters on the board so that they can check their work.

Tricky word "be": This is tricky because although the ‹b› is written as it sounds, the sound /ee/ is written with only one ‹e›. Work this out with the students and ask them to underline the tricky part in purple. Pin up the Tricky Word Wall Flower.

Developing accuracy and fluency: The students take home a sound book to read with their parents and bring back the next day. If available, start using the Jolly Phonics Little Word Books with students who can independently blend simple regular words.

Further ideas: Use the Jolly Song and Wall Frieze section for /oi/. Make boats out of tinfoil. Do coin rubbings with paper and crayons.

Letter Sound /ue/

Flashcards: Review the tricky words *I, the, he, she, me, we, be* and the letter sounds already taught: /s/, /a/, /t/, /i/, /p/, /n/, /c/, /k/, /e/, /h/, /r/, /m/, /d/, /g/, /o/, /u/, /l/, /f/, /b/, /ai/, /j/, /oa/, /ie/, /ee/, /or/, /z/, /w/, /ng/, /v/, /oo/, /oo/, /y/, /x/, /ch/, /sh/, /th/, /th/, /qu/, /ou/, /oi/.

Introducing the letter sound: (Which is really two sounds blended together: /yoo/.) Use a story such as the one below, along with the action.

Samuel is having a birthday party with his friends. They are going to have a barbecue, but first they play musical chairs and watch a magic show. The magician uses a magic wand and is very amusing. He has a big magic box with a unicorn on the side. He stands next to it and does a few card tricks. Then he asks for someone to come and help him. "You," he says, pointing at Samuel. "You are the birthday boy. Will you come and help me?" "Me?" asks Samuel. "You!" shout the children. Samuel helps the magician do a trick. He has to wave the magic wand and say, "ue, ue, ue, ue." Suddenly, a rabbit pops out from under the magician's table, right on cue!

Action: The students point to each other, saying *ue, ue, ue, ue*.

Letter formation: The sound /ue/ is written with two letters. When two letters make one sound it is called a digraph. Remind the class how both letters are formed. The students form the letters for the digraph in the air and then practice writing ‹ue›, ‹th›, ‹qu›, ‹ou›, and ‹oi› in their books.

Blending: Blend the words on the lesson page with the class: *fuel, value, statue, continue.* The students point to the dot underneath each sound as they say it. In words like *blue* and *glue*, the ‹ue› says the long /oo/ sound. In blending, it helps to remember the saying: If one way does not work, try the other.

Identifying the sounds: The students look at the three pictures at the bottom of the lesson page and say the sounds in each word. Then they write ‹ue› in the correct sound dot for the first two words and write all the sounds for the third *[c-**ue**; b-ar-b-e-c-**ue**; **r-e-s-c-ue**]*.

Word bank: *cue, hue, fuel, value, rescue, statue; a quick rescue; The fuel was good value.* Use the word bank regularly to practice blending and auditory segmenting.

Dictation: Dictate the letter sounds /ue/, /oi/, /ou/, /qu/ and the words *cue, fuel, value, statue*. Afterward, sound out each word for the students, writing the letters on the board so that they can check their work.

Tricky word "was": This is tricky because the ‹as› says /oz/. To help remember the spelling, say it as it sounds, pronouncing *was* to rhyme with *mass*. Work this out with the students and ask them to underline the tricky part in purple. Pin up the Tricky Word Wall Flower.

Developing accuracy and fluency: The students take home a sound book to read with their parents and bring back the next day. If available, start using the Jolly Phonics Little Word Books with students who can independently blend simple regular words.

Further ideas: Use the Jolly Song and Wall Frieze section for /ue/. Draw pictures of a rescue. Make small statues from modeling clay.

Letter Sound /er/

Flashcards: Review the tricky words *I, the, he, she, me, we, be, was* and the letter sounds already taught: /s/, /a/, /t/, /i/, /p/, /n/, /c/, /k/, /e/, /h/, /r/, /m/, /d/, /g/, /o/, /u/, /l/, /f/, /b/, /ai/, /j/, /oa/, /ie/, /ee/, /or/, /z/, /w/, /ng/, /v/, /oo/, /oo/, /y/, /x/, /ch/, /sh/, /th/, /th/, /qu/, /ou/, /oi/, /ue/.

Introducing the letter sound: Use a story such as the one below, along with the action.

Today, Bert's teacher, Mr. Bird, read The Gingerbread Man to his class. When Bert gets home from school, he asks if he and his sister, Jennifer, can make some gingerbread for supper. They whisk up some eggs and then weigh the butter, sugar, and flour before putting them in a bowl with a spoonful of ground ginger. Then they give the ingredients a good stir: "er-er-er-er," goes the mixer. Next, Bert and Jennifer roll out the mixture, cut out the gingerbread shapes, and bake them in the oven. When the gingerbread has cooked and cooled, they decorate it with frosting and currants. Bert makes a special gingerbread man for Mr. Bird and gives it to him the next day.

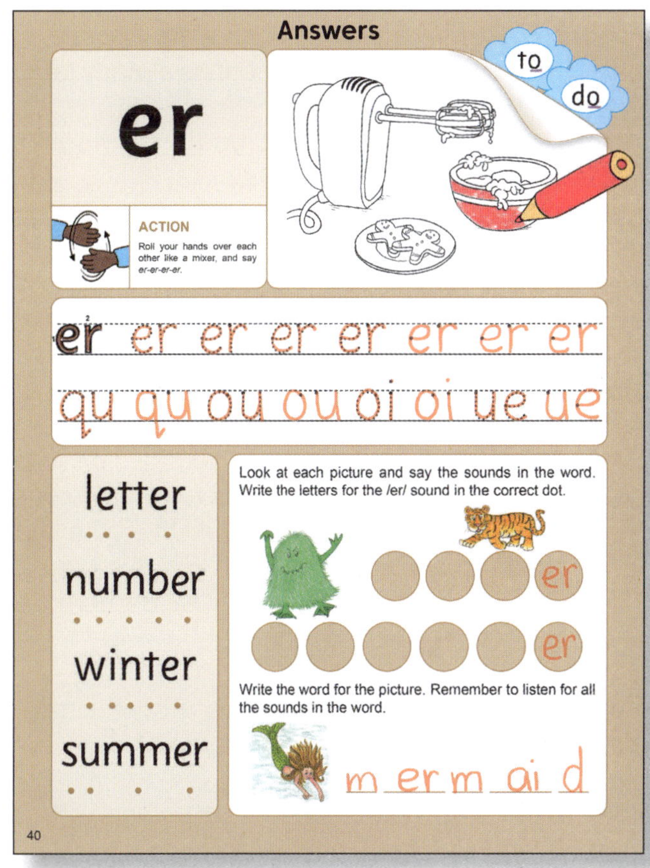
Answers

to

do

er

ACTION

Roll your hands over each other like a mixer, and say *er-er-er-er*.

er er er er er er er er

qu qu ou ou oi oi ue ue

letter

number

winter

summer

Look at each picture and say the sounds in the word. Write the letters for the /er/ sound in the correct dot.

er

er

Write the word for the picture. Remember to listen for all the sounds in the word.

m er m ai d

40

Action: The students roll their hands over each other like a mixer and say *er-er-er-er*.

Letter formation: The sound /er/ is written with two letters. When two letters make one sound it is called a digraph. Remind the class how both letters are formed. The students form the letters for the digraph in the air and then practice writing ‹er›, ‹qu›, ‹ou›, ‹oi›, and ‹ue› in their books.

Blending: Blend the words on the lesson page with the class: *letter, number, winter, summer.* The students point to the dot underneath each sound as they say it.

Identifying the sounds: The students look at the three pictures at the bottom of the lesson page and say the sounds in each word. Then they write ‹er› in the correct sound dot for the first two words and write all the sounds for the third *[t-i-g-**er**; m-o-n-s-t-**er**; **m-er-m-ai-d**]*.

Word bank: *her, fern, herd, jerk, perm, term, verb, perch, mixer, butter, dinner, hammer, ladder, letter, litter, pepper, stern, summer, corner, deeper, singer, waiter, chatter, duster, expert, jester, number, silver, sister, winter, mermaid, blender, monster, printer, helicopter, understand, thunderstorm; a big bad monster; I will do the dinner; Her sister sent a letter to me.*

Dictation: Dictate the letter sounds /er/, /ue/, /oi/, /ou/ and the words *her, fern, sister, waiter*. Afterward, sound out each word for the students, writing the letters on the board so that they can check their work.

Tricky words "to" and "do": These are tricky because although the ‹t› in *to* and ‹d› in *do* are written as they sound, the sound /oo/ in both words is written with only one ‹o›. Work this out with the students and ask them to underline the tricky parts in purple. Pin up the Tricky Word Wall Flowers.

Developing accuracy and fluency: The students take home a sound book to read with their parents and bring back the next day. If available, start using the Jolly Phonics Little Word Books with students who can independently blend simple regular words.

Further ideas: Use the Jolly Song and Wall Frieze section for /er/. Make summer and winter collages. Create gingerbread-family mobiles, cut out of card.

Letter Sound /ar/

Flashcards: Review the tricky words *I, the, he, she, me, we, be, was, to, do* and the letter sounds already taught.

Introducing the letter sound: Use a story such as the one below, along with the action.

The Smart family is on vacation by the ocean. Charlie, Carla, and Barbara are having a great time. So far, they have visited the farm and looked for starfish on the beach. They have even been to see the sharks at the aquarium. Today, Mrs. Smart and the girls are going to the market to buy souvenirs, while Dad and Charlie go down to the harbor. There, Charlie sees a sign with a seal painted on it. "They do boat trips to see the seals," says Dad. We could go tomorrow." Just then, they hear a loud, "ar, ar, ar, ar!" Over on the rocks is a big seal, flapping its flippers. "Wait till Carla and Barbara hear about this," beams Charlie.

Action: The students pretend to be a seal, clapping their hands loosely and saying *ar, ar, ar, ar*.

Letter formation: The sound /ar/ is written with two letters. When two letters make one sound it is called a digraph. Remind the class how both letters are formed. The students form the letters for the digraph in the air and then practice writing them in their books.

Blending: Blend the words on the lesson page with the class: *jar, dark, shark, farmer.*

Identifying the sounds: The students look at the three pictures at the bottom of the lesson page and say the sounds in each word. Then they write ‹ar› in the correct sound dot for the first two words and write all the sounds for the third *[**ar**-m; s-c-**ar**-f; **s-t-ar**]*.

Word bank: *ark, arm, art, bar, car, far, jar, tar, arch, bark, barn, card, cart, dark, dart, farm, hard, harm, harp, mark, park, part, scar, star, tart, yard, argue, charm, chart, harsh, march, marsh, shark, sharp, scarf, smart, spark, start, barber, farmer, larder, sharper, artist, cartoon, darling, garlic, partner, darkroom, farmyard, starfish, starling; ten sharks with sharp teeth; All the coins are in a jar; The sheep are in the barn.*

Dictation: Dictate the letter sounds /ar/, /er/, /ue/, /oi/ and the words *arch, barn, yard, smart*. Afterward, sound out each word for the students, writing the letters on the board so that they can check their work.

Tricky words "are" and "all": The word *are* is tricky because the ‹e› on the end is silent; *all* is tricky because the sound /o/ is written using the alternative spelling ‹al›. Work this out with the students and ask them to underline the tricky parts in purple. Once students know the word *all*, they can read words like *ball, call, fall, hall,* and *tall*. Pin up the Tricky Word Wall Flowers.

Developing accuracy and fluency: The students take home a sound book to read with their parents and bring back the next day. If available, start using the Jolly Phonics Little Word Books with students who can independently blend simple regular words.

Further ideas: Use the Jolly Song and Wall Frieze section for /ar/. Decorate jars or cards with stars. Find out about different types of sharks.

Extra support: Remember to assess and identify any students who are struggling, and provide them with the extra support they need. (See pages 29 to 33.)

Further Practice

Further Practice Activities

Once the students have been taught the letter sounds and know the first set of tricky words, it is important that they continue to review the tricky words and practice their blending and segmenting skills. The activities at the end of Step 1 provide fun and engaging ways to consolidate and extend the students' learning before starting Step 2. The answer sheets are provided on the following two pages.

Tricky Words

The first two pages in this section review the twelve tricky words taught toward the end of Step 1 and introduce the tricky word spelling routine as a reliable way to practice writing the tricky words. There is a row for each tricky word, split into four columns. The students look at the word in the first column and think about which part of the spelling is tricky. They then do the following: copy the word in the next column, writing over the dotted letters; cover up all instances of the word on the page and write it independently; uncover the words and check the spelling; finally, cover the words again and try writing the word one more time. This method is used regularly in Steps 2 and 3, but only after the word has been read and the tricky part has been identified.

Reading and Writing

These activities have been carefully graded to build the students' skills in blending and segmenting. The activities progress from reading and writing simple consonant-vowel-consonant words to activities with words that have digraphs and consonant blends. The progression continues with simple sentences for the students to read, which use the tricky words taught so far. There are also simple reading comprehension activities, such as word and picture matching, or read and draw. Whenever the students are expected to write a word, a line is provided for each sound in that word, with a longer line indicating that a digraph is required. This reminds the students that they have to listen for all the sounds in a word in order to write it. At this point, the students are only expected to write single words. The last page is a review page: the students can practice reading the tricky words and writing all the letter sounds. Once the activities in this section have been completed, the students are ready to begin Step 2.

Decodable Readers

The letter-sound skills that are taught in Step 1 enable the students to tackle their first reading books. Once the /ar/ lesson has been completed, any students who are able to decode regular words independently and know the first twelve tricky words can start reading decodable books. If the Jolly Phonics Readers are available, these students can be given books from the Red Level. Any students who are not confident or fluent in their reading, would be better to start with the Orange Level. In this level, there are three books matched to each letter-sound group and the decodable words in these books only use the letter sounds for that group and below. This makes the books easier for the students to read.

Further Practice: Answers

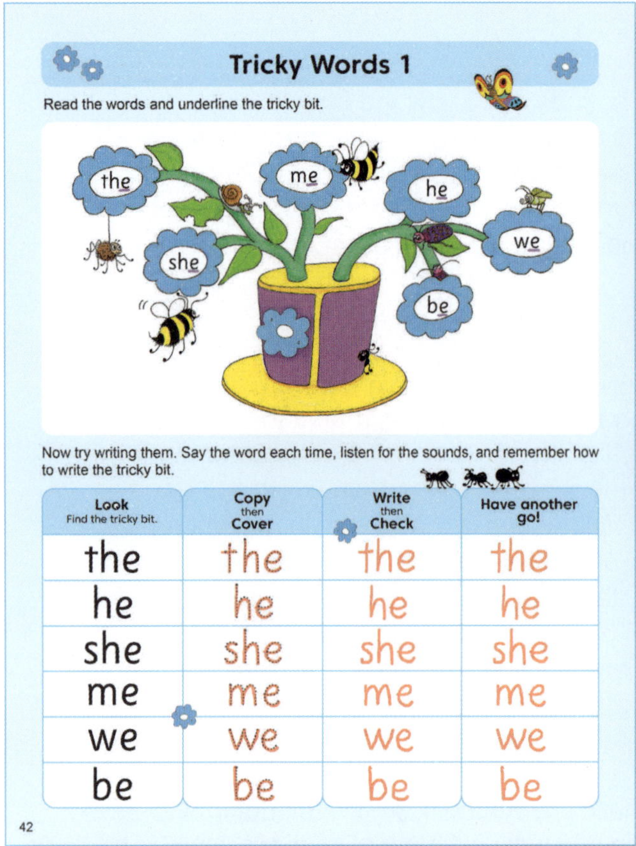

Tricky Words 1

Read the words and underline the tricky bit.

Now try writing them. Say the word each time, listen for the sounds, and remember how to write the tricky bit.

Look Find the tricky bit.	Copy then Cover	Write then Check	Have another go!
the	the	the	the
he	he	he	he
she	she	she	she
me	me	me	me
we	we	we	we
be	be	be	be

42

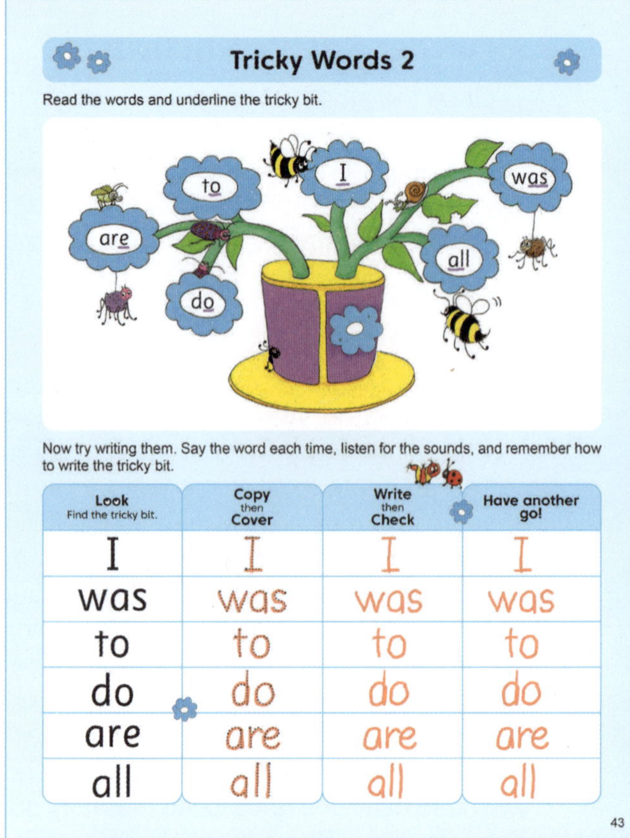

Tricky Words 2

Read the words and underline the tricky bit.

Now try writing them. Say the word each time, listen for the sounds, and remember how to write the tricky bit.

Look Find the tricky bit.	Copy then Cover	Write then Check	Have another go!
I	I	I	I
was	was	was	was
to	to	to	to
do	do	do	do
are	are	are	are
all	all	all	all

43

Reading and Writing

1 Read the words and draw a picture for each one.

ant van cup

2 Choose the right word and write it underneath the picture. Color the pictures in.

met mat man mat	log dig dog dog	sun run fun sun
pet hen pen pen	net nut not net	fix six fox six
three trick tree tree	boot book boat book	shark arm farm shark

44

3 Read each word and match it to the right picture. Color the pictures in.

4 Read these tricky words. Can you find them hidden below?

a	r	e	n	b	e
c	h	e	d	o	f
a	l	l	s	h	e
m	e	y	w	a	s
j	t	o	g	w	e
t	h	e	q	u	I

45

Further Practice: Answers

Teaching Step 2

Weekly Units in Step 2

Jolly Phonics Step 2 has 13 weekly units, each with four lessons on the following topics: Alternatives, Handwriting, Tricky Words, and Words and Sentences. These lessons consolidate and extend the skills taught in Step 1. This means the students regularly practice the basic letter sounds and tricky words that they have already learned, but they are also introduced to the main alternative vowel spellings and new tricky words, as well as capital letters, the alphabet and model sentence writing. The regular blending activities in Further Practice encourage the students toward greater fluency in their reading and the various writing activities help them to become independent and confident writers.

The lessons are taught over four days of the week, leaving a day for other areas of literacy learning. Each topic follows a pattern and the following types of activities are included on a regular basis.

1. Alternatives

In Step 1, the students are taught one way of writing each sound. However, one of the complexities of English spelling is the fact that there are various ways that certain sounds, particularly the vowel sounds, can be written. These alternative spellings also need to be taught.

Step 2
Unit 1
y as /ee/
In these words the ‹y› at the end makes an /ee/ sound.
silly happy muddy jelly
party funny daddy spotty
Read the words in the logs. Match each word to the right picture.
sunny
body
puppy
teddy
sandy
holly
51

To begin with, the students should only be expected to recognize the alternative letter-sound spellings when reading; they should not be expected to use them consistently in their writing. However, the more students are exposed to words with these spellings, the more likely they are to remember how to write these words later on. Therefore it is important that the students have plenty of practice blending words with the alternative spellings.

Every lesson in Step 2 has a Further Practice section, providing words and sentences that contain the alternatives taught so far, along with the tricky words that the students have learned. This section is also useful for blending words that are not strictly regular, but which can be read with a little adjustment, such as words with the schwa sound, words with the ‹nk› spelling, or words in which the letter ‹s› says /z/. The students do not usually find this adjustment difficult in their blending, especially if the word is in their vocabulary.

The following alternative letter-sound spellings are introduced in Step 2:

- ‹y› making the sound /ee/ at the end of a word, as in *holly*.
- ‹ck› making the sound /c k/ in words with a short vowel sound, as in *back*.
- double letters in words with short vowels, as in *rabbit*.
- the hop-over ‹e› digraphs (also known as split digraphs) that are found in words such as *cake, eve, kite, rope,* and *mule*.
- the ‹ay› spelling for the sound /ai/, as in *day*.
- the ‹oy› spelling for the sound /oi/, as in *boy*.
- the ‹ea› spelling for the sound /ee/, as in *leaf*.
- the ‹y› and ‹igh› spellings of the sound /ie/, as in *my* and *high*.
- the ‹ow› spelling, which can make the sound /oa/ (as in *snow*) and the sound /ou/ (as in *owl*).
- the ‹ir› and ‹ur› spellings of the sound /er/, as in *bird* and *curl*.
- the ‹aw›, ‹au›, and ‹al› spellings of the sound /o/.

2. Handwriting

Letter formation

Letter formation is very important and it is worth taking the time to get it right. It is much easier to ensure that the students are using the right formation at the start than try to correct it later on. In Step 1, letter formation focuses on the lower-case letters. In Step 2, the students are taught how to write the capital letters. However, it should not be assumed that the students have now mastered writing all the lower-case letters, and regular practice is required. For more information on letter formation, see pages 14 to 16 of the Introduction.

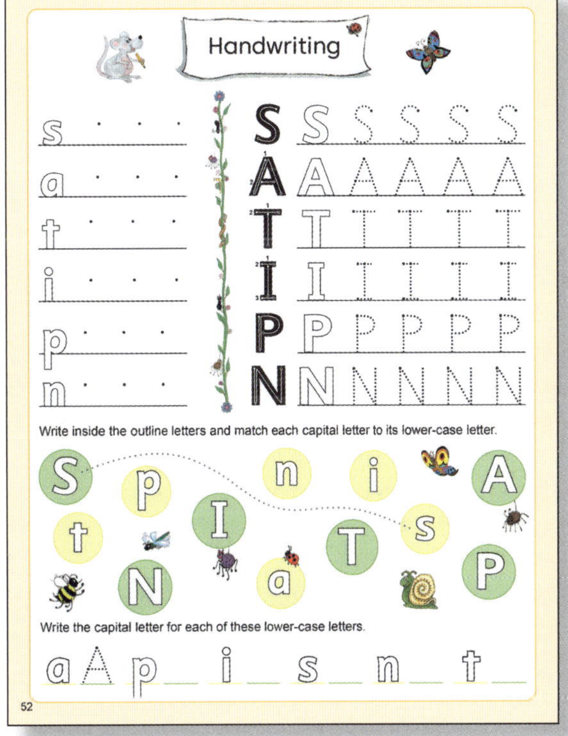

Lower-case letter review

In the first half of Step 2, the lower-case letters are reviewed alongside their capital letters. In the later units, the students review the letters again and are reminded how, for example, to write tall letters, letters that have a tail that goes down under the line, and caterpillar /c/ letters.

Capital letters

Capital letters are taught and practiced across Step 2, first in their letter-sound groups, and then in the four alphabet sections. Flashcards are a useful resource for practicing capitals. They can be used for short review sessions or in matching games such as Snap or Pairs. (Such games are also useful for practicing the tricky words.) There are also regular review activities, based on variations of matching lower- and upper-case letters.

Capital letter and word diction

Dictation of words and capital letters is also a regular activity in the Handwriting lessons. When dictating capital letters, call out the sound, rather than the name of the letter; it is important that the students associate the capital letter with its sound so that they are able to read and write sentences and proper nouns correctly. For more information on dictation, see page 25 of the Introduction.

The alphabet

Reciting the alphabet is a regular activity in Step 2, as it is a useful way to introduce the students to the letter names, and also prepares them for using a dictionary later on. There is a copy of the alphabet on page 72 of Student Book 1 and page 66 of Student Book 2 for the students' reference.

3. Tricky Words

In Step 1, the students are introduced to the first twelve tricky words. In Step 2, regular lessons teach and review the next 28 tricky words:

- *you, your, come, some, said, here, there, they, go, no, so, my* (yellow flowers)
- *one, by, only, old, like, have, live, give, little, down, what, when* (red flowers)
- *why, where, who, which* (green flowers)

To teach the tricky words, encourage the students to listen to the word, blend the sounds, work out which part(s) of the spelling are tricky, and underline the tricky part in purple in their books. The students then practice writing the tricky words in their books, following the tricky word spelling routine introduced in Step 1. Once the students have practiced writing the words several times, the new tricky words can be dictated to them. For more information on tricky words, see pages 27 to 28 of the Introduction.

4. Words and Sentences

In Step 2, this topic focuses on helping the students to start writing independently. Each unit provides a writing topic and a model sentence to get them started. At the beginning, the students will need plenty of help and guidance. Use the picture in the students' books to help initiate a class discussion and ask some of them to say a sentence about it. Then call out the words suggested in the lesson plan to segment and blend. These words are relevant to the lesson topic and some appear in the model sentence. Write the model sentence on the board and use it to explain the main elements of basic sentence structure: Sentences start with a capital letter; Capital letters are always tall; Listen for the sounds in a word to write it; Leave a space between each word; Do not forget the period at the end. If there are tricky words, ask the students how to write them, and point out any spellings that need attention. For example, remind the class of the spelling for *a,* which tends to be swallowed in speech, rather than said with a clear /a/ sound, or pronounced as /ai/ when it is stressed. Other spellings to point out are the letter ‹s› saying /z/ (as in *is, has,* and *woods*) and the different ways to write the /c k/ sound (as in ***c**loa**k**, che**ck**,* and *pi**c**ni**c***). Remind the class that short English words rarely end in ‹c› and that ‹ck› usually comes after a short vowel sound, so *cloak* – which has the long vowel sound /oa/ – is spelled with a kicking /k/. The students then copy the sentence into their books and attempt to do some writing of their own.

Some students will be able to write independently at an early stage, but others may take more time. At this stage, the students are not expected to use the alternative spellings in their writing, so their spelling will not always be accurate but their work can be read. Spelling gradually improves through reading many books and learning to use the alternative spellings correctly in words.

There is a related word and picture matching activity for Units 1 to 6. This can be found in the Extension Activities section at the back of Student Book 1. This section also has other activities for the students to complete, relating to the short and long vowels and tricky words, plus a copy of the alphabet for the students' reference.

Decodable Readers

Once Step 2 Unit 4 has been taught, the students who are ready can move on to the Yellow Level of the Jolly Phonics Readers.

Unit 1: Alternatives

Answers

Step 2

Unit 1

y as /ee/

In these words the ‹y› at the end makes an /ee/ sound.

silly happy muddy jelly

party funny daddy spotty

Read the words in the logs. Match each word to the right picture.

sunny

body

puppy

teddy

sandy

holly

51

Review

- Use flashcards to review the 42 letter sounds taught in Step 1.
- Call out some of the sounds and ask the students to write the letter(s) for each one.

Alternatives: <y> as /ee/

- Write the following words on the board and review the way to write the sound /y/: *yak, yap, yes, yum, yell, yuck, yelp* and *yard*.
- Then say the word *yummy* and write it on the board. Underline the letter ‹y› at the beginning and end of the word and ask the class what sound it is making each time *[/y/ and /ee/]*.
- Explain that the letter ‹y› only says /y/ when it is at the beginning of a word, or sometimes in the middle (as in *beyond)*. When it comes at the end of longer words like *yummy,* it is nearly always pronounced /ee/.
- Write some more words on the board – *jolly, cherry, stormy, windy, rainy, cloudy, chilly, lucky, sleepy* and *quickly* – and blend them with the students. Underline the ‹y› making the sound /ee/ at the end of each one.
- The students then read the words *silly, happy, muddy, jelly, party, funny, daddy,* and *spotty* in their books and underline the alternative spelling in each one.
- Note: Remind the class that when two letters which make the same sound are next to each other, the sound is only said once.

Word and picture matching

- Show the students the words and pictures in their books: *sunny, body, puppy, teddy, sandy, holly.*
- The students read the words in the logs and join each one to the frog with the matching picture.
- The students then color the pictures.

FURTHER PRACTICE

It is important to practice the skills needed for reading and writing on a regular basis.

Blending and segmenting

at, dip, jog, peg, kick,
cart, swam, count, sheep, cobweb

- Call out each word. The students say the sounds, holding up a finger for each one. Write the letters on the board as they do so and blend the word.
- Practice blending the words with the class (as well as in pairs or individually, if extra practice is needed).

Reading sentences

- Write these sentences on the board for the class to read. Point out the tricky words and blend any unknown words with the students:
  1. Do sheep sleep in beds?
  2. The farmyard was a mess.
  3. The shark swam in the reef.
  4. Did she do her job well?

Unit 1: Handwriting

The alphabet (See page 136)

- Show the students the alphabet at the back of their books (Student Book 1, page 72).
- Point out that there are no digraphs in the alphabet because it is a way of ordering the single letters. This means that when we say the alphabet, we use the letter names and not the sounds.
- Say the alphabet, pointing to each letter as you say it. Pause between the sections: A–E; F–M; N–S; T–Z.
- Say it again, asking the students to join in. Over time, the students should be able to say the alphabet on their own.

Handwriting

- Show the students the lesson page in their books. Review the sounds and formation for the letters ‹s›, ‹a›, ‹t›, ‹i›, ‹p›, and ‹n›.
- Remind the students that ‹t› is tall and that ‹p› goes under the line.
- Teach the students how to write the capital letters ‹S›, ‹A›, ‹T›, ‹I›, ‹P›, and ‹N›.
- Explain that all capital letters are tall, and that they start at or near the top. None of the capitals go down under the line.
- The students trace inside the outline capitals and then write over the dotted letters.

Capitals and lower-case letters

- The students write inside the outline letters, using a different color for each pair. Then they join the matching pairs of upper- and lower-case letters in their books.
- Finally, the students write the capital letter for each of the lower-case letters at the bottom of the page.

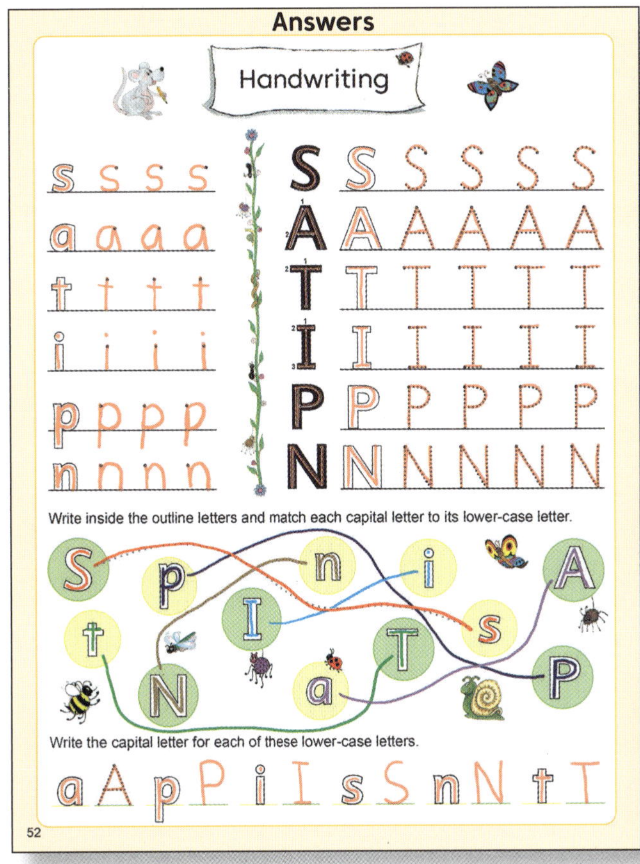

Dictation

- Call out the following words: *cat, dog, hen, step, drum, chin, than, sheep, rain, cobweb.* The students listen for the sounds and write the words.
- Call out the sounds for ‹S›, ‹A›, ‹T›, ‹I›, ‹P›, and ‹N› and ask the students to write the capital letters.

FURTHER PRACTICE

It is important to practice the skills needed for reading and writing on a regular basis.

Blending and segmenting

it, pat, bin, set, hill,
wind, coast, grain, punch, chimpanzee

- Call out each word. The students say the sounds, holding up a finger for each one. Write the letters on the board as they do so and blend the word.
- Practice blending the words with the class (as well as in pairs or individually, if extra practice is needed).

Reading sentences

- Write these sentences on the board for the class to read. Point out the tricky words and blend any unknown words with the students:
  1. We do not jump on the bed.
  2. The big dog has black spots.
  3. Her coat was pink and red.
  4. He brushes his teeth in the morning.

Unit 1: Tricky Words

Flashcards

- Review the 12 tricky words taught in Step 1: *I, the, he, she, me, we, be, was, to, do, are, all.*

Tricky words: you, your

- Remind the class that some words are tricky because they cannot be worked out fully by listening for the sounds. They have an irregular part or an alternative spelling that has to be learned.
- Show the students the words in the yellow flowers at the top of their lesson page. Say each one and ask the students to blend the sounds. Then help the class to work out the tricky parts:
  - The ‹ou› in *you* is tricky because it makes the long /oo/ sound, not /ou/.
  - In *your*, the ‹our› is tricky because it says /or/.
- To help the students remember the spelling, point out that *your* is written the same way as *you*, but it has a letter ‹r› at the end.
- The students write inside the outline letters using a yellow pencil and underline the tricky parts in purple.

Tricky word spelling routine

- Writing the tricky words several times will help the students remember the spelling.
- Show the students the table in their books. They look at the word *you* in the first column and identify the tricky parts. The students then copy the word in the next column, writing over the dotted letters.
- Next, they cover up all instances of the word on the page and write it again by themselves.
- Finally, the students uncover the words and check that the spelling is correct, before covering them again and writing the word one more time.

- The students repeat these steps with the word *your*.

Dictation

- Say the words *you* and *your*. The students listen for the sounds in each word, think about how the tricky parts are spelled, and write the words.

FURTHER PRACTICE

It is important to practice the skills needed for reading and writing on a regular basis.

Blending and segmenting

on, pop, had, cut, deck,
hunch, moist, farmer, shark, shouting

- Call out each word. The students say the sounds, holding up a finger for each one. Write the letters on the board as they do so and blend the word.
- Practice blending the words with the class (as well as in pairs or individually, if extra practice is needed).

Reading sentences

- Write these sentences on the board for the class to read. Point out the tricky words and blend any unknown words with the students:
  1. You will get your wish.
  2. Is your scarf red or green?
  3. This is the bag for your shopping.
  4. You must stop and cross the road.

Unit 1: Words and Sentences

Review

- Use flashcards to review some of the 42 letter sounds, including ‹y› as /y/ and /ee/.
- Call out some of the sounds and ask the students to write the letter(s) for each one.

Talk about the picture: The hen

- Show the students the picture of the hen in their books (see opposite) and discuss it with the class.
- Ask a few students to say a sentence about the picture: for example, *I can see a hen; The chick is on the hen's back; The hen is on her nest.*

Word focus

- In turn, call out the words *hen, eggs, nest, chicks,* and *her*. The students say the sounds in each word, holding up a finger for each one. Write the letters on the board as they do so and blend the sounds with the class to read the word.
  - Remind the students that although the sound at the end of a plural word is often /z/, it is always written as ‹s›, as in *eggs*.
  - Point out the double letters in *eggs* and the ‹ck› spelling in *chicks*. Remind the students that when two letters making the same sound are next to each other, the sound is only said once.

Sentence modeling

- Write the following sentence on the board:
  - *A hen just sits on her nest.*
- Discuss the sentence as you write it. Encourage the students to call out the sounds of each word before you write it and to blend the word afterward.
- Point out the following:
  - Sentences start with a capital letter.
  - Capital letters are always tall.
  - Listen for the sounds in a word to write it.
  - We tend to swallow the word *a* rather than use a clear /a/ sound. When the word is stressed, it says /ai/.
  - Leave a space between each word.
  - Do not forget the period at the end.
- Once the sentence has been modeled, read it with the students. All the students copy the sentence into their books and color the picture.

Free writing

- Those students who are able to write independently can write some more sentences of their own.
- At this stage the students are not expected to use the alternative spellings, so their writing will not always be accurate but the work can be read. Spelling gradually improves through reading many books and learning to apply the alternative letter-sound spellings.

Word and picture matching (See page 136)

- The students go to page 70 of their books and look at the first row of words and pictures: *chick, hen, nest, egg*. They read each word and join it to the matching picture.

Decodable books

- Send the students home with a book that matches their independent reading level (see page 21 for more information).

FURTHER PRACTICE

It is important to practice the skills needed for reading and writing on a regular basis.

Blending and segmenting

in, red, map, rid, fell,
pump, foam, crunch, painter, boiling

- Call out each word. The students say the sounds, holding up a finger for each one. Write the letters on the board as they do so and blend the word.
- Practice blending the words with the class (as well as in pairs or individually, if extra practice is needed).

Reading sentences

- Write these sentences on the board for the class to read. Point out the tricky words and blend any unknown words with the students:
  1. We all went swimming.
  2. Did he look at the books?
  3. I swam ten lengths in the pool.
  4. Can you join us in the park?

Unit 2: Alternatives

Review

- Use flashcards to review some of the 42 letter sounds, including /a/, /e/, /i/, /o/, /u/, and ‹y› as /y/ and /ee/.
- Call out some of the sounds and ask the students to write the letter(s) for each one.

The short vowel sounds

- Show the students the five large letters in their books. Explain that they are special letters called vowels and that there is at least one vowel sound in every word.
- Say the sounds with the class – /a/, /e/, /i/, /o/, /u/ – and tell the students that these are known as the short vowel sounds.
- Read the short vowel words at the top of the page with the class and point out the short vowel in each one: *bag, net, bin, box,* and *mug.*
- Now look at the pictures of the containers and ask the students to find Inky Mouse. Point out where she is, emphasising the short vowel each time:
  - **A**t the side of the b**a**g,
  - On the **e**dge of the n**e**t,
  - **I**n the b**i**n,
  - **O**n t**o**p of the b**o**x, and
  - **U**nder the m**u**g.
- The students trace inside the outline vowel letters, using a blue pencil or pen. They say the sound as they write each letter.

Short vowel words

- Show the students the pictures underneath the vowel containers. Look at the first picture and say the word: *box.* Ask the class to say all the sounds, holding up a finger for each one: /b-o-x/.
- Ask the students to say the sounds again, listening carefully for the short vowel sound */o/.*
- The students then circle the sound /o/ above the picture and write over the dotted letters on the lines below.
- The students repeat these steps with the other pictures. This time there are no dotted letters to help them. The students can then color the pictures.

Answers

Find the short vowels (See page 136)

- The students go to page 69 of their books and find the short vowels in the grid.

FURTHER PRACTICE

It is important to practice the skills needed for reading and writing on a regular basis.

Blending and segmenting

up, ran, hat, pot, sock,
boil, moth, messy, rescue, foghorn

- Call out each word. The students say the sounds, holding up a finger for each one. Write the letters on the board as they do so and blend the word.
- Practice blending the words with the class (as well as in pairs or individually, if extra practice is needed).

Reading sentences

- Write these sentences on the board for the class to read. Point out the tricky words and blend any unknown words with the students:
  1. Can you help me?
  2. I went to the dentist.
  3. Sam had a desk in his bedroom.
  4. You must be good for your granny.

Unit 2: Handwriting

The alphabet (See page 136)

- Ask the students to look at the alphabet at the back of their books (Student Book 1, page 72).
- Remind them that when we say the alphabet, we use the letter names and not the sounds.
- Say the alphabet, pointing to each letter as you say it. Pause between the sections: A–E; F–M; N–S; T–Z.
- Say it again, asking the students to join in. Over time, the students should be able to say the alphabet on their own.

Handwriting

- Show the students the lesson page in their books. Review the sounds and formation for the letters ‹c›, ‹k›, ‹e›, ‹h›, ‹r›, ‹m›, and ‹d›.
- Remind the students that the letters ‹k›, ‹h›, and ‹d› are tall and that ‹r› and ‹m› both begin by going down, up, and over. Also point out that ‹e› starts halfway up the letter and ‹d› starts with a caterpillar /c/.
- Teach the students how to write the capital letters ‹C›, ‹K›, ‹E›, ‹H›, ‹R›, ‹M›, and ‹D›. Remind them that all capital letters are tall and start at or near the top. None of the capitals go down under the line.
- The students trace inside the outline capitals and then write over the dotted letters.

Capitals and lower-case letters

- The students write inside the outline letters, using a different color for each pair. Then they join the matching pairs of upper- and lower-case letters in their books.
- Finally, the students write the capital letter for each of the lower-case letters at the bottom of the page.

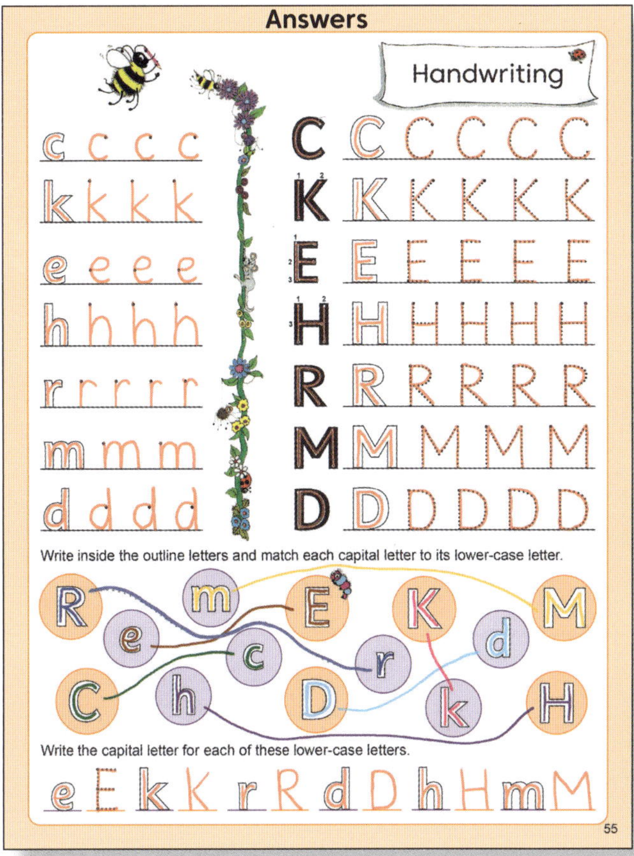

Dictation

- Call out the following words: *cap, dot, men, stop, drip, boat, chip, thin, shoot, nutmeg.* The students listen for the sounds and write the words.
- Ask the students to write the capital letter for the following sounds: caterpillar /c/, kicking /k/, /e/, /h/, /r/, /m/, and /d/.

FURTHER PRACTICE

It is important to practice the skills needed for reading and writing on a regular basis.

Blending and segmenting

ant, cot, ram, fin, peck,
good, sleepy, harm, queen, understand

- Call out each word. The students say the sounds, holding up a finger for each one. Write the letters on the board as they do so and blend the word.
- Practice blending the words with the class (as well as in pairs or individually, if extra practice is needed).

Reading sentences

- Write these sentences on the board for the class to read. Point out the tricky words and blend any unknown words with the students:
  1. Do you need a drink?
  2. He must be very happy.
  3. Your sister has a floppy hat.
  4. We will sit and wait for the bus.

Step 2 Jolly Phonics Student Book 1: Page 56

Unit 2: Tricky Words

Flashcards

- Review the tricky words *he, she, me, we, be, was, to, do, are, all, you, your.*

Tricky words: come, some

- Remind the class that some words are tricky because they cannot be worked out fully by listening for the sounds. They have an irregular part or an alternative spelling that has to be learned.
- Show the students the words in the yellow flowers at the top of their lesson page. Say each one and ask the students to blend the sounds. Then help the class to work out the tricky parts. In both these words it is the letters ‹o› and ‹e› that are tricky because the ‹o› makes the sound /u/ and the ‹e› is silent.
- To help the students remember the spelling, point out that the only difference is the first letter in each word.
- The students write inside the outline letters using a yellow pencil and underline the tricky parts in purple.

Tricky word spelling routine

- Writing the tricky words several times will help the students remember the spelling.
- Show the students the table in their books. They look at the word *come* in the first column and identify the tricky parts.
- The students then copy the word in the next column, writing over the dotted letters.
- Next, they cover up all instances of the word on the page and write it again by themselves.
- Finally, the students uncover the words and check that the spelling is correct, before covering them again and writing the word one more time.
- The students repeat these steps with the word *some*.

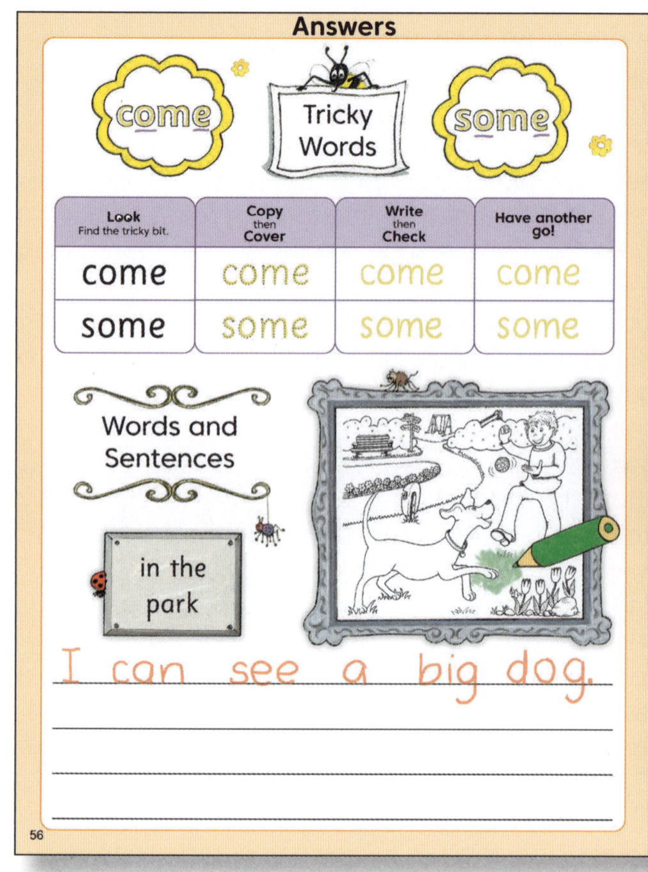

Dictation

Say the words *come* and *some*. The students listen for the sounds in each word, think about how the tricky parts are spelled, and write the words.

FURTHER PRACTICE

It is important to practice the skills needed for reading and writing on a regular basis.

Blending and segmenting

tap, mug, bag, kid, tell,
main, went, soapy, three, shampoo

- Call out each word. The students say the sounds, holding up a finger for each one. Write the letters on the board as they do so and blend the word.
- Practice blending the words with the class (as well as in pairs or individually, if extra practice is needed).

Reading sentences

- Write these sentences on the board for the class to read. Point out the tricky words and blend any unknown words with the students:
  1. Did you see all the horses?
  2. Some cats are greedy.
  3. Dad had a smart green tie.
  4. Can we come to your party?

Unit 2: Words and Sentences

Review

- Use flashcards to review some of the 42 letter sounds, including ‹y› as /y/ and /ee/, and the short vowels /a/, /e/, /i/, /o/, /u/.

Talk about the picture: In the park

- Show the students the picture of the park in their books (see opposite) and discuss it with the class.
- Ask a few students to say a sentence about the picture: for example, *I can see a boy; The dog is in the park; He is playing with a ball.*

Word focus

- In turn, call out the words *I, see, big, dog,* and *park*. The students say the sounds in each word, holding up a finger for each one. Write the letters on the board as they do so and blend the sounds with the class to read the word.
  - Remind the students that *I* is a tricky word and ask them how to spell it.
  - Point out the ‹k› spelling in *park*. Explain that short English words rarely end in ‹c›, and ‹ck› usually comes at the end of a short word with a short vowel sound, so words like *park* are spelled with a kicking /k/.

Sentence modeling

- Write the following sentence on the board:
  - *I can see a big dog.*
- Discuss the sentence as you write it. Encourage the students to call out the sounds of each word before you write it and to blend the word afterward.
- Point out the following:
  - Sentences start with a capital letter.
  - Capital letters are always tall.
  - Listen for the sounds in a word to write it.
  - *I* is a tricky word. How is it spelled?
  - We tend to swallow the word *a* rather than use a clear /a/ sound. When the word is stressed, it says /ai/.
  - Leave a space between each word.
  - Do not forget the period at the end.
- Once the sentence has been modeled, read it with the students. All the students copy the sentence into their books and color the picture.

Free writing

- Those students who are able to write independently can write some more sentences of their own.
- At this stage the students are not expected to use the alternative spellings, so their writing will not always be accurate but the work can be read. Spelling gradually improves through reading many books and learning to apply the alternative letter-sound spellings.

Word and picture matching (See page 136)

- The students go to page 70 of their books and look at the second row of words and pictures: *dog, tree, swing, picnic*. They read each word and join it to the matching picture.

Decodable books

- Send the students home with a book that matches their independent reading level (see page 21 for more information).

FURTHER PRACTICE

It is important to practice the skills needed for reading and writing on a regular basis.

Blending and segmenting

dot, yes, bob, hip, neck,
clock, west, proof, frosty, splinter

- Call out each word. The students say the sounds, holding up a finger for each one. Write the letters on the board as they do so and blend the word.
- Practice blending the words with the class (as well as in pairs or individually, if extra practice is needed).

Reading sentences

- Write these sentences on the board for the class to read. Point out the tricky words and blend any unknown words with the students:
  1. Your dog has muddy feet.
  2. Will you come fishing with us?
  3. Some children are having a picnic.
  4. The man was rescued in a helicopter.

Unit 3: Alternatives

Review

- Use flashcards to review some of the 42 letter sounds, including ‹y› as /y/ and /ee/, and the short vowels /a/, /e/, /i/, /o/, /u/.
- Call out some of the sounds and ask the students to write the letter(s) for each one.

Alternatives: short vowels and <ck>

- Write the following words on the board and read them with the class: *back, deck, pick, lock* and *tuck*.
- Ask the students what the words have in common. *[They all have a short vowel sound and end in ‹ck›]*. Explain that when the sound /c/ comes at the end of a short word with a short vowel, it is usually spelled with both a caterpillar /c/ and a kicking /k/.
- Write some more words on the board – *lick, stuck, shock, pack, speck, chick, block, cluck, fleck* and *snack* – and read them with the students. Underline the ‹ck› spelling in each one and identify the short vowel sound it follows.
- The students then read the words *luck, check, sack, peck, truck, rock, jacket, tick, kick,* and *clock* in their books and underline the alternative spelling in each one.

Rockets

- The students read the dotted words in the rockets: *stick, black, socks, neck, rocket, brick,* and *duck.*
- They write over the first dotted word, *stick*, and draw a picture of this word in the rocket.
- They then do the same with the rest of the words.

Note: <ck> and <k>

- Short English words rarely end in a letter ‹c›. If the word has a short vowel sound, the spelling for the sound /c k/ is usually ‹ck›. If the word does not have a short vowel sound, the spelling is usually ‹k›, as in the words *lake, week, book, cloak, fork,* and *park.*

FURTHER PRACTICE

It is important to practice the skills needed for reading and writing on a regular basis.

Blending and segmenting

pet, lip, dam, van, gull,
breezy, trench, still, raincoat, tinfoil

- Call out each word. The students say the sounds, holding up a finger for each one. Write the letters on the board as they do so and blend the word.
- Practice blending the words with the class (as well as in pairs or individually, if extra practice is needed).

Reading sentences

- Write these sentences on the board for the class to read. Point out the tricky words and blend any unknown words with the students:
  1. She has three pet rabbits.
  2. Dad poaches eggs for our lunch.
  3. Come and feed the ducks with me.
  4. Pack all your things in the trunk.

Unit 3: Handwriting

The alphabet (See page 136)

- Ask the students to look at the alphabet at the back of their books (Student Book 1, page 72).
- Remind them that when we say the alphabet, we use the letter names and not the sounds.
- Say the alphabet, pointing to each letter as you say it. Pause between the sections: A–E; F–M; N–S; T–Z.
- Say it again, asking the students to join in. Over time, the students should be able to say the alphabet on their own.

Handwriting

- Show the students the lesson page in their books. Review the sounds and formation for the letters ‹g›, ‹o›, ‹u›, ‹l›, ‹f›, and ‹b›.
- Remind the students that the letters ‹l›, ‹f›, and ‹b› are tall and that ‹g› has a tail that goes down under the line. The letter ‹b› goes down the "bat" and bounces up and around the "ball."
- Teach the students how to write the capital letters ‹G›, ‹O›, ‹U›, ‹L›, ‹F›, and ‹B›. Remind them that all capital letters are tall and start at or near the top. None of the capitals go down under the line.
- The students trace inside the outline capitals and then write over the dotted letters.

Capitals and lower-case letters

- The students write inside the outline letters, using a different color for each pair. Then they join the matching pairs of upper- and lower-case letters in their books.
- Finally, the students write the capital letter for each of the lower-case letters at the bottom of the page.

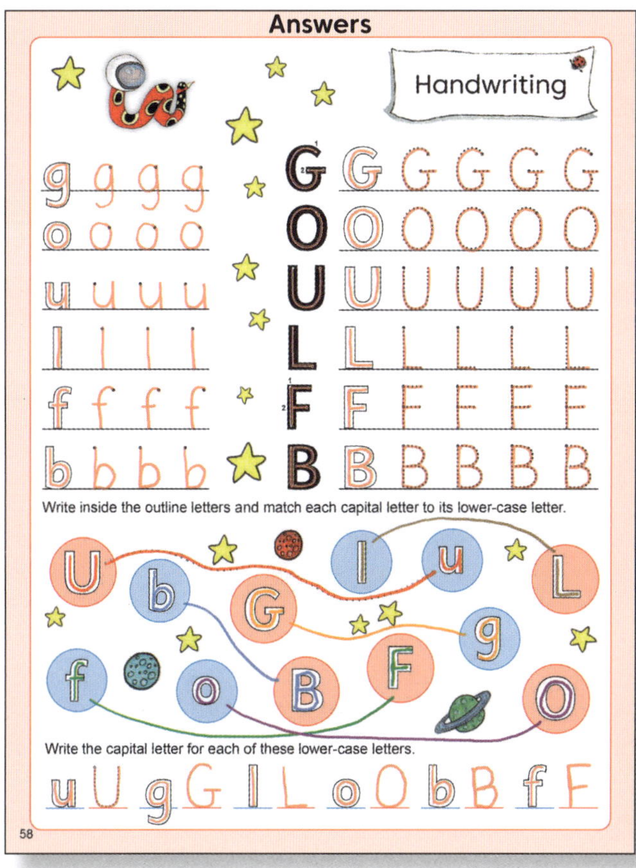

Dictation

- Call out the following words: *set, hit, box, plum, snap, port, sharp, chop, quiz, redwood.* The students listen for the sounds and write the words.
- Call out the sounds for ‹G›, ‹O›, ‹U›, ‹L›, ‹F›, and ‹B› and ask the students to write the capital letters.

FURTHER PRACTICE

It is important to practice the skills needed for reading and writing on a regular basis.

Blending and segmenting

dad, sun, pad, cog, rock,
clump, ping, next, greedy, raindrops

- Call out each word. The students say the sounds, holding up a finger for each one. Write the letters on the board as they do so and blend the word.
- Practice blending the words with the class (as well as in pairs or individually, if extra practice is needed).

Reading sentences

- Write these sentences on the board for the class to read. Point out the tricky words and blend any unknown words with the students:
  1. The clock was on the shelf.
  2. You are very clever indeed.
  3. Did you get a book for me?
  4. We left out some nuts for the squirrels.

Unit 3: Tricky Words

Flashcards

- Review the tricky words *me, we, be, was, to, do, are, all, you, your, come, some.*

Tricky words: said, here, there

- Remind the class that some words are tricky because they cannot be worked out fully by listening for the sounds. They have an irregular part or an alternative spelling that has to be learned.
- Show the students the words in the yellow flowers at the top of their lesson page. Say each one and ask the students to blend the sounds. Then help the class to work out the tricky parts:
  - The ‹ai› in *said* is tricky because it makes the sound /e/ rather than saying /ai/.
  - In the other two words, the ‹ere› is tricky because it says /air/ in *there* and /ier/ in *here*. The sound /air/ is introduced in Step 3 Unit 13.
- To help the students remember the spelling of *here* and *there,* point out that the only difference is that one starts with ‹h› for /h/ and the other with ‹th› for /th/.
- The students write inside the outline letters using a yellow pencil and underline the tricky parts in purple.

Tricky word spelling routine

- Writing the tricky words several times will help the students remember the spelling.
- Show the students the table in their books. They look at the word *said* in the first column and identify the tricky parts. The students then copy the word in the next column, writing over the dotted letters.
- Next, they cover up all instances of the word on the page and write it again by themselves.
- Finally, the students uncover the words and check that the spelling is correct, before covering them again and writing the word one more time.
- Repeat these steps with the words *here* and *there*.

Dictation

- Say the words *said, here* and *there*. The students listen for the sounds in each word, think about how the tricky parts are spelled, and write the words.

FURTHER PRACTICE

It is important to practice the skills needed for reading and writing on a regular basis.

Blending and segmenting

tan, cup, bed, mop, bell,
worn, chest, dusty, liquid, crossing

- Call out each word. The students say the sounds, holding up a finger for each one. Write the letters on the board as they do so and blend the word.
- Practice blending the words with the class (as well as in pairs or individually, if extra practice is needed).

Reading sentences

- Write these sentences on the board for the class to read. Point out the tricky words and blend any unknown words with the students:
  1. Here is a red toadstool.
  2. I am sitting on a wooden bench.
  3. Dad said that he will do the cooking.
  4. There are some fluffy chicks in the barn.

Unit 3: Words and Sentences

Review

- Use flashcards to review some of the 42 letter sounds and alternative spellings, including ‹y› as /y/ and /ee/, ‹ck›, and the short vowels /a/, /e/, /i/, /o/, /u/.
- Call out some of the sounds and ask the students to write the letter(s) for each one.

Talk about the picture: On the pond

- Show the students the picture of the pond in their books (see opposite) and discuss it with the class.
- Ask a few students to say a sentence about the picture: for example, *The pond is big; A duckling quacks at the frog; I can see a boat.*

Word focus

- In turn, call out the words *boat, sails, pond, frogs,* and *ducklings*. The students say the sounds in each word, holding up a finger for each one. Write the letters on the board as they do so and blend the sounds with the class to read the word.
  - Remind the students that although the sound at the end of a plural word is often /z/, it is always written as ‹s›, as in *sails, frogs,* and *ducklings*.
  - Point out the short vowel sound /u/ in *ducklings* and ask the students how to spell the sound /c k/ before writing ‹ck›. (Although this is a long word, its root word is *duck*.)

Sentence modeling

- Write the following sentence on the board:
  - *A boat sails on the pond.*
- Discuss the sentence as you write it. Encourage the students to call out the sounds of each word before you write it and to blend the word afterward.
- Point out the following:
  - Sentences start with a capital letter.
  - Capital letters are always tall.
  - Listen for the sounds in a word to write it.
  - We tend to swallow the word *a* rather than use a clear /a/ sound. When the word is stressed, it says /ai/.
  - *The* is a tricky word. How is it spelled?
  - Leave a space between each word.
  - Do not forget the period at the end.
- Once the sentence has been modeled, read it with the students. All the students copy the sentence into their books and color the picture.

Free writing

- Those students who are able to write independently can write some more sentences of their own.
- At this stage the students are not expected to use the alternative spellings, so their writing will not always be accurate but the work can be read. Spelling gradually improves through reading many books and learning to apply the alternative letter-sound spellings.

Word and picture matching (See page 136)

- The students go to page 70 of their books and look at the third row of words and pictures: *toad, boat, duckling, rocks*. They read each word and join it to the matching picture.

Decodable books

- Send the students home with a book that matches their independent reading level (see page 21 for more information).

FURTHER PRACTICE

It is important to practice the skills needed for reading and writing on a regular basis.

Blending and segmenting

cat, mud, job, win, loss,
sling, pinch, shrug, munch, grumpy

- Call out each word. The students say the sounds, holding up a finger for each one. Write the letters on the board as they do so and blend the word.
- Practice blending the words with the class (as well as in pairs or individually, if extra practice is needed).

Reading sentences

- Write these sentences on the board for the class to read. Point out the tricky words and blend any unknown words with the students:
  1. Shall we sing a song?
  2. Here is an empty box.
  3. He said his truck is black.
  4. There is a crack in this cup.

Unit 4: Alternatives

Review

- Use flashcards to review some of the 42 letter sounds and alternative spellings, including ‹y› as /y/ and /ee/, ‹ck›, and the short vowels /a/, /e/, /i/, /o/, /u/.
- Call out some of the sounds and ask the students to write the letter(s) for each one.

Alternatives: short vowels and double letters

- Write the following words on the board and read them with the class: *jazz, mess, ill, odd* and *fluff.* Remind the students that when two letters which make the same sound are next to each other, the sound is only said once.
- Ask the students what the words have in common. *[They all have a short vowel sound followed by a double letter].* Explain that letters that are not vowel letters (consonants) are often doubled if they follow a short vowel sound, or if they come between two vowel letters.
- Write some more words on the board – *smell, drill, ladder, puffin, otter, hammer, hiss, tennis, butter,* and *offer* – and read them with the students. Underline the double letters in each one and identify the short vowel sound they follow.
- The students then read the words *parrot, egg, bell, add, button, kitten, buzz, toffee, doll,* and *miss* in their books and underline the double letters in each one.

Double letter rabbit

- Show the students the large rabbit in their books. Ask them to read the word *rabbit* and color in the small picture.
- Explain that they are going to read the other words and draw a picture for each one.

Answers

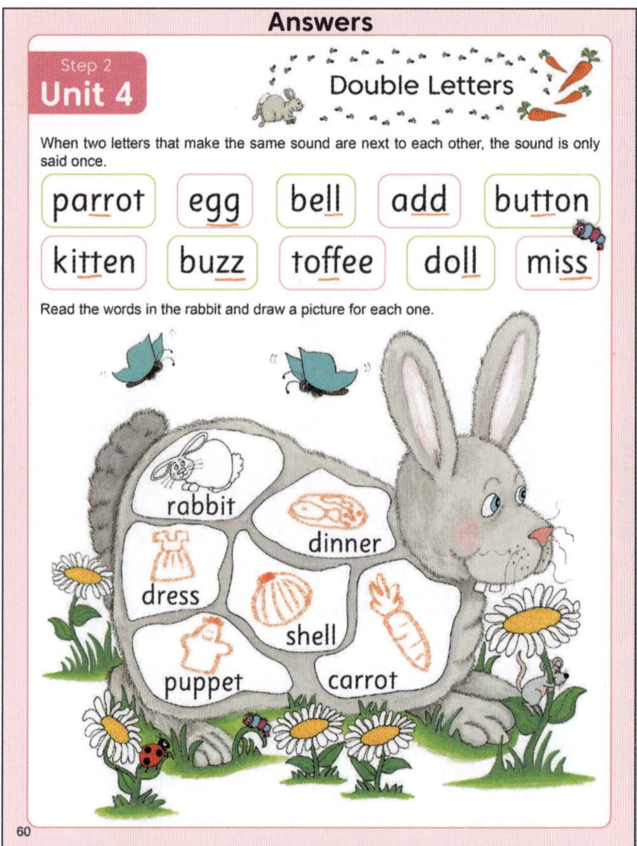

- **Note:** The second vowel letter in *parr**o**t, butt**o**n, kitt**e**n* and *carr**o**t* makes a schwa sound. (This is a swallowed, or neutral sound.) This is not usually a problem for blending, but it makes the spelling more difficult. The more students read a word with a schwa, the more likely it is that they will remember the spelling.

FURTHER PRACTICE

It is important to practice the skills needed for reading and writing on a regular basis.

Blending and segmenting

nip, run, rot, sat, buzz,
short, spoil, letter, suffer, tricking

- Call out each word. The students say the sounds, holding up a finger for each one. Write the letters on the board as they do so and blend the word.
- Practice blending the words with the class (as well as in pairs or individually, if extra practice is needed).

Reading sentences

- Write these sentences on the board for the class to read. Point out the tricky words and blend any unknown words with the students:
  1. All your dresses are here.
  2. She found some duck eggs.
  3. He said he had sent you a letter.
  4. There are green bugs under this log.

Unit 4: Handwriting

The alphabet (See page 136)

- Ask the students to look at the alphabet at the back of their books (Student Book 1, page 72).
- Remind them that when we say the alphabet, we use the letter names and not the sounds.
- Say the alphabet with the class, pausing between the sections: A–E; F–M; N–S; T–Z. The students point to each letter as they say it.
- Call out some of the letters and ask the students to point to them in their books. Ask them whether these letters are red, yellow, green, or blue.

Handwriting

- Show the students the lesson page in their books.
- Review the formation of the letter(s) that make the sounds /j/, /ai/, /oa/, /ie/, /ee/, and /or/. Remind the students that the letter ‹j› has a tail that goes down under the line.
- Teach the students how to write the capital letter ‹J›. Remind them that all capital letters are tall and start at or near the top. None of the capitals go down under the line.
- The students trace inside the outline capital ‹J› and write over the dotted letters.

Capitals and lower-case letters

- The students write inside the outline letters, using a different color for each pair. Then they join the matching pairs of upper- and lower-case letters in their books.
- Finally, the students write the capital letter for each of the lower-case letters at the bottom of the page.

Answers

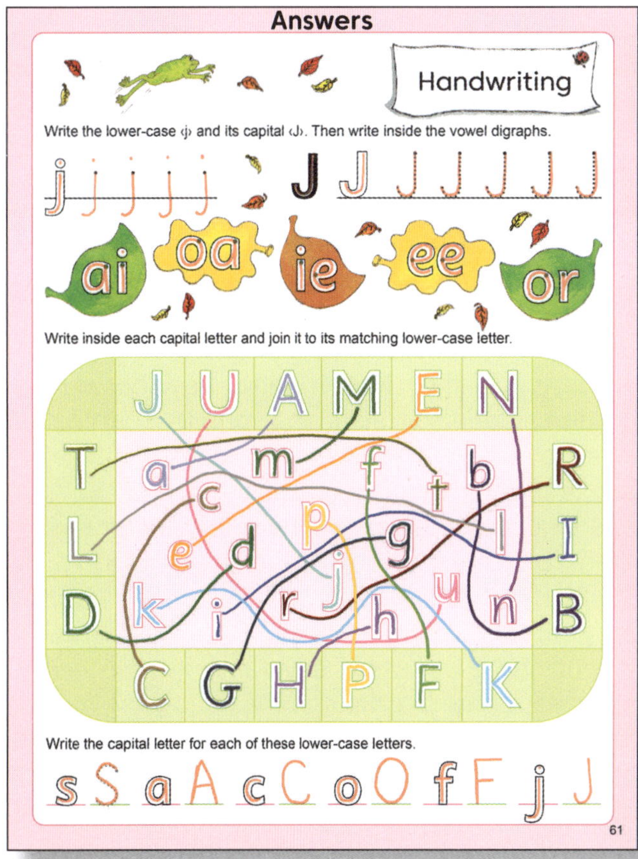

Dictation

- Call out the following words: *bat, let, cup, swim, flat, much, coin, loud, teeth, herself.* The students listen for the sounds and write the words.
- Call out the sound for ‹J› and ask the students to write its capital letter. Do the same with some of the other capitals the students have learned so far.

FURTHER PRACTICE

It is important to practice the skills needed for reading and writing on a regular basis.

Blending and segmenting

rat, hug, gap, mid, dull,
suck, food, poach, cracking, bookshelf

- Call out each word. The students say the sounds, holding up a finger for each one. Write the letters on the board as they do so and blend the word.
- Practice blending the words with the class (as well as in pairs or individually, if extra practice is needed).

Reading sentences

- Write these sentences on the board for the class to read. Point out the tricky words and blend any unknown words with the students:
  1. The bees buzz happily.
  2. Your cat has such a long tail.
  3. She has a scarf around her neck.
  4. Meg said she had lost the umbrella.

Unit 4: Tricky Words

Flashcards

- Review the tricky words *was, to, do, are, all, you, your, come, some, said, here, there.*

Tricky words: they

- Remind the class that some words are tricky because they cannot be worked out fully by listening for the sounds. They have an irregular part or an alternative spelling that has to be learned.
- Show the students the word *they* in the yellow flower at the top of their lesson page. Say the word and ask the students to blend the sounds. Then help the class to work out the tricky parts. In this word, the ‹ey› is tricky because it makes the sound /ai/.
- The students write inside the outline letters using a yellow pencil and underline the tricky parts in purple.

Tricky word spelling routine

- Writing the tricky word several times will help the students remember the spelling.
- Show the students the table in their books. They look at the word *they* in the first column and identify the tricky parts. The students then copy the word in the next column, writing over the dotted letters.
- Next, they cover up all instances of the word on the page and write it again by themselves.
- Finally, the students uncover the words and check that the spelling is correct, before covering them again and writing the word one more time.

Dictation

Say the word *they*. The students listen for the sounds in the word, think about how the tricky part is spelled, and write the word.

Wordsearch (See page 136)

- The students go to page 71 of their books and do the wordsearch at the bottom of the page. They read the tricky words in the flowers and try to find them in the grid.

FURTHER PRACTICE

It is important to practice the skills needed for reading and writing on a regular basis.

Blending and segmenting

rim, cod, nap, pup, mill,
pool, cluck, brook, cheek, sheriff

- Call out each word. The students say the sounds, holding up a finger for each one. Write the letters on the board as they do so and blend the word.
- Practice blending the words with the class (as well as in pairs or individually, if extra practice is needed).

Reading sentences

- Write these sentences on the board for the class to read. Point out the tricky words and blend any unknown words with the students:
  1. They do not drop litter.
  2. There is a doll on her bed.
  3. Your hands are very grubby.
  4. Can they come to dinner?

Unit 4: Words and Sentences

Review

- Use flashcards to review some of the 42 letter sounds and alternative spellings, including ‹y› as /y/ and /ee/, ‹ck›, and the short vowels /a/, /e/, /i/, /o/, /u/.
- Call out some of the sounds and ask the students to write the letter(s) for each one.

Talk about the picture: The fox

- Show the students the picture of the fox in their books (see opposite) and discuss it with the class.
- Ask a few students to say a sentence about the picture: for example, *I can see a fox; The bat is flying; The moon and stars are shining.*

Word focus

- In turn, call out the words *fox, looks, moon, trees,* and *bats*. The students say the sounds in each word, holding up a finger for each one. Write the letters on the board as they do so and blend the sounds with the class to read the word.
  - Point out the sound /c k/ in *looks* and ask the students how to spell it before writing it on the board. Remind them that short English words rarely end in ‹c›, and ‹ck› usually comes after a short vowel sound, so *looks* is spelled with a kicking /k/.
  - Remind the students that although the sound at the end of a plural word is often /z/, it is always written as ‹s›, as in *trees*.

Sentence modeling

- Write the following sentence on the board:
  - *The fox looks up at the moon.*
- Discuss the sentence as you write it.
- Encourage the students to call out the sounds of each word before you write it and to blend the word afterward.
- Point out the following:
  - Sentences start with a capital letter.
  - Capital letters are always tall.
  - Listen for the sounds in a word to write it.
  - *The* is a tricky word. How is it spelled?
  - *Looks* has a /c k/ sound. Which spelling should it be?
  - Leave a space between each word.
  - Do not forget the period at the end.
- Once the sentence has been modeled, read it with the students. All the students copy the sentence into their books and color the picture.

Free writing

- Those students who are able to write independently can write some more sentences of their own.
- At this stage the students are not expected to use the alternative spellings, so their writing will not always be accurate but the work can be read. Spelling gradually improves through reading many books and learning to apply the alternative letter-sound spellings.

Word and picture matching (See page 136)

- The students go to page 70 of their books and look at the fourth row of words and pictures: *red, tail, fox, bat.* They read each word and join it to the matching picture.

Jolly Phonics readers

Students who have finished the Red Level Readers and who know the alternative spellings and tricky words taught so far can start the Yellow Level.

FURTHER PRACTICE

It is important to practice the skills needed for reading and writing on a regular basis.

Blending and segmenting

log, bet, lid, pal, kill,
flock, clang, finch, gloomy, chopsticks

- Call out each word. The students say the sounds, holding up a finger for each one. Write the letters on the board as they do so and blend the word.
- Practice blending the words with the class (as well as in pairs or individually, if extra practice is needed).

Reading sentences

- Write these sentences on the board for the class to read. Point out the tricky words and blend any unknown words with the students:
  1. The puppets are kept here.
  2. Are your socks too big for you?
  3. They need some butter and flour.
  4. They said the trip to the zoo was fun.

Unit 5: Alternatives

Review

- Use flashcards to review some of the 42 letter sounds and alternative spellings, including /ai/, /ee/, /ie/, /oa/, /ue/; ‹y› as /y/ and /ee/; ‹ck› and the short vowels /a/, /e/, /i/, /o/, /u/.
- Call out some of the sounds and ask the students to write the letter(s) for each one.

Alternatives: the long vowel sounds

- Write the vowels letters on the board and say their short sounds with the class: /a/, /e/, /i/, /o/, /u/. Explain that these letters also have long vowel sounds: /ai/, /ee/, /ie/, /oa/, /ue/.
- Remind the students that they already know one way to write the long vowel sounds. Write the digraphs on the board and say the sounds with the class.
- Point out that the spelling of each short and long vowel sound starts with the same letter, but in the short vowels this letter says its sound and in the long vowels it says its name.
- Explain that this is because vowels are "magic" and when two of them are close together in a word, the second vowel can influence the way the first vowel is pronounced. This is why we say *When two vowels go walking, the first does the talking*.
- Now show the students the spellings in their books – ‹a_e›, ‹e_e›, ‹i_e›, ‹o_e›, ‹u_e› – and explain that these are another way to write the long vowel sounds. They are still digraphs, but the two vowel letters are separated by a consonant letter, represented by a dash. (This is why they are sometimes referred to as split digraphs.) The second vowel in these spellings does not say its sound; instead, it uses its magic to hop back and turn the short vowel sound into a long one. This is why it is known as magic ‹e›.

Answers

Step 2
Unit 5

Magic e

The final ‹e› in the spellings below does not say its sound. Instead, it uses its magic to hop back over the consonant and turns the short vowel into a long vowel sound.

a_e e_e i_e o_e u_e

Add a magic ‹e› to complete each word. Then color the pictures.

bike rose mule

gate Eve five

mole cake cube

63

Magic <e>

- The students write inside the outline spellings and say the long vowel sounds: /ai/, /ee/, /ie/, /oa/, /ue/.
- They then sound out the incomplete words below, starting with /b-i-k/. They add magic ‹e› and blend it again to say /b-ie-k/. They do the same with the other words and then color the pictures.

FURTHER PRACTICE

It is important to practice the skills needed for reading and writing on a regular basis.

Blending and segmenting

sip, lap, big, top, fizz,
chill, roast, spotty, mermaid, lunchbox

- Call out each word. The students say the sounds, holding up a finger for each one. Write the letters on the board as they do so and blend the word.
- Practice blending the words with the class (as well as in pairs or individually, if extra practice is needed).

Reading sentences

- Write these sentences on the board for the class to read. Point out the tricky words and blend any unknown words with the students:
    1. The goat ate some oats.
    2. Your puppy is very cute.
    3. She lent me her skates.
    4. They keep bees in a hive.

Unit 5: Handwriting

The alphabet (See page 136)

- Ask the students to look at the alphabet at the back of their books (Student Book 1, page 72).
- Remind them that when we say the alphabet, we use the letter names and not the sounds.
- Say the alphabet with the class, pausing between the sections: A–E; F–M; N–S; T–Z. The students point to each letter as they say it.
- Call out some of the letters and ask the students to point to them in their books. Ask them whether these letters are red, yellow, green, or blue.

Handwriting

- Show the students the lesson page in their books.
- Review the sounds and formation for the letters ‹z›, ‹w›, and ‹v› and teach the students how to write the capitals for these letters.
- Remind the students that all capital letters are tall and start at or near the top. None of them go down under the line.
- The students trace inside the outline capitals ‹Z›, ‹W›, and ‹V›, and then write over the dotted letters.

Capitals and lower-case letters

- The students look at the clouds and write inside each outline letter.
- If the outline letter is lower case, the students write the matching capital letter next to it. If the outline letter is a capital, the students write the matching lower-case letter next to it.

Dictation

- Call out the following words: *hid, hum, ant, from, slip, shed, them, chain, harp, mushroom.* The students listen for the sounds and write the words.
- Call out the sounds for ‹Z›, ‹W›, and ‹V› and ask the students to write the capital letters.

Answers

FURTHER PRACTICE

It is important to practice the skills needed for reading and writing on a regular basis.

Blending and segmenting

men, rod, bit, hop, fill,
stool, fussy, paint, clever, broomstick

- Call out each word. The students say the sounds, holding up a finger for each one. Write the letters on the board as they do so and blend the word.
- Practice blending the words with the class (as well as in pairs or individually, if extra practice is needed).

Reading sentences

- Write these sentences on the board for the class to read. Point out the tricky words and blend any unknown words with the students:
  1. Will you bake me a cake?
  2. They had some cherry pie.
  3. Steve and Jane never argue.
  4. The queen sat on her throne.

Unit 5: Tricky Words

Flashcards

- Review the tricky words *to, do, are, all, you, your, come, some, said, here, there, they.*

Tricky words: go, no, so

- Remind the class that some words are tricky because they cannot be worked out fully by listening for the sounds. They have an irregular part or an alternative spelling that has to be learned.
- Show the students the words in the yellow flowers at the top of their lesson page. Say each one and ask the students to blend the sounds. Then help the class to work out the tricky parts. In these words it is the letter ‹o› that is tricky because it makes its long vowel sound, /oa/, rather than its short vowel sound, /o/.
- As a general rule for reading, it helps the students to remember that *If the short vowel sound does not work, try the long one*.
- The students write inside the outline letters using a yellow pencil and underline the tricky parts in purple.

Tricky word spelling routine

- Writing the tricky words several times will help the students remember the spelling.
- Show the students the table in their books. They look at the word *go* in the first column and identify the tricky parts.
- The students then copy the word in the next column, writing over the dotted letters.
- Next, they cover up all instances of the word on the page and write it again by themselves.
- Finally, the students uncover the words and check that the spelling is correct, before covering them again and writing the word one more time.

- The students repeat these steps with the words *no* and *so*.

Dictation

Say the words *go, no* and *so*. The students listen for the sounds in each word, think about how the tricky parts are spelled, and write the words.

FURTHER PRACTICE

It is important to practice the skills needed for reading and writing on a regular basis.

Blending and segmenting

pan, job, beg, mad, ill,
oats, train, muddy, shock, bookmark

- Call out each word. The students say the sounds, holding up a finger for each one. Write the letters on the board as they do so and blend the word.
- Practice blending the words with the class (as well as in pairs or individually, if extra practice is needed).

Reading sentences

- Write these sentences on the board for the class to read. Point out the tricky words and blend any unknown words with the students:
  1. Your jokes are so funny.
  2. They like to go camping.
  3. Kate is waiting for the train.
  4. There are no fish in this lake.

Unit 5: Words and Sentences

Review
- Use flashcards to review some of the 42 letter sounds and alternative spellings, including ‹y› as /y/ and /ee/; ‹ck›, the short vowels, and the hop-over ‹e› digraphs.
- Call out some of the letter sounds and ask the students to write the different spellings for each one.

Talk about the picture: The fish
- Show the students the picture of the fish in their books (see opposite) and discuss it with the class.
- Ask a few students to say a sentence about the picture: for example, *I can see a crab; The fish is swimming; There is a shell in the weeds.*

Word focus
- In turn, call out the words *fish, long, tail, weed,* and *crab*. The students say the sounds in each word, holding up a finger for each one. Write the letters on the board as they do so and blend the sounds with the class to read the word. All these words are straightforward to blend and segment.

Sentence modeling
- Write the following sentence on the board:
  - *That fish has a long tail.*
- Discuss the sentence as you write it. Encourage the students to call out the sounds of each word before you write it and to blend the word afterward.
- Point out the following:
  - Sentences start with a capital letter.
  - Capital letters are always tall.
  - Listen for the sounds in a word to write it.
  - Although the sound at the end of *has* is /z/, it is written as ‹s›.
  - We tend to swallow the word *a* rather than use a clear /a/ sound. When the word is stressed, it says /ai/.
  - Leave a space between each word.
  - Do not forget the period at the end.
- Once the sentence has been modeled, read it with the students. All the students copy the sentence into their books and color the picture.

Free writing
- Those students who are able to write independently can write some more sentences of their own.
- At this stage the students are not expected to use the alternative spellings, so their writing will not always be accurate but the work can be read. Spelling gradually improves through reading many books and learning to apply the alternative letter-sound spellings.

Word and picture matching (See page 136)
- The students go to page 71 of their books and look at the first row of words and pictures: *starfish, flatfish, eel, catfish*. They read each word and join it to the matching picture.
- If the students are unfamiliar with these animals, show them the pictures first and talk about them. Explain that the names *starfish, catfish,* and *flatfish* relate to the way each animal looks.

Decodable books
- Send the students home with a book that matches their independent reading level (see page 21 for more information).

FURTHER PRACTICE
It is important to practice the skills needed for reading and writing on a regular basis.

Blending and segmenting
hit, rag, dig, rip, huff,
vain, flex, yard, rocky, eggshell
- Call out each word. The students say the sounds, holding up a finger for each one. Write the letters on the board as they do so and blend the word.
- Practice blending the words with the class (as well as in pairs or individually, if extra practice is needed).

Reading sentences
- Write these sentences on the board for the class to read. Point out the tricky words and blend any unknown words with the students:
  1. She spoke to them so quickly.
  2. There are no mules on the farm.
  3. They tied the rope around the tree.
  4. We go shopping three times a week.

Unit 6: Alternatives

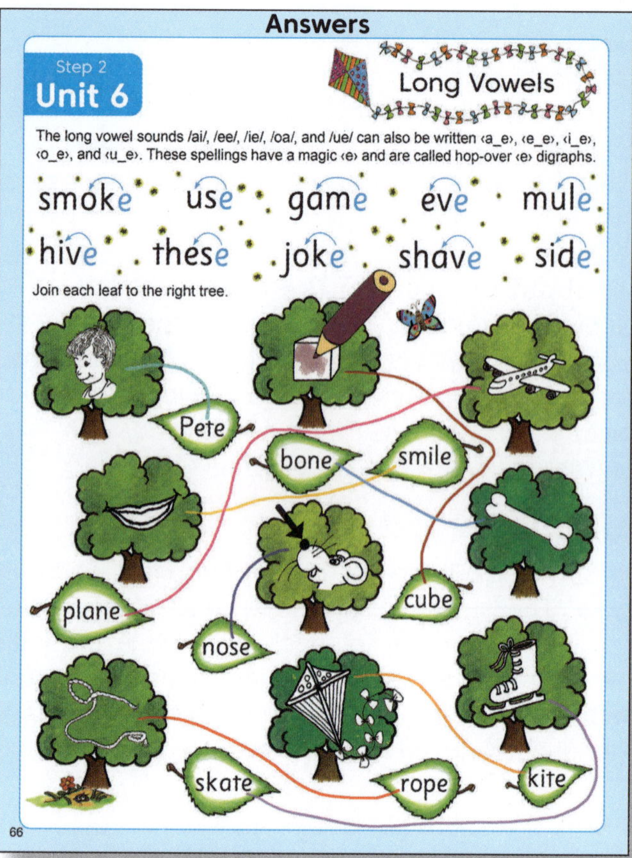

Review

- Use flashcards to review some of the 42 letter sounds and alternative spellings, including /ai/, /ee/, /ie/, /oa/, /ue/; ‹y› as /y/ and /ee/; ‹ck› and the short vowels /a/, /e/, /i/, /o/, /u/.
- Call out some of the letter sounds and ask the students to write the different spellings for each one.

Alternatives: long vowels and magic <e>

- Write the long vowel spellings ‹a_e›, ‹e_e›, ‹i_e›, ‹o_e›, and ‹u_e› on the board. Remind the students that these are an alternative way of writing the long vowel sounds /ai/, /ee/, /ie/, /oa/, /ue/.
- Now show the students the magic ‹e› words at the top of their lesson page and remind them that *When two vowels go walking, the first does the talking*. In these words this means that the ‹e› at the end of each word does not say its sound; instead, it uses its magic to hop back over the consonant letter and turn the short vowel sound into a long one. This is why these spellings are also known as hop-over ‹e› digraphs.
- Look at the first word and cover up the magic ‹e›. Ask the students to blend the sounds they can see: /s-m-o-k/. Now uncover the magic ‹e› and blend it again, this time saying /s-m-oa-k/. Remind the students that the magic ‹e› changes the short vowel /o/ into the long vowel /oa/. Repeat these steps with the other words.

Vowel forest trees

- The students read the word in each leaf, pointing to the two letters making the long vowel sound.
- Next, they join each leaf to the tree with the matching picture. When the students have finished, they can color the pictures in.
- The students then go to page 69 in their books. They read each pair of short- and long-vowel words at the bottom of the page and write the correct word under each picture (See page 136).

FURTHER PRACTICE

It is important to practice the skills needed for reading and writing on a regular basis.

Blending and segmenting

gas, did, hen, ban, yell,
march, prize, indeed, drench, mushroom

- Call out each word. The students say the sounds, holding up a finger for each one. Write the letters on the board as they do so and blend the word.
- Practice blending the words with the class (as well as in pairs or individually, if extra practice is needed).

Reading sentences

- Write these sentences on the board for the class to read. Point out the tricky words and blend any unknown words with the students:
  1. We will go outside soon.
  2. Did you see the statue?
  3. I rode the boat on the lake.
  4. There are no books on the shelf.

Unit 6: Handwriting

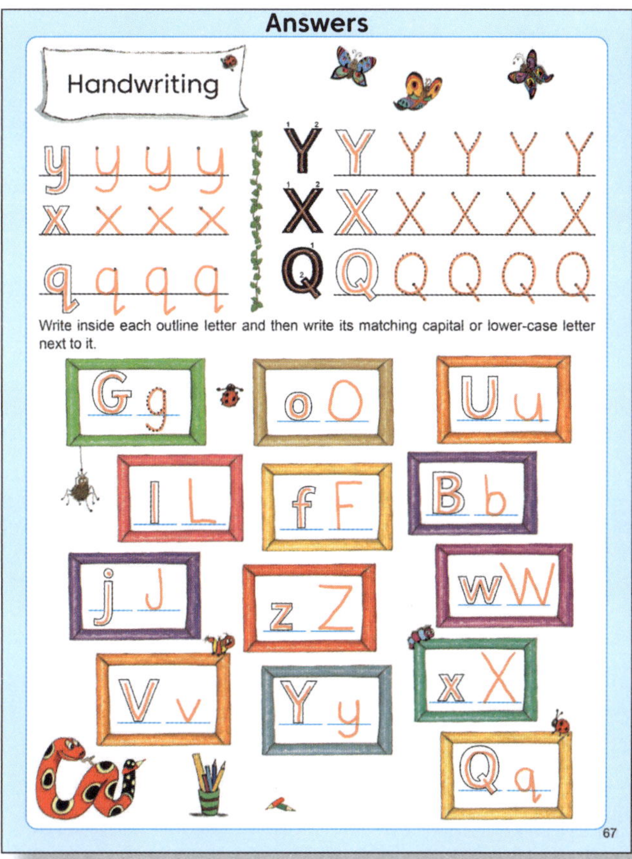

The alphabet (See page 136)

- Ask the students to look at the alphabet at the back of their books (Student Book 1, page 72).
- Remind them that when we say the alphabet, we use the letter names and not the sounds.
- Say the alphabet with the class, pausing between the sections: A–E; F–M; N–S; T–Z. The students point to each letter as they say it.
- Call out some of the letters and ask the students to point to them in their books. Ask them whether these letters are red, yellow, green, or blue.

Handwriting

- Show the students the lesson page in their books. Review the sounds and formation for the letters ‹y›, ‹x›, and ‹q›. Remind the students that the letters ‹y› and ‹q› have tails that go down under the line.
- Teach the students how to write the capitals letters ‹Y›, ‹X›, and ‹Q›. Remind them that all capital letters are tall and start at or near the top. None of the capitals go down under the line.
- The students trace inside the outline capitals and then write over the dotted letters.

Capitals and lower-case letters

- The students look at the picture frames and write inside each outline letter.
- If the outline letter is a capital, the students write the matching lower-case letter next to it. If the outline letter is lower case, the students write the matching capital next to it.

Dictation

- Call out the following words: *van, jug, yes, west, jump, shin, thud, cheep, quilt, starfish.* The students listen for the sounds and write the words.
- Call out the sounds for ‹Y›, ‹X›, and ‹Q› and ask the students to write the capital letters.

FURTHER PRACTICE

It is important to practice the skills needed for reading and writing on a regular basis.

Blending and segmenting

pin, got, kit, cap, bill,
bench, stung, blame, boxing, woodpecker

- Call out each word. The students say the sounds, holding up a finger for each one. Write the letters on the board as they do so and blend the word.
- Practice blending the words with the class (as well as in pairs or individually, if extra practice is needed).

Reading sentences

- Write these sentences on the board for the class to read. Point out the tricky words and blend any unknown words with the students:
  1. It is so windy here.
  2. We use the same shampoo.
  3. No, you cannot go out alone.
  4. Moles make holes in the ground.

Unit 6: Tricky Words

Flashcards

- Review the tricky words *all, you, your, come, some, said, here, there, they, go, no, so.*

Tricky words: my, one, by

- Remind the class that some words are tricky because they cannot be worked out fully by listening for the sounds. They have an irregular part or an alternative spelling that has to be learned.
- Show the students the words in the yellow and red flowers at the top of their lesson page. Say each one and ask the students to blend the sounds. Then help the class to work out the tricky parts:
  - The ‹y› in *my* and *by* is tricky because it it is an alternative spelling of the sound /ie/.
  - The word *one* is irregular because it says /wun/. Saying the word as it sounds will help the class to remember the spelling.
- The students write inside the outline letters using a yellow pencil for *my* and a red pencil for *one* and *by*. They underline the tricky parts in purple.

Tricky word spelling routine

- Writing the tricky words several times will help the students remember the spelling.
- Show the students the table in their books. They look at the word *my* in the first column and identify the tricky parts. The students then copy the word in the next column, writing over the dotted letters.
- Next, they cover up all instances of the word on the page and write it again by themselves.
- Finally, the students uncover the words and check that the spelling is correct, before covering them again and writing the word one more time.

- Repeat these steps with the words *one* and *by*.

Dictation

- Say the words *my, one* and *by*. The students listen for the sounds in each word, think about how the tricky parts are spelled, and write the words.

FURTHER PRACTICE

It is important to practice the skills needed for reading and writing on a regular basis.

Blending and segmenting

get, lit, den, bib, miss,
smoke, mister, smarter, slither, armband

- Call out each word. The students say the sounds, holding up a finger for each one. Write the letters on the board as they do so and blend the word.
- Practice blending the words with the class (as well as in pairs or individually, if extra practice is needed).

Reading sentences

- Write these sentences on the board for the class to read. Point out the tricky words and blend any unknown words with the students:
  1. Can we go by plane?
  2. Take one cake with you.
  3. My family had a barbecue.
  4. Did you invite my sister too?

Unit 6: Words and Sentences

Review

- Use flashcards to review some of the 42 letter sounds and alternative spellings, including ‹y› as /y/ and /ee/; ‹ck›, the short vowels, and the hop-over ‹e› digraphs.
- Call out some of the letter sounds and ask the students to write the different spellings for each one.

Talk about the picture: In the dark

- Show the students the night-time picture in their books (see opposite) and discuss it with the class.
- Ask a few students to say a sentence about the picture: for example, *I can see an owl; A bat is flying; The moon shines in the dark.*

Word focus

- In turn, call out the words *moth, stars, tree, twig,* and *wing*. The students say the sounds in each word, holding up a finger for each one. Write the letters on the board as they do so and blend the sounds with the class to read the word.
- Remind the students that although the sound at the end of a plural word is often /z/, it is always written as ‹s›, as in *stars*.

Sentence modeling

- Write the following sentence on the board:
  - *The moth is on the tree.*
- Discuss the sentence as you write it. Encourage the students to call out the sounds of each word before you write it and to blend the word afterward.
- Point out the following:
  - Sentences start with a capital letter.
  - Capital letters are always tall.
  - Listen for the sounds in a word to write it.
  - *The* is a tricky word. How is it spelled?
  - Although the sound at the end of *is* is /z/, it is written as ‹s›.
  - Leave a space between each word.
  - Do not forget the period at the end.
- Once the sentence has been modeled, read it with the students. All the students copy the sentence into their books and color the picture.

Free writing

- Those students who are able to write independently can write some more sentences of their own.
- At this stage the students are not expected to use the alternative spellings, so their writing will not always be accurate but the work can be read. Spelling gradually improves through reading many books and learning to apply the alternative letter-sound spellings.

Word and picture matching (See page 136)

- The students go to page 71 of their books and look at the second row of words: *star, moon, moth, sleeping*. They read each word and join it to the matching picture.

Decodable books

- Send the students home with a book that matches their independent reading level (see page 21 for more information).

FURTHER PRACTICE

It is important to practice the skills needed for reading and writing on a regular basis.

Blending and segmenting

mat, pit, net, bad, lick,
cute, fling, fox, stoop, toadstool

- Call out each word. The students say the sounds, holding up a finger for each one. Write the letters on the board as they do so and blend the word.
- Practice blending the words with the class (as well as in pairs or individually, if extra practice is needed).

Reading sentences

- Write these sentences on the board for the class to read. Point out the tricky words and blend any unknown words with the students:
  1. I will ride my bike.
  2. There is no one here.
  3. They run by the river.
  4. My dog has a red collar.

Step 2 Jolly Phonics Student Book 2: Page 2

Unit 7: Alternatives

Review

- Use flashcards to review some of the 42 letter sounds and alternative spellings, including ‹ai› and ‹oi›; ‹a_e›, ‹e_e›, ‹i_e›, ‹o_e›, ‹u_e›; ‹y› as /y/ and /ee/; ‹ck› and the short vowels.
- Call out some of the letter sounds and ask the students to write the different spellings for each one.

Alternatives: ‹ay› and ‹oy›

- Write the digraphs ‹ai› and ‹oi› on the board and ask the students to say the sounds. Point out that both spellings end in the letter ‹i›.
- Look at some examples of words with these spellings, such as *aim, nail, oil,* and *foil.* Point out that the spellings are either at the beginning of the words, or in the middle, but not at the end.
- Explain that the reason for this is that the letter ‹i› is very shy and does not like to come at the end of English words. If the sounds /ai/ or /oi/ come at the end of a word, toughy ‹y› takes shy ‹i›'s place.
- Go back to the ‹ai› and ‹oi› spellings on the board and replace the ‹i› in both digraphs with a ‹y›. Explain that ‹ay› is an alternative way of writing the sound /ai/ and that ‹oy› is an alternative way of writing the sound /oi/.
- Write the following words on the board and read them with the class: *day, say, play, joy, enjoy, annoy, stay,* and *way.* Underline the ‹ay› or ‹oy› spelling at the end of each word.

Which spelling should it be?

- Ask the students to look at their books and write inside the outline digraphs ‹ai› and ‹ay›.
- They then say the word for each picture, listen to where the sound /ai/ comes in the word and decide whether to write ‹ai› or ‹ay› to complete the word.
- The students do the same again with the next set of pictures, this time listening for the sound /oi/.

Animal anagrams (See page 137)

- The students go to page 24 in their books. They look at the top row of anagrams, unscramble the letters, and write the words.

FURTHER PRACTICE

It is important to practice the skills needed for reading and writing on a regular basis.

Blending and segmenting

jig, luck, pie, see, lump,
port, flesh, value, bother, stripes

- Call out each word. The students say the sounds, holding up a finger for each one. Write the letters on the board as they do so and blend the word.
- Practice blending the words with the class (as well as in pairs or individually, if extra practice is needed).

Reading sentences

- Write these sentences on the board for the class to read. Point out the tricky words and blend any unknown words with the students:
  1. Is this the way home?
  2. My sister is very annoying.
  3. One day, the boy ran away.
  4. We are playing with our toys.

Unit 7: Handwriting

The alphabet (See page 136)

- Show the students the alphabet at the back of their books (Student Book 2, page 66).
- The students say the alphabet, pointing to each letter as they say it. Encourage them to pause between the sections: A–E; F–M; N–S; T–Z.
- Call out some of the letters and ask the students to point to them in their books. Ask them whether these letters are red, yellow, green, or blue.
- **Note:** Knowing which letters are in each section will help the students find words more quickly when they start using a dictionary.

Handwriting

- Show the students the capital letters on their lesson page. Point out that the capitals are in alphabetical order in the four colored sections.
- Remind the students that all capital letters are tall and start at or near the top. None of them go down under the line.
- The students complete each section of the alphabet. They write inside the outline letters, using a red pencil for A to E, a yellow pencil for F to M, a green pencil for N to S, and a blue pencil for T to Z.

Capitals and lower-case letters

- The students write the lower-case letter next to each capital letter, using a red, yellow, green, or blue pencil to complete the alphabet.

Dictation

- Call out the following words: *log, jam, bat, loft, hunt, shut, chest, tooth, tree, oilcan*. The students listen for the sounds and write the words.

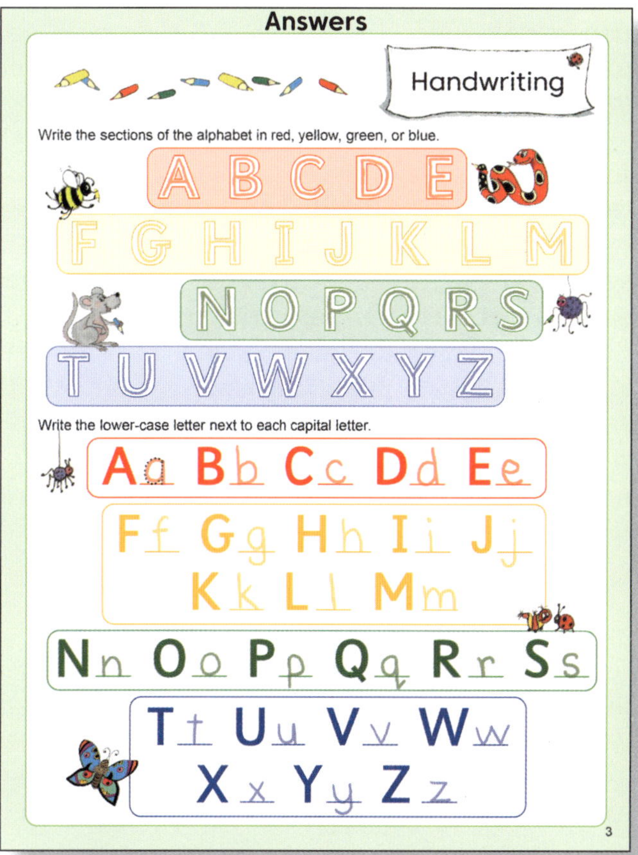

- Call out the sounds for some of the alphabet letters and ask the students to write the capital letters.

FURTHER PRACTICE

It is important to practice the skills needed for reading and writing on a regular basis.

Blending and segmenting

can, back, for, pain, help,
stamp, scarf, brake, rusty, bedroom

- Call out each word. The students say the sounds, holding up a finger for each one. Write the letters on the board as they do so and blend the word.
- Practice blending the words with the class (as well as in pairs or individually, if extra practice is needed).

Reading sentences

- Write these sentences on the board for the class to read. Point out the tricky words and blend any unknown words with the students:
  1. Roy and Joy are twins.
  2. The hay is kept in the barn.
  3. He enjoys cooking very much.
  4. They went to the park on Sunday.

Unit 7: Tricky Words

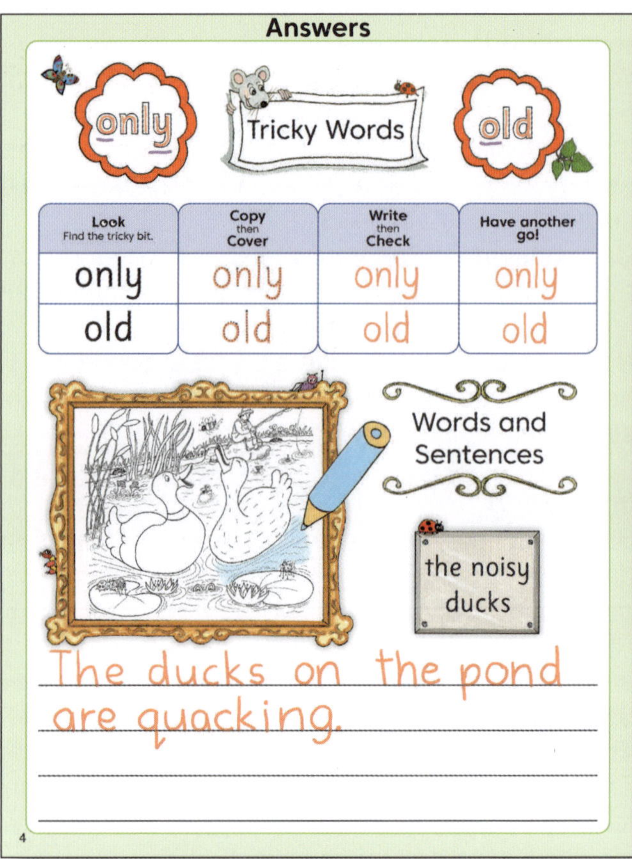

Flashcards

- Review the tricky words *come, some, said, here, there, they, go, no, so, my, one, by.*

Tricky words: only, old

- Remind the class that some words are tricky because they cannot be worked out fully by listening for the sounds. They have an irregular part or an alternative spelling that has to be learned.
- Show the students the words in the red flowers at the top of their lesson page. Say each one and ask the students to blend the sounds. Then help the class to work out the tricky parts:
  - In both these words, the ‹o› is tricky because it makes its long vowel sound, /oa/, rather than its short vowel sound, /o/.
  - The students also have to remember the ‹y› as /ee/ spelling in *only*.
- As a general rule for reading, it helps the students to remember that *If the short vowel sound does not work, try the long one*.
- The students write inside the outline letters using a red pencil and underline the tricky parts in purple.

Tricky word spelling routine

- Writing the tricky words several times will help the students remember the spelling.
- Show the students the table in their books. They look at the word *only* in the first column and identify the tricky parts. The students then copy the word in the next column, writing over the dotted letters.
- Next, they cover up all instances of the word on the page and write it again by themselves.
- Finally, the students uncover the words and check that the spelling is correct, before covering them again and writing the word one more time.
- The students repeat these steps with the word *old*.

Dictation

- Say the words *only* and *old*. The students listen for the sounds in each word, think about how the tricky parts are spelled, and write the words.

FURTHER PRACTICE

It is important to practice the skills needed for reading and writing on a regular basis.

Blending and segmenting

hum, will, goat, corn, mend,
snail, took, chomp, brave, weeping

- Call out each word. The students say the sounds, holding up a finger for each one. Write the letters on the board as they do so and blend the word.
- Practice blending the words with the class (as well as in pairs or individually, if extra practice is needed).

Reading sentences

- Write these sentences on the board for the class to read. Point out the tricky words and blend any unknown words with the students:
  1. I can only say thank you.
  2. Denmark has a royal family.
  3. Can we stay with you today?
  4. Her old teddy is in the toy box.

Unit 7: Words and Sentences

Review

- Use flashcards to review some of the 42 letter sounds and alternative spellings taught so far.
- Call out some of the letter sounds and ask the students to write the different spellings for each one.

Talk about the picture: The noisy ducks

- Show the students the picture of the ducks in their books (see opposite) and discuss it with the class.
- Ask a few students to say a sentence about the picture: for example, *I can see some ducks; The ducks are quacking; The man is fishing.*

Word focus

- In turn, call out the words *ducks, pond, quacking, reeds,* and *fishing*.
- The students say the sounds in each word, holding up a finger for each one. Write the letters on the board as they do so and blend the sounds with the class to read the word.
  - Point out the sound /c k/ in *ducks* and *quacking* and ask the students how to spell it before writing it on the board. Remind them that ‹ck› usually comes after a short vowel sound, so here the sound /c k/ is written with a caterpillar /c/ and a kicking /k/.
  - Remind the students that although the sound at the end of a plural word is often /z/, it is always written as ‹s›, as in *reeds*.

Sentence modeling

- Write the following sentence on the board:
  - *The ducks on the pond are quacking.*
- Discuss the sentence as you write it. Encourage the students to call out the sounds of each word before you write it and to blend the word afterward.
- Point out the following:
  - Sentences start with a capital letter.
  - Capital letters are always tall.
  - Listen for the sounds in a word to write it.
  - *The* and *are* are tricky words. How are they spelled?
  - *Ducks* and *quacking* have a /c k/ sound. How is it spelled?
  - Leave a space between each word.
  - Do not forget the period at the end.
- Once the sentence has been modeled, read it with the students. All the students copy the sentence into their books and color the picture.

Free writing

- Those students who are able to write independently can write some more sentences of their own.
- At this stage the students are not expected to use the alternative spellings, so their writing will not always be accurate but the work can be read. Spelling gradually improves through reading many books and learning to apply the alternative letter-sound spellings.

Decodable books

- Send the students home with a book that matches their independent reading level (see page 21 for more information).

FURTHER PRACTICE

It is important to practice the skills needed for reading and writing on a regular basis.

Blending and segmenting

hot, puff, rich, boat, lift,
stove, poppy, croak, butter, morning

- Call out each word. The students say the sounds, holding up a finger for each one. Write the letters on the board as they do so and blend the word.
- Practice blending the words with the class (as well as in pairs or individually, if extra practice is needed).

Reading sentences

- Write these sentences on the board for the class to read. Point out the tricky words and blend any unknown words with the students:
  1. His old dog is very loyal.
  2. There are only three pens left.
  3. He will be joining the Boy Scouts.
  4. The waiter brings us drinks on a tray.

Unit 8: Alternatives

Answers

Step 2
Unit 8

ea as /ee/

As well as ‹ee›, ‹y›, and ‹e_e›, the /ee/ sound can be written as ‹ea›.

ee | seal | teeth | tea | ea
leaf | feet | sheep
tree | read | sea

Read the words at the top of the page and write the correct word under each picture.

sheep	leaf	seal
sea	read	teeth
feet	tree	tea

5

Review

- Use flashcards to review some of the 42 letter sounds and alternative spellings, including ‹ee›, ‹ay› and ‹oy›; ‹a_e›, ‹e_e›, ‹i_e›, ‹o_e›, ‹u_e›; ‹y› as /y/ and /ee/; ‹ck› and the short vowels.
- Call out some of the letter sounds and ask the students to write the different spellings for each one.

Alternatives: ‹ea› as /ee/

- Write the words *free* and *eve* on the board and review the ‹ee› and ‹e_e› spellings for the long vowel sound /ee/.
- Now say the words *eat* and *peas* and write them on the board. Explain that ‹ea› is another way to write the sound /ee/.
- Underline the three spellings on the board – ‹ee›, ‹e_e›, and ‹ea› – and remind the students that *When two vowels go walking, the first does the talking*.
- Write some more words on the board and read them with the class: *clean, meat, bean, each, heat, stream, teach,* and *peanut.* Underline the ‹ea› spelling in each word.

‹ee› or ‹ea›?

- Ask the students to look at their books and write inside the outline digraphs ‹ee› and ‹ea›.
- Read the words with the class and discuss which spelling of the sound /ee/ is used in each one. The students underline the alternative spelling in each word.
- They then match these words to the pictures below, writing the correct word under each picture.
- There is a line for each sound in the word. A longer line indicates that a digraph is needed.

Animal anagrams (See page 137)

- The students go to page 24 in their books. They look at the second row of anagrams, unscramble the letters, and write the words.

FURTHER PRACTICE

It is important to practice the skills needed for reading and writing on a regular basis.

Blending and segmenting

dog, cuff, bang, loaf, rust,
toy, stray, pound, playing, wagging

- Call out each word. The students say the sounds, holding up a finger for each one. Write the letters on the board as they do so and blend the word.
- Practice blending the words with the class (as well as in pairs or individually, if extra practice is needed).

Reading sentences

- Write these sentences on the board for the class to read. Point out the tricky words and blend any unknown words with the students:
  1. We had tea and cake on a tray.
  2. He only eats meat on Sundays.
  3. We planted some peas and beans.
  4. They took a trip on an old steam train.

Unit 8: Handwriting

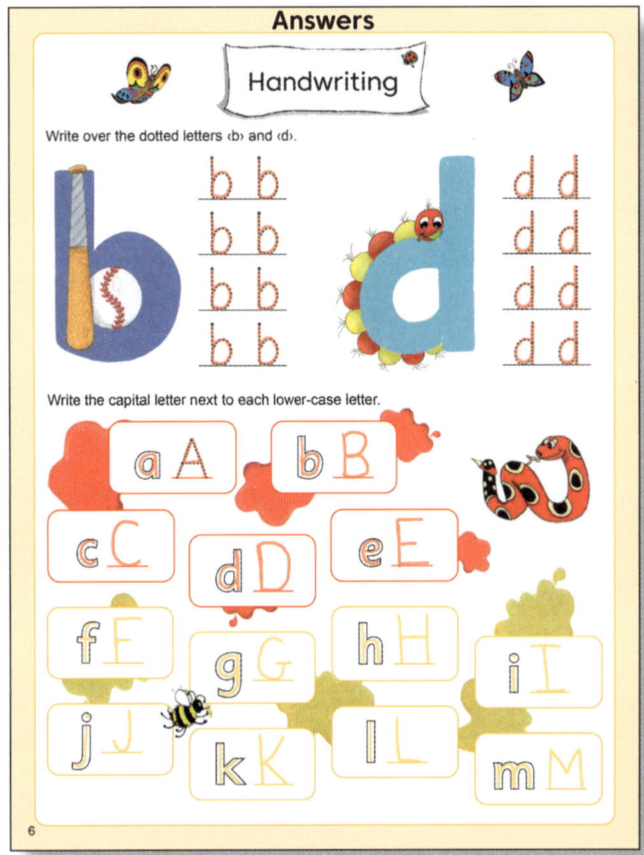
Answers

Handwriting

Write over the dotted letters ‹b› and ‹d›.

b b
b b
b b
b b

d d
d d
d d
d d

Write the capital letter next to each lower-case letter.

a A, b B, c C, d D, e E, f F, g G, h H, i I, j J, k K, l L, m M

6

The alphabet (See page 136)

- The students go to page 66 at the back of their books and say the alphabet. They point to each letter as they say it and pause between the sections: A–E; F–M; N–S; T–Z.
- Call out some of the letters and ask the students to point to them in their books. Ask them whether these letters are red, yellow, green, or blue.
- **Note:** Knowing which letters are in each section will help the students find words more quickly when they start using a dictionary.

Handwriting

- The letters ‹b› and ‹d› are often confused by young students so it is important to review the formation regularly.
- Show the students the large letters in their books and remind them of the following:
  - The letter ‹b› is tall. It starts at the top and goes down the "bat" and bounces up and around the "ball."
  - The letter ‹d› is also tall, but, it starts with a cater-pillar /c/.
- The students form the letters in the air before writing them in their books. They write over the dotted letters, taking care to begin at each starting dot.

Capitals and lower-case letters

- The students practice writing the first half of the alphabet. They write inside each outline lower-case letter and then write the matching capital letter next to it. They use a red pencil for A to E and a yellow pencil for F to M.
- Remind the students that all capital letters are tall and start at or near the top. None of them go down under the line.

Dictation

- Call out the following words: *big, bag, men, sand, belt, wish, north, lunch, sort, without.* The students listen for the sounds and write the words.
- Call out the sounds for some of the letters in the first two alphabet sections and ask the students to write the capitals.

FURTHER PRACTICE

It is important to practice the skills needed for reading and writing on a regular basis.

Blending and segmenting

him, boss, fork, moon, pond,
fray, oyster, hound, charm, boyish

- Call out each word. The students say the sounds, holding up a finger for each one. Write the letters on the board as they do so and blend the word.
- Practice blending the words with the class (as well as in pairs or individually, if extra practice is needed).

Reading sentences

- Write these sentences on the board for the class to read. Point out the tricky words and blend any unknown words with the students:
  1. The seals bark on the rocks.
  2. Each leaf is very interesting.
  3. I met my old teacher yesterday.
  4. Dad will only make tea in a teapot.

Unit 8: Tricky Words

Flashcards

- Review the tricky words *said, here, there, they, go, no, so, my, one, by, only, old.*

Tricky words: like, have

- Remind the class that some words are tricky because they cannot be worked out fully by listening for the sounds. They have an irregular part or an alternative spelling that has to be learned.
- Show the students the words in the red flowers at the top of their lesson page. Say each one and ask the students to blend the sounds. Then help the class to work out the tricky parts:
  - *Like* is tricky because the class have to remember the ‹k› spelling of the /c k/ sound and the alternative speling ‹i_e›.
  - *Have* is tricky because it has a silent ‹e›.
- The students write inside the outline letters using a red pencil and underline the tricky parts in purple.

Tricky word spelling routine

- Writing the tricky words several times will help the students remember the spelling.
- Show the students the table in their books. They look at the word *like* in the first column and identify the tricky parts.
- The students then copy the word in the next column, writing over the dotted letters.
- Next, they cover up all instances of the word on the page and write it again by themselves.
- Finally, the students uncover the words and check that the spelling is correct, before covering them again and writing the word one more time.
- The students repeat these steps with the word *have.*

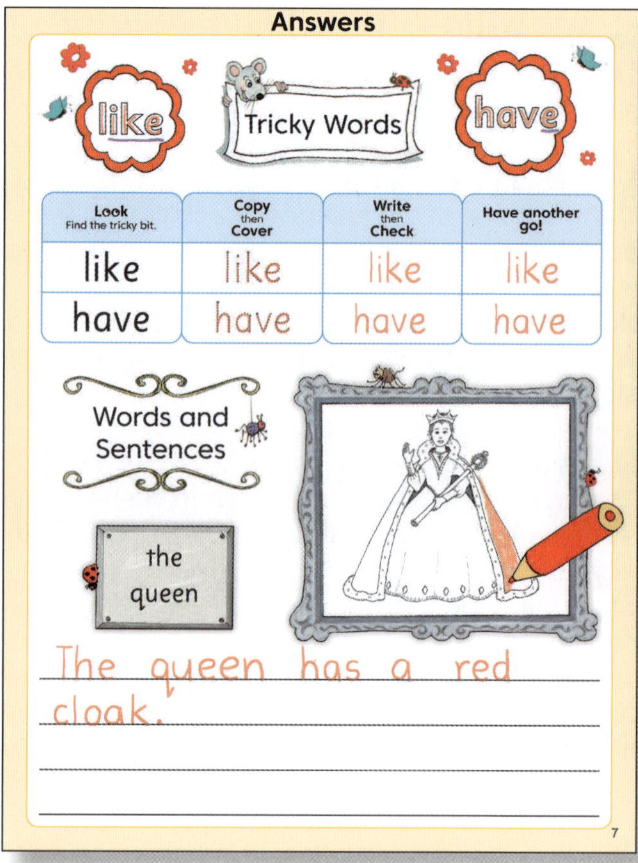

Dictation

- Say the words *like* and *have*. The students listen for the sounds in each word, think about how the tricky parts are spelled, and write the words.

Wordsearch (See page 137)

- The students go to page 23 of their books and do the wordsearch at the top of the page. They read the tricky words in the flowers and try to find them in the grid.

FURTHER PRACTICE

It is important to practice the skills needed for reading and writing on a regular basis.

Blending and segmenting

pen, dell, chin, toad, jump,
clay, part, fuel, quench, scrapbook

- Call out each word. The students say the sounds, holding up a finger for each one. Write the letters on the board as they do so and blend the word.
- Practice blending the words with the class (as well as in pairs or individually, if extra practice is needed).

Reading sentences

- Write these sentences on the board for the class to read. Point out the tricky words and blend any unknown words with the students:
  1. Parrots have big beaks.
  2. They like to read books.
  3. Dean looks just like his dad.
  4. Have you ever eaten oysters?

Unit 8: Words and Sentences

Review

- Use flashcards to review some of the 42 letter sounds and alternative spellings taught so far.
- Call out some of the letter sounds and ask the students to write the different spellings for each one.

Talk about the picture: The queen

- Show the students the picture of the queen in their books (see opposite) and discuss it with the class.
- Ask a few students to say a sentence about the picture: for example, *I can see a queen; She is wearing a long dress; The queen has a golden crown.*

Word focus

- In turn, call out the words *queen, red, cloak, dress,* and *stand*. The students say the sounds in each word, holding up a finger for each one. Write the letters on the board as they do so and blend the sounds with the class to read the word.
  - Point out the sound /c k/ in *cloak* and ask the students how to spell it before writing it on the board. Remind them that short English words rarely end in ‹c›, and ‹ck› usually comes after a short vowel sound, so *cloak* is spelled with a kicking /k/.
  - Also remind the students that a consonant letter is often doubled when it comes directly after a short vowel sound, as in *dress*.

Sentence modeling

- Write the following sentence on the board:
  - *The queen has a red cloak.*
- Discuss the sentence as you write it. Encourage the students to call out the sounds of each word before you write it and to blend the word afterward.
- Point out the following:
  - Sentences start with a capita letter.
  - Capital letters are always tall.
  - Listen for the sounds in a word to write it.
  - *The* is a tricky word. How is it spelled?
  - Although the sound at the end of *has* is /z/, it is written as ‹s›.
  - We tend to swallow the word *a* rather than use a clear /a/ sound. When the word is stressed, it says /ai/.
  - *Cloak* has a /c k/ sound. How is it spelled?
  - Leave a space between each word.
  - Do not forget the period at the end.
- Once the sentence has been modeled, read it with the students. All the students copy the sentence into their books and color the picture.

Free writing

- Those students who are able to write independently can write some more sentences of their own.
- At this stage the students are not expected to use the alternative spellings, so their writing will not always be accurate but the work can be read. Spelling gradually improves through reading many books and learning to apply the alternative letter-sound spellings.

Decodable books

- Send the students home with a book that matches their independent reading level (see page 21 for more information).

FURTHER PRACTICE

It is important to practice the skills needed for reading and writing on a regular basis.

Blending and segmenting

sag, dock, aim, lie, nest,
flag, boy, shatter, slipper, monster

- Call out each word. The students say the sounds, holding up a finger for each one. Write the letters on the board as they do so and blend the word.
- Practice blending the words with the class (as well as in pairs or individually, if extra practice is needed).

Reading sentences

- Write these sentences on the board for the class to read. Point out the tricky words and blend any unknown words with the students:
  1. I like eating peaches.
  2. We will have a tea party.
  3. Do you like roasted peanuts?
  4. Beavers have very strong teeth.

Unit 9: Alternatives

Review

- Use flashcards to review some of the 42 letter sounds and alternative spellings, including ‹ie›, ‹ea›, ‹ay›, ‹oy›; ‹a_e›, ‹e_e›, ‹i_e›, ‹o_e›, ‹u_e›; ‹y› as /y/ and /ee/; ‹ck› and the short vowels.
- Call out some of the letter sounds and ask the students to write the different spellings for each one.

Alternatives: ‹y› and ‹igh› as /ie/

- Write the words *die* and *five* on the board and review the ‹ie› and ‹i_e› spellings for the long vowel sound /ie/. Remind the students that *When two vowels go walking, the first does the talking.*
- Now say the words *dry* and *sigh* and write them on the board. Explain that ‹y› and ‹igh› are two more ways that the long vowel sound /ie/ can be written. Underline the four spellings on the board: ‹ie›, ‹i_e›, ‹y›, and ‹igh›.
- Write some more words on the board and read them with the class: *by, fry, cry, sight, thigh, bright, flying and lightning.* Underline the ‹y› or ‹igh› spelling in each one.

Reading words

- Show the students the words at the top of their lesson page. They read the words and underline the spelling of the sound /ie/ in each one.
- Remind the students that *my* is one of the tricky words. When they write it, they have to remember to spell the sound /ie/ with a ‹y›.

Read and draw

- The students read the word in each star and draw a picture for each one in the adjoining moon.

Answers

Animal anagrams (See page 137)

- The students go to page 24 in their books. They look at the third row of anagrams, unscramble the letters, and write the words.

FURTHER PRACTICE

It is important to practice the skills needed for reading and writing on a regular basis.

Blending and segmenting

gum, pick, coat, long, soft,
tram, weak, crust, spark, cleaner

- Call out each word. The students say the sounds, holding up a finger for each one. Write the letters on the board as they do so and blend the word.
- Practice blending the words with the class (as well as in pairs or individually, if extra practice is needed).

Reading sentences

- Write these sentences on the board for the class to read. Point out the tricky words and blend any unknown words with the students:
  1. Bats like flying at night.
  2. The kite flies high in the sky.
  3. I have a slight pain in my neck.
  4. The moth flutters its wings in the moonlight.

Unit 9: Handwriting

The alphabet (See page 136)

- The students go to page 66 at the back of their books and say the alphabet. They point to each letter as they say it and pause between the sections: A–E; F–M; N–S; T–Z.
- Call out some of the letters and ask the students to point to them in their books. Ask them whether these letters are red, yellow, green, or blue.
- **Note:** Knowing which letters are in each section will help the students find words more quickly when they start using a dictionary.

Handwriting

- Show the students the letters ‹r›, ‹n›, ‹m›, and ‹h› on their lesson page. Remind them that these letters all start in the same way: they begin at the top, go down to the line, come straight back up, and then go over. The letter ‹h› is a tall letter.
- The students practice writing the letters. They trace inside the outline letters and then write over the dotted letters.

Capitals and lower-case letters

- The students practice writing the second half of the alphabet. They write inside each outline lower-case letter and then write the matching capital letter next to it. They use a green pencil for N to S and a blue pencil for T to Z.
- Remind the students that all capital letters are tall and start at or near the top. None of them go down under the line.

Dictation

- Call out the following words: *dug, mix, leg, help, soft, rang, this, shout, coach, raindrop.* The students listen for the sounds and write the words.
- Call out the sounds for some of the letters in the last two alphabet sections and ask the students to write the capitals.

Answers

Handwriting

Practice writing these letters. Remember to start at the top and go down. Then come straight back up and over.

Write the capital letter next to each lower-case letter.

FURTHER PRACTICE

It is important to practice the skills needed for reading and writing on a regular basis.

Blending and segmenting

rug, pack, cork, seed, pest,
foot, sweep, reading, number, woodland

- Call out each word. The students say the sounds, holding up a finger for each one. Write the letters on the board as they do so and blend the word.
- Practice blending the words with the class (as well as in pairs or individually, if extra practice is needed).

Reading sentences

- Write these sentences on the board for the class to read. Point out the tricky words and blend any unknown words with the students:
    1. My sister is very shy.
    2. They fight like cats and dogs.
    3. The sun shines brightly.
    4. Do you have the right time?

Unit 9: Tricky Words

Flashcards

- Review the tricky words *there, they, go, no, so, my, one, by, only, old, like, have.*

Tricky words: live, give

- Remind the class that some words are tricky because they cannot be worked out fully by listening for the sounds. They have an irregular part or an alternative spelling that has to be learned.
- Show the students the words in the red flowers at the top of their lesson page. Say each one and ask the students to blend the sounds. Then help the class to work out the tricky parts. In both these words, the ‹e› is tricky because it is silent.
- Remind the students that the tricky word *have* shares a similar spelling. This is because English words rarely end in the letter ‹v›.
- The students write inside the outline letters using a red pencil and underline the tricky parts in purple.
- **Note:** The word *live* has two meanings and two pronunciations; the students must work out which is meant from the context of the sentence.

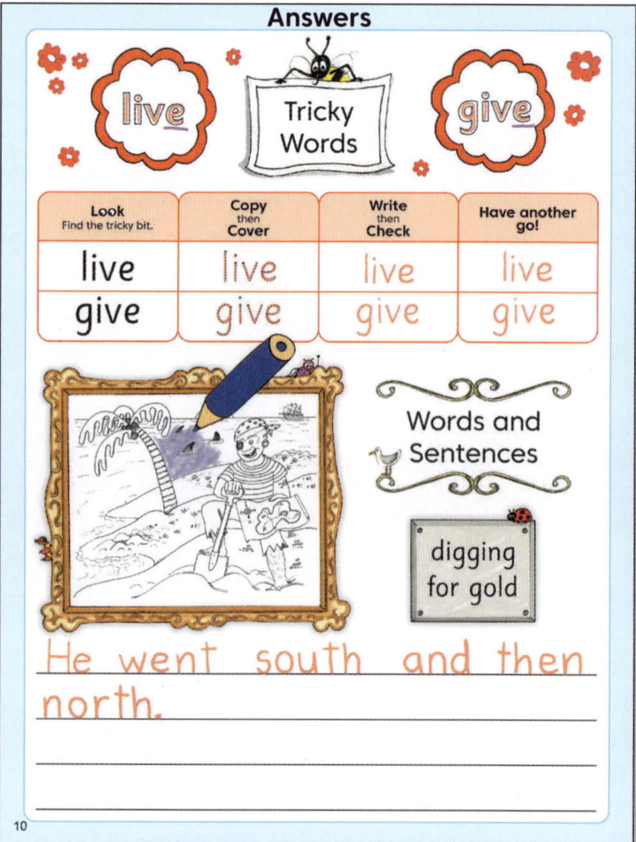

Tricky word spelling routine

- Writing the tricky words several times will help the students remember the spelling.
- Show the students the table in their books. They look at the word *live* in the first column and identify the tricky parts. The students then copy the word in the next column, writing over the dotted letters.
- Next, they cover up all instances of the word on the page and write it again by themselves.
- Finally, the students uncover the words and check that the spelling is correct, before covering them again and writing the word one more time.
- The students repeat these steps with the word *give*.

Dictation

- Say the words *live* and *give*. The students listen for the sounds in each word, think about how the tricky parts are spelled, and write the words.

FURTHER PRACTICE

It is important to practice the skills needed for reading and writing on a regular basis.

Blending and segmenting

jab, well, deep, king, sand,
beast, cheeky, teacup, outfit, spoilsport

- Call out each word. The students say the sounds, holding up a finger for each one. Write the letters on the board as they do so and blend the word.
- Practice blending the words with the class (as well as in pairs or individually, if extra practice is needed).

Reading sentences

- Write these sentences on the board for the class to read. Point out the tricky words and blend any unknown words with the students:
    1. They live near the beach.
    2. Did you give him a present?
    3. We lived in Spain for ten years.
    4. Give your sister some lemonade.

Unit 9: Words and Sentences

Review

- Use flashcards to review some of the 42 letter sounds and alternative spellings taught so far.
- Call out some of the letter sounds and ask the students to write the different spellings for each one.

Talk about the picture: Digging for gold

- Show the students the picture of the pirate in their books (see opposite) and discuss it with the class.
- Ask a few students to say a sentence about the picture: for example, *I can see a pirate; The pirate has a map; He is looking for treasure.*

Word focus

- In turn, call out the words *went, north, then, south,* and *map*. The students say the sounds in each word, holding up a finger for each one. Write the letters on the board as they do so and blend the sounds with the class to read the word. All these words are straightforward to blend and sound.

Sentence modeling

- Write the following sentence on the board:
  - *He went south and then north.*
- Discuss the sentence as you write it. Encourage the students to call out the sounds of each word before you write it and to blend the word afterward.
- Point out the following:
  - Sentences start with a capital letter.
  - Capital letters are always tall.
  - Listen for the sounds in a word to write it.
  - *He* is a tricky word. How is it spelled?
  - Leave a space between each word.
  - Do not forget the period at the end.
- Once the sentence has been modeled, read it with the students. All the students copy the sentence into their books and color the picture.

Free writing

- Those students who are able to write independently can write some more sentences of their own.
- At this stage the students are not expected to use the alternative spellings, so their writing will not always be accurate but the work can be read. Spelling gradually improves through reading many books and learning to apply the alternative letter-sound spellings.

Decodable books

- Send the students home with a book that matches their independent reading level (see page 21 for more information).

FURTHER PRACTICE

It is important to practice the skills needed for reading and writing on a regular basis.

Blending and segmenting

vet, duck, oak, shed, band,
steam, chilly, spring, snore, starfish

- Call out each word. The students say the sounds, holding up a finger for each one. Write the letters on the board as they do so and blend the word.
- Practice blending the words with the class (as well as in pairs or individually, if extra practice is needed).

Reading sentences

- Write these sentences on the board for the class to read. Point out the tricky words and blend any unknown words with the students:
  1. Do you live around here?
  2. I spy a dragonfly by the stream.
  3. My older sister still lives at home.
  4. Dad might give me a better bike.

Unit 10: Alternatives

Review

- Use flashcards to review some of the 42 letter sounds and alternative spellings, including ‹oa› and ‹ou›; ‹igh›, ‹ea›, ‹ay›, ‹oy›; ‹a_e›, ‹e_e›, ‹i_e›, ‹o_e›, ‹u_e›; ‹y› as /y/, /ee/, and /ie/; ‹ck› and the short vowels.
- Call out some of the letter sounds and ask the students to write the different spellings for each one.

Alternatives: ‹ow› as /oa/ and /ou/

- Write the words *goat* and *rope* on the board and review the ‹oa› and ‹o_e› spellings for the long vowel sound /oa/. Remind the students that *When two vowels go walking, the first does the talking*.
- Then say the word *show*, add it to the board, and underline the digraph ‹ow›. Explain that this is another way to write the sound /oa/.
- Now say the word *cow* and write it on the board. Read it with the class and ask them what sound the ‹ow› spelling is making now *[/ou/]*.
- Explain that because the digraph ‹ow› has two sounds – /oa/ and /ou/ – the students must try both when reading an unfamiliar word with this spelling.
- Write some more words on the board and read them with the class, trying both sounds: */oa/ glow, rainbow, elbow, shadow; /ou/ now, crowd, down, shower.*

Reading words

- Show the students the words at the top of their lesson page. They read the words and underline the spelling of the sound /oa/ or /ou/ in each one.

Read and draw

- The students read the words in the clouds and boats and draw a picture for each one.

Answers

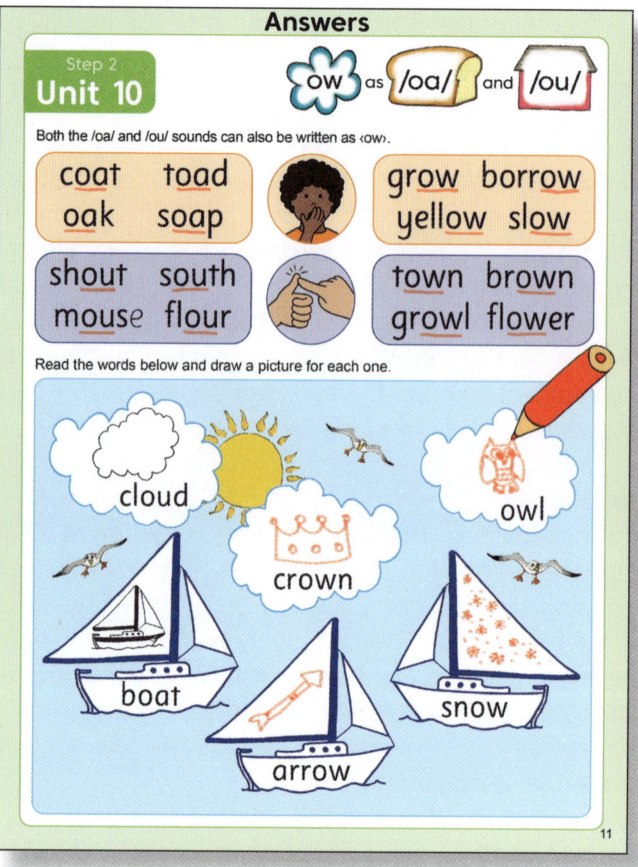

Animal anagrams (See page 137)

- The students go to page 24 in their books. They look at the bottom row of anagrams, unscramble the letters, and write the words.

FURTHER PRACTICE

It is important to practice the skills needed for reading and writing on a regular basis.

Blending and segmenting

wet, mess, sail, cool, vest,
sky, try, smash, sight, smoother

- Call out each word. The students say the sounds, holding up a finger for each one. Write the letters on the board as they do so and blend the word.
- Practice blending the words with the class (as well as in pairs or individually, if extra practice is needed).

Reading sentences

- Write these sentences on the board for the class to read. Point out the tricky words and blend any unknown words with the students:
    1. Granny grows yellow roses.
    2. A brown owl lives in the barn.
    3. Did you throw the pillow at me?
    4. Do not frown and scowl like that.

Unit 10: Handwriting

The alphabet (See page 136)

- The students go to page 66 at the back of their books and say the alphabet. They point to each letter as they say it and pause between the sections: A–E; F–M; N–S; T–Z.
- Call out some of the letters and ask the students to point to them in their books. Ask them whether these letters are red, yellow, green, or blue.
- **Note:** Knowing which letters are in each section will help the students find words more quickly when they start using a dictionary.

Handwriting

- Show the students the letters ‹c›, ‹a›, ‹d›, ‹o›, ‹g›, and ‹q› on their lesson page. Remind them that these letters start with a caterpillar /c/. Knowing this will help the students avoid writing a ‹b› instead of a ‹d›.
- Also remind the students that the letter ‹d› is tall and that the letters ‹g› and ‹q› have tails that go down under the line.
- The students practice writing the letters. They trace inside the outline letters and then write over the dotted letters.

Alphabetical order

- The students put the two sets of letters into alphabetical order. Using the alphabet at the bottom of the page, they look at each letter in turn until they find the first one in the set. They write this on the first line and continue until they have found all four letters.

Dictation

- Call out the following words: *run, bad, lip, just, melt, moth, sang, porch, rescue, magpie.* The students listen for the sounds and write the words.
- Call out the sounds for some of the alphabet letters and ask the students to write the capitals.

FURTHER PRACTICE

It is important to practice the skills needed for reading and writing on a regular basis.

Blending and segmenting

jam, doll, zoo, her, lend,
clamp, thrush, shrimp, igloo, highlight

- Call out each word. The students say the sounds, holding up a finger for each one. Write the letters on the board as they do so and blend the word.
- Practice blending the words with the class (as well as in pairs or individually, if extra practice is needed).

Reading sentences

- Write these sentences on the board for the class to read. Point out the tricky words and blend any unknown words with the students:
  1. I need to blow my nose.
  2. He will give her some flowers.
  3. The crowd is getting very loud.
  4. Can I borrow your brown jacket?

Unit 10: Tricky Words

Flashcards

- Review the tricky words *go, no, so, my, one, by, only, old, like, have, live, give.*

Tricky words: little, down

- Remind the class that some words are tricky because they cannot be worked out fully by listening for the sounds. They have an irregular part or an alternative spelling that has to be learned.
- Show the students the words in the red flowers at the top of their lesson page. Say each one and ask the students to blend the sounds. Then help the class to work out the tricky parts:
  - In the word *little*, the ‹le› is tricky because it says /ool/. The students also have to remember that the letter ‹t› is doubled.
  - *Down* is tricky because ihe students have to remember the alternative spelling ‹ow›.
- The students write inside the outline letters using a red pencil and underline the tricky parts in purple.

Tricky word spelling routine

- Writing the tricky words several times will help the students remember the spelling.
- Show the students the table in their books. They look at the word *little* in the first column and identify the tricky parts. The students then copy the word in the next column, writing over the dotted letters.
- Next, they cover up all instances of the word on the page and write it again by themselves.
- Finally, the students uncover the words and check that the spelling is correct, before covering them again and writing the word one more time.
- The students repeat these steps with the word *down*.

Answers

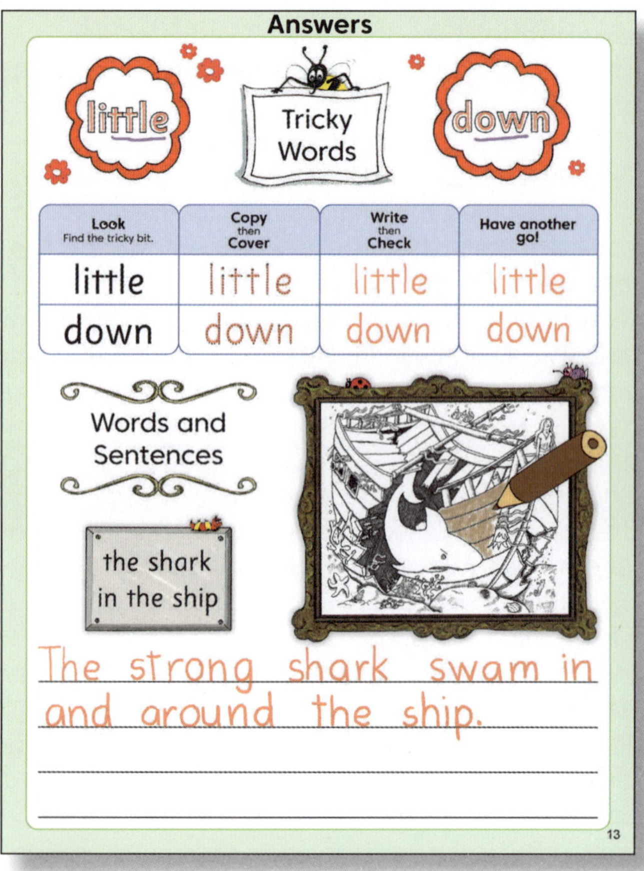

Dictation

- Say the words *little* and *down*. The students listen for the sounds in each word, think about how the tricky parts are spelled, and write the words.

FURTHER PRACTICE

It is important to practice the skills needed for reading and writing on a regular basis.

Blending and segmenting

jug, sack, feet, tie, hand,
Spain, drying, crouch, wigwam, lightning

- Call out each word. The students say the sounds, holding up a finger for each one. Write the letters on the board as they do so and blend the word.
- Practice blending the words with the class (as well as in pairs or individually, if extra practice is needed).

Reading sentences

- Write these sentences on the board for the class to read. Point out the tricky words and blend any unknown words with the students:
  1. The little boy ran down the hill.
  2. She cut up the meat into little bits.
  3. The little tadpoles swim up and down.
  4. Did the tree blow down in the storm?

Unit 10: Words and Sentences

Review

- Use flashcards to review some of the 42 letter sounds and alternative spellings taught so far.
- Call out some of the letter sounds and ask the students to write the different spellings for each one.

Talk about the picture: The shark in the ship

- Show the students the picture of the shark in their books (see opposite) and discuss it with the class.
- Ask a few students to say a sentence about the picture: for example, *I can see a mermaid; The ship has sunk; A shark swims out of the ship.*

Word focus

- In turn, call out the words *strong, shark, swam, ship,* and *mermaid*. The students say the sounds in each word, holding up a finger for each one. Write the letters on the board as they do so and blend the sounds with the class to read the word.
  - Point out the sound /c k/ in *shark* and ask the students how to spell it before writing it on the board. Remind them that short English words rarely end in ‹c›, and ‹ck› usually comes after a short vowel sound, so *shark* is spelled with a kicking /k/.

Sentence modeling

- Write the following sentence on the board:
  - *The strong shark swam in and around the ship.*
- Discuss the sentence as you write it. Encourage the students to call out the sounds of each word before you write it and to blend the word afterward.
- Point out the following:
  - Sentences start with a capital letter.
  - Capital letters are always tall.
  - Listen for the sounds in a word to write it.
  - *The* is a tricky word. How is it spelled?
  - *Shark* has a /c k/ sound. How is it spelled?
  - In the word *around*, we tend to swallow the sound /a/ .
  - Leave a space between each word.
  - Do not forget the period at the end.
- Once the sentence has been modeled, read it with the students. All the students copy the sentence into their books and color the picture.

Free writing

- Those students who are able to write independently can write some more sentences of their own.
- At this stage the students are not expected to use the alternative spellings, so their writing will not always be accurate but the work can be read. Spelling gradually improves through reading many books and learning to apply the alternative letter-sound spellings.

Decodable books

- Send the students home with a book that matches their independent reading level (see page 21 for more information).

FURTHER PRACTICE

It is important to practice the skills needed for reading and writing on a regular basis.

Blending and segmenting

web, sick, beef, with, left,
drain, supper, quack, brightly, skylight

- Call out each word. The students say the sounds, holding up a finger for each one. Write the letters on the board as they do so and blend the word.
- Practice blending the words with the class (as well as in pairs or individually, if extra practice is needed).

Reading sentences

- Write these sentences on the board for the class to read. Point out the tricky words and blend any unknown words with the students:
  1. I live in a little town.
  2. A little old dog is lying down.
  3. The snow is slowing down now.
  4. The little mole lives deep down underground.

Unit 11: Alternatives

Review

- Use flashcards to review some of the 42 letter sounds and alternative spellings, including ‹er›, ‹ow›, ‹igh›, ‹ea›, ‹ay›, ‹oy›; ‹a_e›, ‹e_e›, ‹i_e›, ‹o_e›, ‹u_e›; ‹y› as /y/, /ee/, and /ie/; ‹ck› and the short vowels.
- Call out some of the letter sounds and ask the students to write the different spellings for each one.

Alternatives: ‹ir› and ‹ur› as /er/

- Write the words *her and fern* on the board and read them with the class.
- Now say the words *stir* and *fur* and write them on the board. Explain that there are three main ways to write the sound /er/ – ‹er›, ‹ir›, and ‹ur› – and underline the spelling in each word.
- Write some more words on the board – *turn, twirl, thirty, turban, thirsty, surfing, birthday, and Saturday* – and read them with the class. Underline the ‹ir› or ‹ur› spelling in each word.

Reading words

- Show the students the words at the top of their lesson page. They read the words and underline the spelling of the sound /er/ in each one.
- Point out that the ‹e› in *purple* is shown in light type because the ‹e› is silent. The same is true of the words *nurse* and *purse* in the next activity.

Read and draw

- The students write inside the outline digraphs ‹er›, ‹ir›, and ‹ur› in the pictures of the gingerbread man, bird, and turkey.
- They then read the words and draw a picture for each one.

Animal anagrams (See page 137)

- The students go to page 25 in their books. They look at the top rows of anagrams, unscramble the letters, and write the words.

FURTHER PRACTICE

It is important to practice the skills needed for reading and writing on a regular basis.

Blending and segmenting

jet, jazz, quiz, cue, gift,
trust, joke, snowing, mixing, mailbox

- Call out each word. The students say the sounds, holding up a finger for each one. Write the letters on the board as they do so and blend the word.
- Practice blending the words with the class (as well as in pairs or individually, if extra practice is needed).

Reading sentences

- Write these sentences on the board for the class to read. Point out the tricky words and blend any unknown words with the students:
  1. The little kitten has brown fur.
  2. I had a surprise birthday party.
  3. A bird is chirping in the fir tree.
  4. Will dad burn the burgers again?

Unit 11: Handwriting

The alphabet (See page 136)

- The students go to page 66 at the back of their books and say the alphabet. They point to each letter as they say it and pause between the sections: A–E; F–M; N–S; T–Z.
- Call out some of the letters and ask the students to point to them in their books. Ask them whether these letters are red, yellow, green, or blue.
- **Note:** Knowing which letters are in each section will help the students find words more quickly when they start using a dictionary.

Handwriting

- Show the students the letters ‹b›, ‹d›, ‹h›, ‹k›, ‹l›, and ‹f› on their lesson page. Remind them that these letters are tall. They all start at the top, except for ‹d›, which starts with a caterpillar /c/. Knowing this will help the students not to confuse ‹b› and ‹d›.
- The students practice writing the letters. They trace inside the outline letters and then write over the dotted letters.

Writing the alphabet

- The students complete each section of the alphabet writing the capital letters. They write inside the outline letters and fill in the missing letters, using a different color pencil for each section: red (A–E), yellow (F–M), green (N–S), and blue (T–Z).
- Remind the students that all capital letters are tall and start at or near the top. None of them go down under the line.

Dictation

- Call out the following words: *can, hen, pit, best, went, wing, chart, three, tried, toadstool.* The students listen for the sounds and write the words.
- Call out the sounds for some of the alphabet letters and ask the students to write the capitals.

Answers

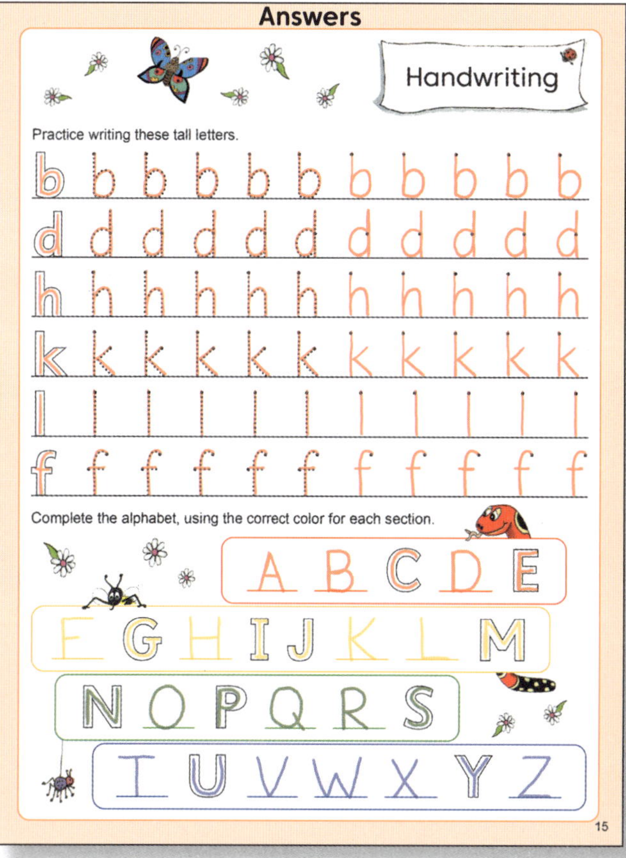

FURTHER PRACTICE

It is important to practice the skills needed for reading and writing on a regular basis.

Blending and sounding

wig, kiss, barn, tail, desk,
bloom, string, cried, lonely, frowning

- Call out each word. The students say the sounds, holding up a finger for each one. Write the letters on the board as they do so and blend the word.
- Practice blending the words with the class (as well as in pairs or individually, if extra practice is needed).

Reading sentences

- Write these sentences on the board for the class to read. Point out the tricky words and blend any unknown words with the students:
  1. The little girl twirls her skirt.
  2. He fell down and hurt his elbow.
  3. Dad grows marrows and turnips.
  4. Can you come swimming on Saturday?

Unit 11: Tricky Words

Flashcards
- Review the tricky words *so, my, one, by, only, old, like, have, live, give, little, down.*

Tricky words: what, when
- Remind the class that some words are tricky because they cannot be worked out fully by listening for the sounds. They have an irregular part or an alternative spelling that has to be learned.
- Show the students the words in the red flowers at the top of their lesson page. Say each one and ask the students to blend the sounds. Then help the class to work out the tricky parts:
  - In both words, the ‹wh› is tricky because it says the sound /w/.
  - In the word *what*, the ‹a› is also tricky because it says the sound /o/.
- The students write inside the outline letters using a red pencil and underline the tricky parts in purple.
- **Note:** ‹wh› is another spelling for /w/, which is used in question words like *what, when, why, where,* and *which*.

Tricky word spelling routine
- Writing the tricky words several times will help the students remember the spelling.
- Show the students the table in their books. They look at the word *what* in the first column and identify the tricky parts. The students then copy the word in the next column, writing over the dotted letters.
- Next, they cover up all instances of the word on the page and write it again by themselves.
- Finally, the students uncover the words and check that the spelling is correct, before covering them again and writing the word one more time.
- The students repeat these steps with the word *when*.

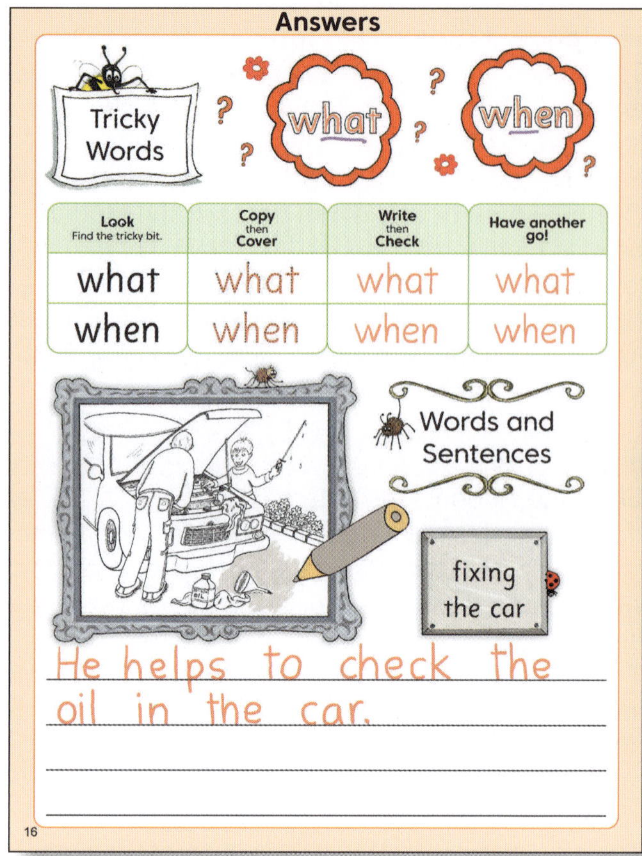

Dictation
- Say the words *what* and *when*. The students listen for the sounds in each word, think about how the tricky parts are spelled, and write the words.

FURTHER PRACTICE
It is important to practice the skills needed for reading and writing on a regular basis.

Blending and segmenting
dim, mass, ring, sort, yelp,
row, south, slope, lower, herself
- Call out each word. The students say the sounds, holding up a finger for each one. Write the letters on the board as they do so and blend the word.
- Practice blending the words with the class (as well as in pairs or individually, if extra practice is needed).

Reading sentences
- Write these sentences on the board for the class to read. Point out the tricky words and blend any unknown words with the students:
  1. Tell me when to turn right.
  2. I can see what is happening.
  3. What made the balloon burst?
  4. When did you burn your shirt?

Unit 11: Words and Sentences

Review

- Use flashcards to review some of the 42 letter sounds and alternative spellings taught so far.
- Call out some of the letter sounds and ask the students to write the different spellings for each one.

Talk about the picture: Fixing the car

- Show the students the picture of the car in their books (see opposite) and discuss it with the class.
- Ask a few students to say a sentence about the picture: for example, *I can see a car; The car has broken down; The boy is helping his dad.*

Word focus

- In turn, call out the words *helps, check, oil, car,* and *dad*. The students say the sounds in each word, holding up a finger for each one. Write the letters on the board as they do so and blend the sounds with the class to read the word.
    - Point out the sound /c k/ in *check* and ask the students how to spell it before writing it on the board. Remind them that ‹ck› usually comes after a short vowel sound, so *check* is spelled with both a caterpillar /c/ and a kicking /k/.

Sentence modeling

- Write the following sentence on the board:
    - *He helps to check the oil in the car.*
- Discuss the sentence as you write it. Encourage the students to call out the sounds of each word before you write it and to blend the word afterward.
- Point out the following:
    - Sentences start with a capital letter.
    - Capital letters are always tall.
    - Listen for the sounds in a word to write it.
    - *He, to,* and *the* are tricky words. How are they spelled?
    - *Check* has a /c k/ sound. How is it spelled?
    - Leave a space between each word.
    - Do not forget the period at the end.
- Once the sentence has been modeled, read it with the students. All the students copy the sentence into their books and color the picture.

Free writing

- Those students who are able to write independently can write some more sentences of their own.
- At this stage the students are not expected to use the alternative spellings, so their writing will not always be accurate but the work can be read. Spelling gradually improves through reading many books and learning to apply the alternative letter-sound spellings.

Decodable books

- Send the students home with a book that matches their independent reading level (see page 21 for more information).

FURTHER PRACTICE

It is important to practice the skills needed for reading and writing on a regular basis.

Blending and segmenting

yap, fuss, thin, jeep, dust,
snort, sixty, freezer, flagpole, suntan

- Call out each word. The students say the sounds, holding up a finger for each one. Write the letters on the board as they do so and blend the word.
- Practice blending the words with the class (as well as in pairs or individually, if extra practice is needed).

Reading sentences

- Write these sentences on the board for the class to read. Point out the tricky words and blend any unknown words with the students:
    1. Show me what the problem is.
    2. I drink a lot when I am thirsty.
    3. When can they come on Thursday?
    4. What is the first thing you remember?

Unit 12: Alternatives

Review

- Use flashcards to review some of the 42 letter sounds and alternative spellings, including ‹ue›, ‹ir›, ‹ur›, ‹ow›, ‹igh›, ‹ea›, ‹ay›, ‹oy›; ‹a_e›, ‹e_e›, ‹i_e›, ‹o_e›, ‹u_e›; ‹y› as /y/, /ee/, and /ie/; ‹ck› and the short vowels.
- Call out some of the letter sounds and ask the students to write the different spellings for each one.

Alternatives: <ew> as /ue/

- Write the words *fuel* and *cute* on the board and review the ‹ue› and ‹u_e› spellings for the long vowel sound /ue/. Remind the students that *When two vowels go walking, the first does the talking*.
- Now say the word *few* and write it on the board. Underline the digraph ‹ew› and explain that this is another way to write the sound /ue/.
- **Note:** In Step 3 the students learn that these spellings say the long /oo/ sound in words like *blue, rule,* and *chew*, In blending, it helps to remember this saying: *If one way does not work, try the other.*

<ue>, <u_e>, or <ew>?

- Show the students the words at the top of their lesson page and point out the silent ‹e› in the word *ewe*.
- The students write inside the outline digraphs ‹ue›, ‹u_e›, and ‹ew› and read the words for each spelling.
- They then match the words to the pictures below, writing the correct one under each picture.
- There is a line for each sound in the word. A longer line indicates that a digraph is needed.

Animal anagrams (See page 137)

- The students go to page 25 in their books. They look at the second row of anagrams, unscramble the letters, and write the words.

Answers

FURTHER PRACTICE

It is important to practice the skills needed for reading and writing on a regular basis.

Blending and segmenting

led, pill, rain, frill, lamp,
swirl, strip, murmur, thirsty, windmill

- Call out each word. The students say the sounds, holding up a finger for each one. Write the letters on the board as they do so and blend the word.
- Practice blending the words with the class (as well as in pairs or individually, if extra practice is needed).

Reading sentences

- Write these sentences on the board for the class to read. Point out the tricky words and blend any unknown words with the students:
  1. What is the mule's name?
  2. I can use the silver spoons
  3. When was the statue made?
  4. The church pews are very old.

Unit 12: Handwriting

The alphabet (See page 136)

- The students go to page 66 at the back of their books and say the alphabet. They point to each letter as they say it and pause between the sections: A–E; F–M; N–S; T–Z.
- Call out some of the letters and ask the students to point to them in their books. Ask them whether these letters are red, yellow, green, or blue.
- **Note:** Knowing which letters are in each section will help the students find words more quickly when they start using a dictionary.

Handwriting

- Show the students the letters ‹g›, ‹j›, ‹p›, ‹q›, and ‹y› on their lesson page. Remind them that these letters have tails that go down under the line. The letters ‹g› and ‹q› also start with a caterpillar /c/.
- The students practice writing the letters. They trace inside the outline letters and then write over the dotted letters.

Writing the alphabet

- The students complete each section of the alphabet writing the capital letters. They write inside the outline letters and fill in the missing letters, using a different color pencil for each section: red (A–E), yellow (F–M), green (N–S), and blue (T–Z).
- Remind the students that all capital letters are tall and start at or near the top. None of them go down under the line.

Dictation

- Call out the following words: *rub, man, get, land, test, long, mouth, bench, yard, toothbrush.* The students listen for the sounds and write the words.
- Call out the sounds for some of the alphabet letters and ask the students to write the capitals.

Answers

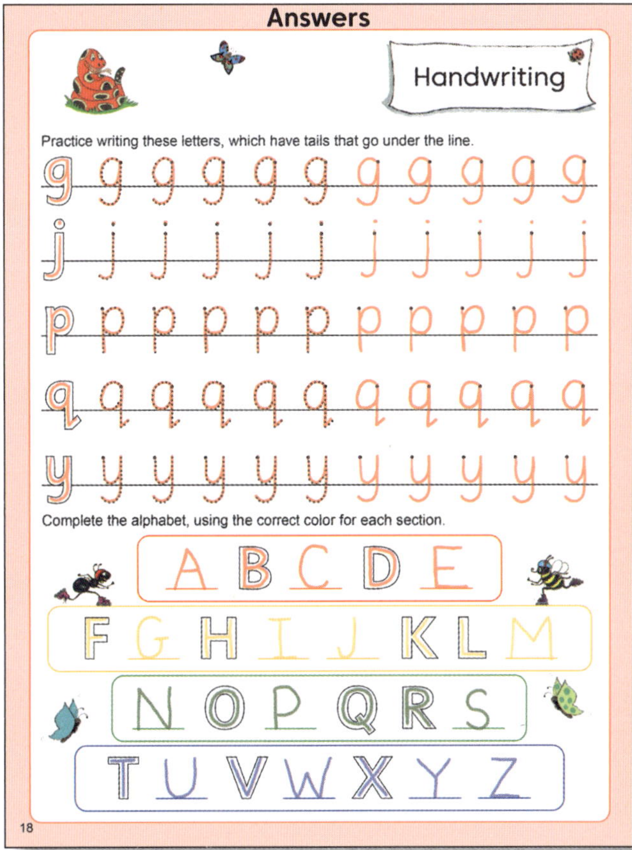
Handwriting

Practice writing these letters, which have tails that go under the line.

g g g g g g g g g g g
j j j j j j j j j j j
p p p p p p p p p p p
q q q q q q q q q q q
y y y y y y y y y y y

Complete the alphabet, using the correct color for each section.

A B C D E
F G H I J K L M
N O P Q R S
T U V W X Y Z

18

FURTHER PRACTICE

It is important to practice the skills needed for reading and writing on a regular basis.

Blending and segmenting

tin, less, card, then, mist,
harder, stir, cannot, perfume, quicksand

- Call out each word. The students say the sounds, holding up a finger for each one. Write the letters on the board as they do so and blend the word.
- Practice blending the words with the class (as well as in pairs or individually, if extra practice is needed).

Reading sentences

- Write these sentences on the board for the class to read. Point out the tricky words and blend any unknown words with the students:
  1. The kittens are so cute.
  2. I continued down the road.
  3. The farmer rescued the goat.
  4. I need some skewers for the barbecue.

Unit 12: Tricky Words

Flashcards

- Review the tricky words *one, by, only, old, like, have, live, give, little, down, what, when.*

Tricky words: why, where

- Remind the class that some words are tricky because they cannot be worked out fully by listening for the sounds. They have an irregular part or an alternative spelling that has to be learned.
- Show the students the words in the green flowers at the top of their lesson page. Say each one and ask the students to blend the sounds. Then help the class to work out the tricky parts:
  - In both words, the ‹wh› is tricky because it says the sound /w/.
  - The word *why* is also tricky because the students have to remember the alternative spelling ‹y›.
  - The word *where* is also tricky because the ‹ere› says /air/, as it does in the tricky word *there.*
- The students write inside the outline letters using a green pencil and underline the tricky parts in purple.
- **Note:** ‹wh› is another spelling for /w/, which is used in question words like *what, when, why, where,* and *which.*

Tricky word spelling routine

- Writing the tricky words several times will help the students remember the spelling.
- Show the students the table in their books. They look at the word *why* in the first column and identify the tricky parts. The students then copy the word in the next column, writing over the dotted letters.
- Next, they cover up all instances of the word on the page and write it again by themselves.
- Finally, the students uncover the words and check that the spelling is correct, before covering them again and writing the word one more time.
- The students repeat these steps with the word *where.*

Dictation

- Say the words *why* and *where*. The students listen for the sounds in each word, think about how the tricky parts are spelled, and write the words.

FURTHER PRACTICE

It is important to practice the skills needed for reading and writing on a regular basis.

Blending and segmenting

zap, lock, join, wood, rest,
drift, squirt, burning, sprinter, twirling

- Call out each word. The students say the sounds, holding up a finger for each one. Write the letters on the board as they do so and blend the word.
- Practice blending the words with the class (as well as in pairs or individually, if extra practice is needed).

Reading sentences

- Write these sentences on the board for the class to read. Point out the tricky words and blend any unknown words with the students:
  1. Stay where you are.
  2. Why are you crying?
  3. Where are my green socks?
  4. Why did the car slow down?

Unit 12: Words and Sentences

Review

- Use flashcards to review some of the 42 letter sounds and alternative spellings taught so far.
- Call out some of the letter sounds and ask the students to write the different spellings for each one.

Talk about the picture: The statue

- Show the students the picture of the statue in their books (see opposite) and discuss it with the class.
- Ask a few students to say a sentence about the picture: for example, *I can see a statue; The farmer is holding a lamb; The sun is shining.*

Word focus

- In turn, call out the words *statue, tie, sun, robin,* and *boots*. The students say the sounds in each word, holding up a finger for each one. Write the letters on the board as they do so and blend the sounds with the class to read the word. All these words are straightforward to blend and segment, but take care to say /statue/ rather than /stachoo/.

Sentence modeling

- Write the following sentence on the board:
  - *The statue has a hat and coat.*
- Discuss the sentence as you write it. Encourage the students to call out the sounds of each word before you write it and to blend the word afterward. Point out the following:
  - Sentences start with a capital letter.
  - Capital letters are always tall.
  - Listen for the sounds in a word to write it.
  - *The* is a tricky word. How is it spelled?
  - Although the sound at the end of *has* is /z/, it is written as ‹s›.
  - We tend to swallow the word *a* rather than use a clear /a/ sound. When the word is stressed, it says /ai/.
  - Leave a space between each word.
  - Do not forget the period at the end.
- Once the sentence has been modeled, read it with the students. All the students copy the sentence into their books and color the picture.

Free writing

- Those students who are able to write independently can write some more sentences of their own.
- At this stage the students are not expected to use the alternative spellings, so their writing will not always be accurate but the work can be read. Spelling gradually improves through reading many books and learning to apply the alternative letter-sound spellings.

Decodable books

- Send the students home with a book that matches their independent reading level (see page 21 for more information).

FURTHER PRACTICE

It is important to practice the skills needed for reading and writing on a regular basis.

Blending and segmenting

tub, hiss, room, shut, test,
forty, unless, juggler, blushing, chatterbox

- Call out each word. The students say the sounds, holding up a finger for each one. Write the letters on the board as they do so and blend the word.
- Practice blending the words with the class (as well as in pairs or individually, if extra practice is needed).

Reading sentences

- Write these sentences on the board for the class to read. Point out the tricky words and blend any unknown words with the students:
  1. Where is my perfume?
  2. Why is it so hot in here?
  3. Where do they live now?
  4. That is why she cannot go.

Unit 13: Alternatives

Review

- Use flashcards to review some of the 42 letter sounds and alternative spellings, including ‹o›, ‹ew›, ‹ir›, ‹ur›, ‹ow›, ‹igh›, ‹ea›, ‹ay›, ‹oy›; ‹a_e›, ‹e_e›, ‹i_e›, ‹o_e›, ‹u_e›; ‹y› as /y/, /ee/, and /ie/; ‹ck› and the short vowels.
- Call out some of the letter sounds and ask the students to write the different spellings for each one.

Alternatives: ‹aw›, ‹au›, and ‹al›

- Say the words *crawl, haul,* and *tall* and write them on the board.
- Underline the digraphs ‹aw›, ‹au›, and ‹al› and ask the students what sound they are making in the words *[/o/].*
- Explain that these are the three main alternative ways to write the sound /o/.
- Write some more words with these spellings on the board and read them with the class:
  - ‹aw› *jaw, draw, shawl, straw, jigsaw*
  - ‹au› *haunt, launch, August, laundry, applaud*
  - ‹al› *all, hall, talk, small, walk.*
- Underline the alternative spelling in each word.

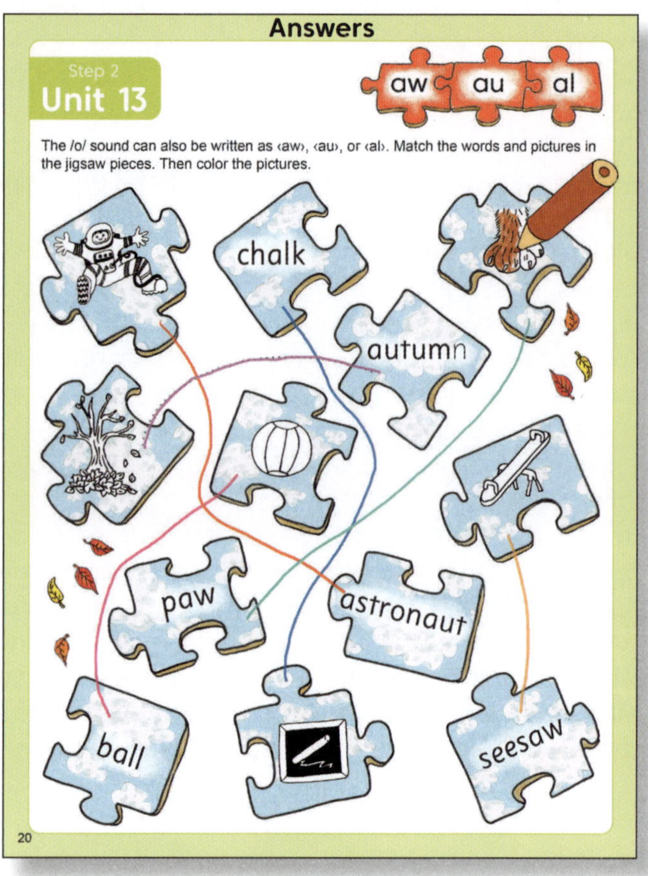
Answers

Step 2
Unit 13

aw au al

The /o/ sound can also be written as ‹aw›, ‹au›, or ‹al›. Match the words and pictures in the jigsaw pieces. Then color the pictures.

chalk
autumn
paw
astronaut
ball
seesaw

20

Word and picture matching

- The students look at the jigsaw pieces in their books. They read the words and join them to the matching pictures.
- Point out the silent ‹n› in the word *autumn*.

Animal anagrams (See page 137)

- The students go to page 25 in their books. They look at the bottom row of anagrams, unscramble the letters, and write the words.

FURTHER PRACTICE

It is important to practice the skills needed for reading and writing on a regular basis.

Blending and segmenting

rob, add, far, wool, quest,
cube, argue, oilcan, smuggler, footprint

- Call out each word. The students say the sounds, holding up a finger for each one. Write the letters on the board as they do so and blend the word.
- Practice blending the words with the class (as well as in pairs or individually, if extra practice is needed).

Reading sentences

- Write these sentences on the board for the class to read. Point out the tricky words and blend any unknown words with the students:
  1. I went for a long walk.
  2. We go camping in August.
  3. Why did she yawn so much?
  4. Where do you keep your chalk?

Unit 13: Handwriting

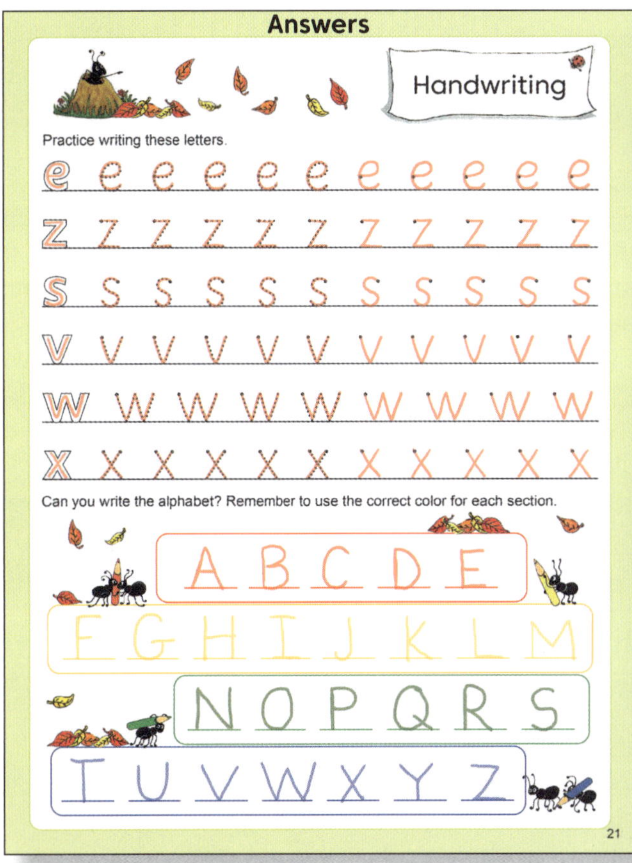

The alphabet (See page 136)

- The students go to page 66 at the back of their books and say the alphabet. They point to each letter as they say it and pause between the sections: A–E; F–M; N–S; T–Z.
- Call out some of the letters and ask the students to point to them in their books. Ask them whether these letters are red, yellow, green, or blue.
- **Note:** Knowing which letters are in each section will help the students find words more quickly when they start using a dictionary.

Handwriting

- Show the students the letters ‹e›, ‹z›, ‹s›, ‹v›, ‹w›, and ‹x› on their lesson page.
- These letters do not start with a vertical stroke or a caterpillar /c/. Instead, ‹e› and ‹z› start by going around or across to the right. The letter ‹s›, like ‹f›, starts by going up and back around just a little before changing direction. The letters ‹v›, ‹w›, and ‹x› start by going diagonally down to the line.
- The students practice writing the letters. They trace inside the outline letters and then write over the dotted letters.

Writing the alphabet

- The students write the capital letters for the four alphabet sections, using a different color for each one: red (A–E), yellow (F–M), green (N–S), and blue (T–Z). Remind them that all capital letters are tall and start at or near the top. None go down under the line.

Dictation

- Call out the following words: *pen, bug, six, pond, gift, rash, south, pinch, queen, raincoat.* The students listen for the sounds and write the words.
- Call out the sounds for some of the alphabet letters and ask the students to write the capitals.

FURTHER PRACTICE

It is important to practice the skills needed for reading and writing on a regular basis.

Blending and segmenting

rib, rack, coil, hint, zest,
mew, value, wobbly, skewer, fantastic

- Call out each word. The students say the sounds, holding up a finger for each one. Write the letters on the board as they do so and blend the word.
- Practice blending the words with the class (as well as in pairs or individually, if extra practice is needed).

Reading sentences

- Write these sentences on the board for the class to read. Point out the tricky words and blend any unknown words with the students:
    1. I need to do the laundry.
    2. Why is the beanstalk so tall?
    3. Come and play on the seesaw.
    4. Where is the strawberry cake?

Unit 13: Tricky Words

Flashcards

- Review the tricky words *only, old, like, have, live, give, little, down, what, when, why, where.*

Tricky words: who, which

- Remind the class that some words are tricky because they cannot be worked out fully by listening for the sounds. They have an irregular part or an alternative spelling that has to be learned.
- Show the students the words in the green flowers at the top of their lesson page. Say each one and ask the students to blend the sounds. Then help the class to work out the tricky parts:
  - *Who* is tricky because the ‹w› is silent and the ‹o› says the long /oo/ sound.
  - W*h*ich is tricky because (like *what, when, why, where,* and *which*) the ‹wh› says the sound /w/.
- The students write inside the outline letters using a green pencil and underline the tricky parts in purple.

Tricky word spelling routine

- Writing the tricky words several times will help the students remember the spelling.
- Show the students the table in their books. They look at the word *who* in the first column and identify the tricky parts.
- The students then copy the word in the next column, writing over the dotted letters.
- Next, they cover up all instances of the word on the page and write it again by themselves.
- Finally, the students uncover the words and check that the spelling is correct, before covering them again and writing the word one more time.
- The students repeat these steps with the word *which.*

Dictation

- Say the words *who* and *which*. The students listen for the sounds in each word, think about how the tricky parts are spelled, and write the words.

Wordsearch (See page 137)

- The students go to page 23 of their books and do the wordsearch at the bottom of the page. They read the tricky words in the flowers and try to find them in the grid.

FURTHER PRACTICE

It is important to practice the skills needed for reading and writing on a regular basis.

Blending and segmenting

elf, jar, span, quill, picnic,
vanish, fewer, selfish, volume, floating

- Call out each word. The students say the sounds, holding up a finger for each one. Write the letters on the board as they do so and blend the word.
- Practice blending the words with the class (as well as in pairs or individually, if extra practice is needed).

Reading sentences

- Write these sentences on the board for the class to read. Point out the tricky words and blend any unknown words with the students:
  1. Which one is smaller?
  2. Which way did she go?
  3. Did you see who it was?
  4. Who was he talking to?

Unit 13: Words and Sentences

Review

- Use flashcards to review some of the 42 letter sounds and alternative spellings taught so far.
- Call out some of the letter sounds and ask the students to write the different spellings for each one.

Talk about the picture: Having a picnic

- Show the students the picture of the picnic in their books (see opposite) and discuss it with the class.
- Ask a few students to say a sentence about the picture: for example, *I can see a picnic; There is a big cake; The knife is long and sharp.*

Word focus

- In turn, call out the words *jam, fork, picnic, food,* and *woods*. The students say the sounds in each word, holding up a finger for each one. Write the letters on the board as they do so and blend the sounds with the class to read the word.
  - Point out the sound /c k/ in *fork* and ask the students how to spell it before writing it on the board. Remind them that short English words rarely end in ‹c›, and ‹ck› usually comes after a short vowel sound, so *shark* is spelled with a kicking /k/.
  - Explain that the word *picnic* does not follow the usual spelling rules because both /c k/ sounds are written with the letter ‹c›.
  - Remind the students that although the sound at the end of a plural word is often /z/, it is always written as ‹s›, as in *woods*.

Sentence modeling

- Write the following sentence on the board:
  - *We had a picnic in the woods.*
- Discuss the sentence as you write it. Encourage the students to call out the sounds of each word before you write it and to blend the word afterward.
- Point out the following:
  - Sentences start with a capital letter.
  - Capital letters are always tall.
  - Listen for the sounds in a word to write it.
  - How do you spell the tricky words *We* and *the*?
  - Although the sound at the end of *woods* is /z/, it is written as ‹s›.
  - We tend to swallow the word *a* rather than use a clear /a/ sound. When the word is stressed, it says /ai/.
  - How are the /c k/ sounds in *picnic* spelled?
  - Leave a space between each word.
  - Do not forget the period at the end.
- Once the sentence has been modeled, read it with the students. All the students copy the sentence into their books and color the picture.

Free writing

- Those students who are able to write independently can write some more sentences of their own.
- At this stage the students are not expected to use the alternative spellings, so their writing will not always be accurate but the work can be read. Spelling gradually improves through reading many books and learning to apply the alternative letter-sound spellings.

Jolly Phonics readers

Students who have finished the Yellow Level Readers and who know the alternative spellings and tricky words taught so far can start the Green Level.

FURTHER PRACTICE

It is important to practice the skills needed for reading and writing on a regular basis.

Blending and segmenting

hut, wail, snug, tusk, speck,
statue, wombat, skew, waiter, underground

- Call out each word. The students say the sounds, holding up a finger for each one. Write the letters on the board as they do so and blend the word.
- Practice blending the words with the class (as well as in pairs or individually, if extra practice is needed).

Reading sentences

- Write these sentences on the board for the class to read. Point out the tricky words and blend any unknown words with the students:
  1. My dog has big paws.
  2. Astronauts are very brave.
  3. Which tree are you drawing?
  4. Who did you call this morning?

Extension Activities: Answers

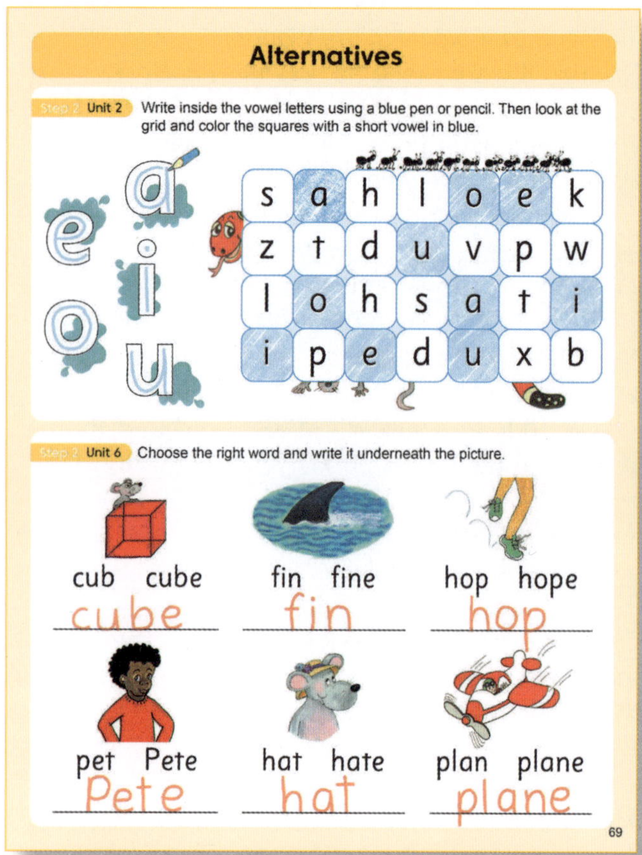

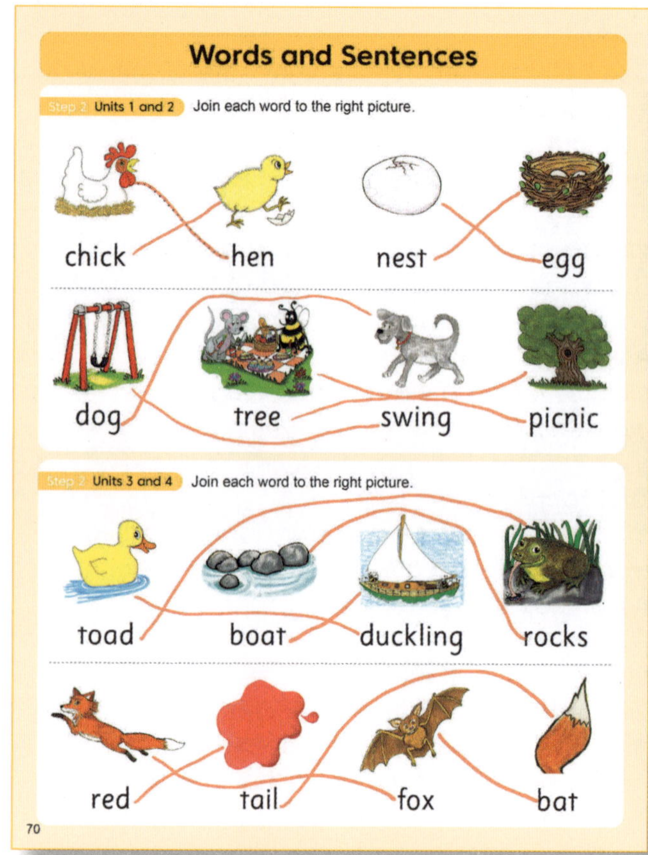

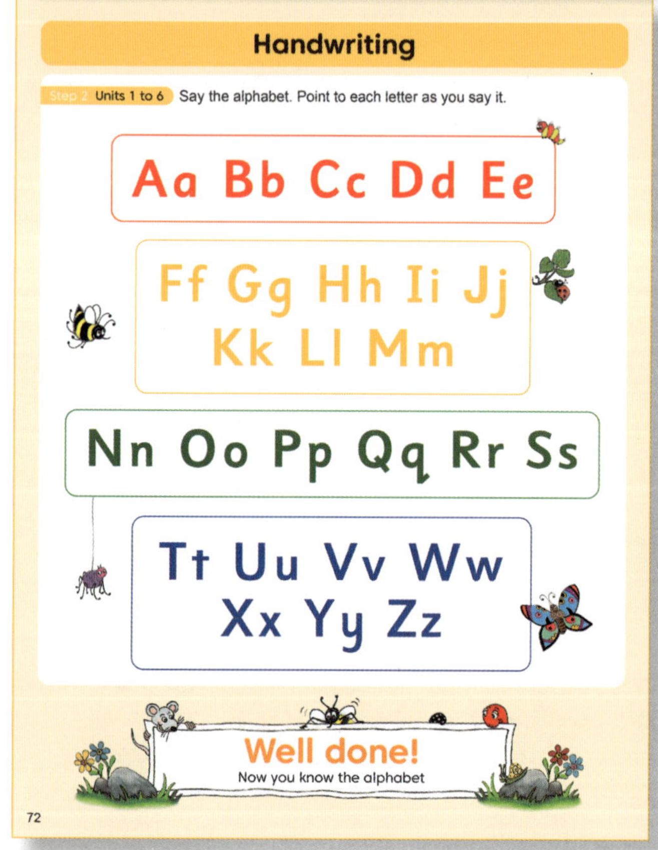

Extension Activities: Answers

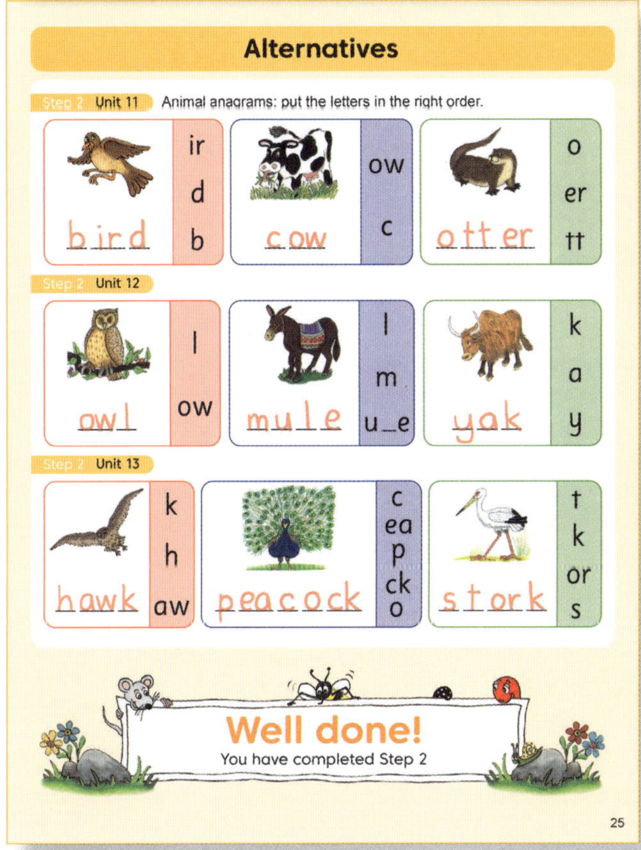

Teaching Step 3

Weekly Units in Step 3

Jolly Phonics Step 3 has 13 weekly units, each with three lessons on the following topics: Alternatives, Tricky Words, and Words and Sentences. Handwriting is still a focus for teaching, but practicing capital letters, digraph formation, and the alphabet is now part of Words and Sentences, under the heading Read, Write, and Review.

The lessons in Step 3 consolidate and extend the skills taught in Steps 1 and 2. This means the students regularly practice the alternative vowel spellings and tricky words that they have already learned, but they are also introduced to new tricky words and some more alternative spellings, including those for the new sound /air/. The regular blending activities in Further Practice encourage the students toward greater fluency in their reading and the various writing activities help them to become independent and confident writers. There is also a strong focus on improving the students' reading comprehension skills in the Words and Sentences lessons.

The teaching content increases in Step 3, particularly in the Tricky Words and Words and Sentences lessons. The students should now be at a stage to cope with the extra learning, but not everything in a lesson has to be done in one session. In particular, the Further Practice activities can be done at any spare moment, and it is important to do some letter-sound review and blending and segmenting every day.

The lessons are taught over three days of the week, leaving two days for further practice and other areas of literacy learning. Each topic follows a pattern and the following types of activities are included on a regular basis.

1. Alternatives

In Step 3, the students are introduced to the sound /air/ and to the following alternative spellings:

- ‹ph› making the sound /f/ in words with a Greek origin, as in *alphabet*.
- soft ‹c› making the sound /s/ before the letters ‹e›, ‹i›, or ‹y›, as in *ice, acid,* and *icy.*
- soft ‹g› making the sound /j/ before the letters ‹e›, ‹i›, or ‹y›, as in *age, magic,* and *energy*.
- ‹ue›, ‹u_e›, and ‹ew› making the sound /oo/ in words like *clue, June,* and *chew.*
- ‹air›, ‹ear›, and ‹are› making the sound /air/ in words like *air, bear,* and *care*.

However, a large part of the teaching is dedicated to consolidating and reinforcing the students' knowledge of the alternative spellings that have already been taught. These spellings are the main alternatives that the students will come across in their reading, so they need to know them well in order to become fluent readers. Like Step 2, every lesson in Step 3 has a Further Practice section, providing words and sentences that contain the alternative spellings, along with the tricky words that the students have learned. This section is also useful for blending longer words and words that are not strictly regular, but which can be read with a little adjustment, such as words with the schwa sound, words with the ‹nk› spelling, or words in which the letter ‹s› says /z/. The students do not usually find this adjustment difficult in their blending, especially if the word is in their vocabulary.

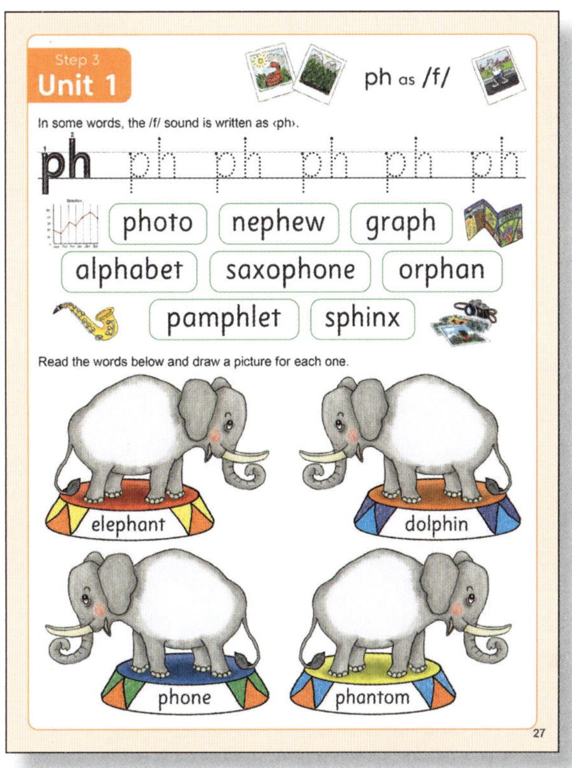

The students are only expected to know the alternative spellings for reading; they should not be expected to use them consistently in their writing. However, by gently introducing some of the basic rules for spelling and regularly reviewing them in the lessons, the students will start to remember them and may gradually apply them in their writing. Some of these rules are first introduced in Step 2. For example, the students are introduced to shy ‹i› and toughy ‹y›, and how this affects the spelling of the sounds /ai/ and /oi/ at the end of a word. They also learn more about the spelling of the /c k/ sound in words with short and long vowels. In Step 3 they go on to learn that the ‹e_e› spelling is far less common than the other spellings for the sound /ee/.

Many spelling rules relate to the short and long vowels. These are practiced regularly in Step 3, using the vowel hand shown in the back of Student Book 2. Say the short vowels – /a/, /e/, /i/, /o/ and /u/ – with the students, while they point to the tip of the thumb for /a/, the tip of the index finger for /e/ and so on. Then say the long vowel sounds – /ai/, /ea/, /ie/, /oa/ and /ue/. This time the students point to the base of the thumb and fingers to indicate the sounds. This activity can be practiced at any spare moment and, once they know it well, the students can try pointing to their own hand instead of the picture. It can also be done while singing a little song, sung to the traditional tune of Skip to my Lou:

/a/, /e/, /i/, /o/, /u/ (Repeat 3 times)
are short vowels that we use!
A vowel is in every word, every word, every word,
A vowel is in every word that we read or write.
/ai/, /ee/, /ie/, /oa/, /ue/ (Repeat 3 times)
are long vowels that we use!

2. Tricky Words

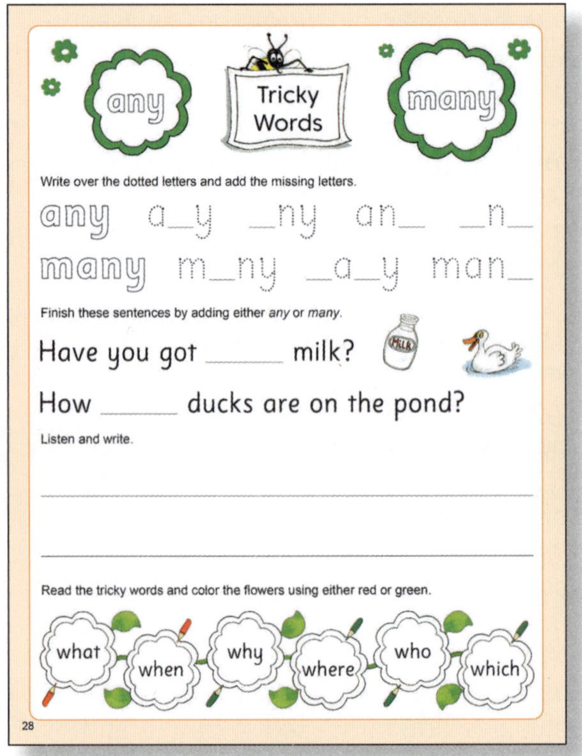

In Step 3, the students are introduced to the remaining tricky words taught in Jolly Phonics

- *any, many, more, before, other, were, because, want* (green flowers)
- *saw, put, could, should, would, right, two, four, goes, does, made, their* (pink flowers)
- *once, upon, always, also, of, eight, love, cover, after, every, mother, father* (brown flowers)

To teach the tricky words, encourage the students to listen to the word, blend the sounds, work out which part(s) of the spelling are tricky, and underline them in purple. The students can then practice writing the tricky words on a separate sheet of paper, following the tricky word spelling routine used in Steps 1 and 2. After that, there are four more activities for the students to do. First, they practice writing the new tricky words by writing inside the outline words and then writing them again, tracing over the dotted letters and filling in the missing letters. Then the students read the sentences in their books, work out which of the tricky words is missing, and, after a class discussion, complete each sentence. The students are now ready to write a sentence from dictation for each of the new tricky words. This gives them the opportunity to write regular words and the tricky words in context. Finally, the students can review some of the tricky words that have already been taught. They read the tricky words in the flowers at the bottom of the page and color the edge of the flowers in the appropriate color. For more information on tricky words, see pages 27 to 28 of the Introduction.

3. Words and Sentences

In Step 3, the Words and Sentences lessons cover a range of activities, all of which aim to improve the students' blending abilities as well as their comprehension skills. There is a strong emphasis on reading comprehension in these lessons and the text the students have to read uses the alternative spellings and tricky words that have been taught so far. The reading comprehension activity for Unit 1 is shown opposite.

Toward the end of the book, more challenging words are sometimes used and these will need to be blended with the students. These words may include the schwa sound, vowel letters saying the long vowel sound, silent letters (shown in light type), or spellings that need a little adjustment to hear the word correctly, such as *water* and *year.* With a little guidance, most students are able to blend these words, especially if the word is in their vocabulary.

Read, write, and review

This section consolidates the students' knowledge of the alphabet and reviews the formation of capital letters and digraphs. In the first half of Step 3, the students recite the alphabet, pointing to the letters in their books as they say them. They also complete a section of the alphabet, writing the capital letters next to the lower-case letters. In the second half of Step 3, the students continue to recite the alphabet, but now they are encouraged to say it without any prompting. They also practice writing the digraphs and then use them in context: first by copying a sentence that has been modeled for them and then by writing three sentences from dictation. Not all of the sentences have to be done in one session; the dictation sentences could be attempted during the week. The space to practice the alphabet, capital letters, and digraphs is found at the back of Student Book 2 in a section called Further Unit Activities. This section also contains the vowel hand, some short and long vowel practice, and wordsearches that give the students some extra practice reading and writing the tricky words.

Free writing

If there is time, either at the end of this lesson or during the week, the students should be given the opportunity to do some writing of their own. An extension activity is suggested in every unit, linked to the lesson topic, but teachers should feel free to use one of their own choosing. At the beginning, the students will need plenty of help and guidance to get them started, so it is important to begin with a class discussion about the topic and to write a few key words on the board for blending. The students then write as much as they are able. Their spelling will not always be accurate, but their work can be read. The students can then illustrate their work and this could be collated into a class book.

Decodable Readers

Students who have finished the Yellow Level of the Jolly Phonics Readers can move on to the Green Level from the beginning of Step 3. Those students who have finished the Green Level are ready to move on to the Blue Level from Unit 10.

Unit 1: Alternatives

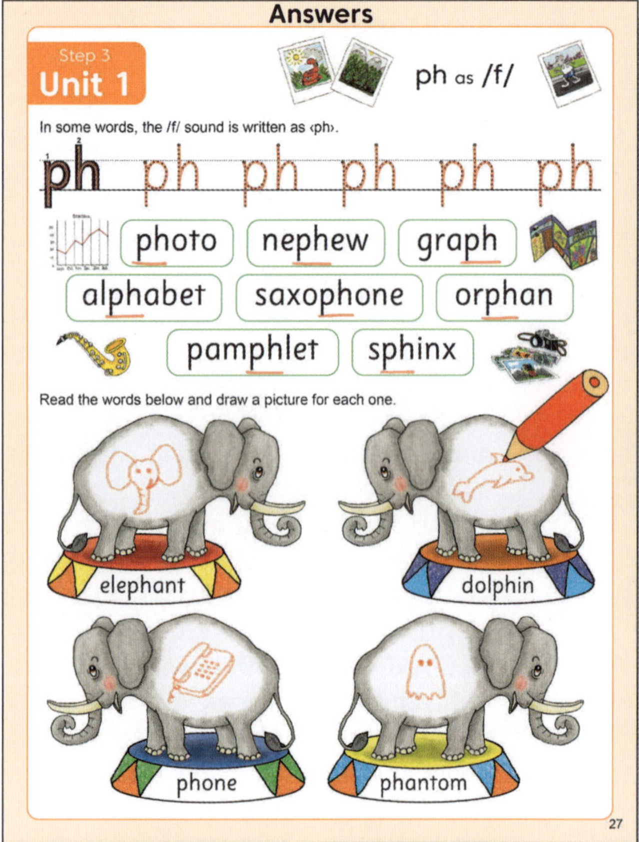

Review

- Use flashcards to review ‹ck› and some of the alternative vowel spellings: ‹ai›, ‹a_e›, ‹ay›; ‹ee›, ‹e_e›, ‹ea›; ‹ie›, ‹i_e›, ‹y›, ‹igh›; ‹oa›, ‹o_e›, ‹ow›; ‹ue›, ‹u_e›, ‹ew›; ‹ou›, ‹ow›; ‹oi›, ‹oy›; ‹er›, ‹ir›, ‹ur›; ‹aw›, ‹au›, ‹al›. Point out that ‹y› can say /y/, /ee/, or /ie/.
- Call out some of the letter sounds and ask the students to write the different spellings for each one.

Vowel hand (See page 182)

- Show the students the vowel hand at the back of their books (Student Book 2, page 72).
- Practice saying the short and long vowel sounds with the class. The students point to the tip of each finger as they say the short vowel sounds and then to the base of each finger as they say the long vowel sounds.
- The students then use their finger to trace inside the outline letters for each sound.

Alternatives: ‹ph› as /f/

- Say the words *dolphin* and *phone,* and write them on the board. Ask the class which letters are making the /f/ sound in each one *[‹ph›]* and explain that some words – ones that are Greek in origin – use this spelling instead of the letter ‹f›. Read the words again with the class and underline the ‹ph› spelling in each one.
- Show the students how to write the digraph ‹ph›. The students form the letters in the air and then practice writing them in their books.

Reading words

- Read the ‹ph› words with the class. Some of the them are quite challenging, so help the students where necessary. The saying *If the short vowel sound does not work, try the long vowel* is helpful for words like *photo*.

Read and draw

- The students read the words under the elephants and draw a picture for each one.

Decodable books: Send the students home with a book that matches their independent reading level.

FURTHER PRACTICE

It is important to practice the skills needed for reading and writing on a regular basis.

Blending and segmenting

peck, rash, twig, stork, poach,
funny, hurry, yummy, carry, simply

- Call out each word. The students say the sounds, holding up a finger for each one. Write the letters on the board as they do so and blend the word.
- Practice blending the words with the class (as well as in pairs or individually, if extra practice is needed).

Reading sentences

- Write these sentences on the board for the class to read. Point out the tricky words and blend any unknown words with the students:
  1. Can you draw a graph?
  2. Dolphins live in the sea.
  3. Who can say the alphabet?
  4. This story is about a phantom.

Unit 1: Tricky Words

Answers

any

Tricky Words

many

Write over the dotted letters and add the missing letters.

any any any any any

many many many many

Finish these sentences by adding either *any* or *many*.

Have you got any milk?

How many ducks are on the pond?

Listen and write.

The farmer had many sheep.

I did not see any chimps at the zoo.

Read the tricky words and color the flowers using either red or green.

what when why where who which

28

Flashcards

- Review the tricky words *like, have, live, give, little, down, what, when, why, where, who, which.*

Tricky words: any, many

- Show the students the words in the green flowers at the top of their lesson page. Say each one and ask the students to blend the sounds. Then help the class to work out the tricky parts:
  - In both words, the ‹a› is tricky because it says the sound /e/. Both words are also tricky because the students have to remember the ‹y› as /ee/ spelling.
- To help the students remember the spelling, point out that *many* is written the same way as *any*, except that it has a letter ‹m› at the beginning.
- The students write inside the outline letters using a green pencil and underline the tricky parts in purple.

Tricky word spelling routine (See page 28)

- The students practice writing the new tricky words on a separate sheet of paper.

Fill in the gaps

- The students write inside the outline letters, write over the dotted letters, and fill in the missing letters.

Any or many?

- Read the sentences with the class and discuss which tricky word should be used in each one.
- Read each sentence back to the students, using their chosen word, and ask them if it makes sense.
- The students complete the sentences, writing the correct word in each one.

Dictation

- Say the following sentences. The students listen carefully and write them in their books:
  - The farmer had many sheep.
  - I did not see any chimps at the zoo.

Reading the tricky words

- The students read the tricky words in the flowers and color the edge of the flowers red or green.

FURTHER PRACTICE

It is important to practice the skills needed for reading and writing on a regular basis.

Blending and segmenting

tell, paid, flat, creep, shook,
west, scrap, muffin, tennis, lollipop

- Call out each word. The students say the sounds, holding up a finger for each one. Write the letters on the board as they do so and blend the word.
- Practice blending the words with the class (as well as in pairs or individually, if extra practice is needed).

Reading sentences

- Write these sentences on the board for the class to read. Point out the tricky words and blend any unknown words with the students:
  1. Do you have any nephews?
  2. We took many photos on our walk.
  3. Do they sell any cheaper phones?
  4. Many children in books are orphans.

Unit 1: Words and Sentences

Review

- Use flashcards to review ‹ph›, ‹ck›, and some of the alternative vowel spellings.
- Call out some of the letter sounds and ask the students to write the different spellings for each one.

Read, write, and review (See page 181)

- The students go to page 66 of their books and say the alphabet. They point to each letter as they say it, pausing between the sections: A–E; F–M; N–S; T–Z.
- Call out some of the letters. The students find them and say whether they are red, yellow, green, or blue.
- Review how to write the capital letters A, B, C, D, E. Remind the students that all the capital letters are tall, that they start at or near the top, and that none of them go down under the line.
- The students trace inside the outline lower-case letters and write the capital letters A, B, C, D, E, using a red pencil.

Out at sea

- Write the following words on the board and read them with the class: *starfish, shark, yellow, seagull, flying, seaweed, sky, waves*. Pay particular attention to the digraphs, double letters, and alternative spellings.
- The students then read the list of items at the bottom of their lesson page and draw them in the picture.

Extension activity

- The students could write a short story about a fish who lives in the sea, using some of the vocabulary from the main activity.
- Go around the class and talk about the different things the students might want to include. Discuss what the title of the story should be and write it on the board.
- The students copy the title onto a sheet of paper and write as much as they are able. The spelling will not always be accurate but it can be read.

FURTHER PRACTICE

It is important to practice the skills needed for reading and writing on a regular basis.

Blending and segmenting

pack, her, blot, plain, brook,
crack, risk, lucky, quicker, quacking

- Call out each word. The students say the sounds, holding up a finger for each one. Write the letters on the board as they do so and blend the word.
- Practice blending the words with the class (as well as in pairs or individually, if extra practice is needed).

Reading sentences

- Write these sentences on the board for the class to read. Point out the tricky words and blend any unknown words with the students:
  1. The singer has a microphone.
  2. Are there many elephants in Africa?
  3. The book has many interesting phrases.
  4. Do you have any pamphlets I can read?

Unit 2: Alternatives

Review

- Use flashcards to review ‹ph›, ‹ck›, and some of the alternative vowel spellings: ‹ai›, ‹a_e›, ‹ay›; ‹ee›, ‹e_e›, ‹ea›; ‹ie›, ‹i_e›, ‹y›, ‹igh›; ‹oa›, ‹o_e›, ‹ow›; ‹ue›, ‹u_e›, ‹ew›; ‹ou›, ‹ow›; ‹oi›, ‹oy›; ‹er›, ‹ir›, ‹ur›; ‹aw›, ‹au›, ‹al›. Point out that ‹y› can say /y/, /ee/, or /ie/.
- Call out some of the letter sounds and ask the students to write the different spellings for each one.

Vowel hand (See page 182)

- The students use the vowel hand at the back of their books (Student Book 2, page 72) to practice saying the short and long vowel sounds.
- They then use their finger to trace inside the outline letters for each sound.

Alternatives: soft ‹c›

- Say the words *nice, city,* and *fancy* and write them on the board. Ask the class which letter is making the /s/ sound in each one *[‹c›].* Explain that when the letter ‹c› is followed by ‹e›, ‹i›, or ‹y›, it usually makes the /s/ sound. When this happens it is called a soft ‹c›.
- Read the words on the board again with the class. Underline the soft ‹c› in each one, along with the ‹e›, ‹i›, or ‹y› that influences it.

Reading words

- Read the soft ‹c› words with the class. Point out that in the word *accident,* only the second ‹c› is soft; the first ‹c› says /c k/.
- The students find the soft ‹c› in each word, together with the ‹e›, ‹i›, or ‹y› that follows it, and underline them both.

Answers

Word and picture matching

- The students read each word and write it under the matching tent. They then color the pictures.
- Remind the class that the letter ‹e› in *circle* and *cycle* is shown in light type because it is silent and has no influence on the rest of the word.

Decodable books

Send the students home with a book that matches their independent reading level.

FURTHER PRACTICE

It is important to practice the skills needed for reading and writing on a regular basis.

Blending and segmenting

dull, hood, swam, bring, bumper, cannot, Philip, hiccup, nephew, grubby

- Call out each word. The students say the sounds, holding up a finger for each one. Write the letters on the board as they do so and blend the word.
- Practice blending the words with the class (as well as in pairs or individually, if extra practice is needed).

Reading sentences

- Write these sentences on the board for the class to read. Point out the tricky words and blend any unknown words with the students:
  1. Did they have a nice time?
  2. I have been ill since Sunday.
  3. Are there many places to sit?
  4. The velvet dress has a lace collar.

Unit 2: Tricky Words

Flashcards

- Review the tricky words *live, give, little, down, what, when, why, where, who, which, any, many.*

Tricky words: more, before

- Show the students the words in the green flowers at the top of their lesson page. Say each one and ask the students to blend the sounds. Then help the class to work out the tricky parts:
  - In both words, the final ‹e› is tricky because it is silent.
  - In the word *before,* the first ‹e› is also tricky because it makes the sound /i/.
- The students write inside the outline letters using a green pencil and underline the tricky parts in purple.

Tricky word spelling routine (See page 28)

- The students practice writing the new tricky words on a separate sheet of paper.

Fill in the gaps

- The students write inside the outline letters, write over the dotted letters, and fill in the missing letters.

More or before?

- Read the sentences with the class and discuss which tricky word should be used in each one.
- Read each sentence back to the students, using their chosen word, and ask them if it makes sense.
- The students complete the sentences, writing the correct word in each one.

Dictation

- Say the following sentences. The students listen carefully and write them in their books:
  - We will swim before lunch.
  - You need much more paint.

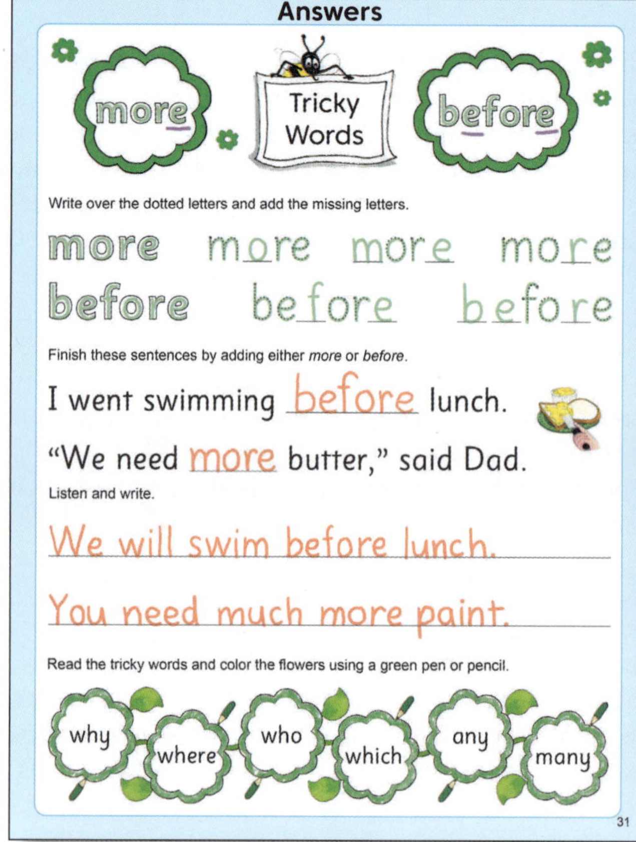
Answers

more | Tricky Words | before

Write over the dotted letters and add the missing letters.

more more more more

before before before

Finish these sentences by adding either *more* or *before*.

I went swimming before lunch.

"We need more butter," said Dad.

Listen and write.

We will swim before lunch.

You need much more paint.

Read the tricky words and color the flowers using a green pen or pencil.

why where who which any many

31

Reading the tricky words

- The students read the tricky words in the flowers and color the edge of the flowers green.

FURTHER PRACTICE

It is important to practice the skills needed for reading and writing on a regular basis.

Blending and segmenting

with, sell, trip, green, eel,
phone, empty, phonic, traffic, dentist

- Call out each word. The students say the sounds, holding up a finger for each one. Write the letters on the board as they do so and blend the word.
- Practice blending the words with the class (as well as in pairs or individually, if extra practice is needed).

Reading sentences

- Write these sentences on the board for the class to read. Point out the tricky words and blend any unknown words with the students:
  1. Do you have any more pencils?
  2. There is no more space in here.
  3. The runners rest before the race.
  4. Clean your face before going to bed.

Unit 2: Words and Sentences

Review

- Use flashcards to review soft ‹c›, ‹ph›, ‹ck›, and some of the alternative vowel spellings.
- Call out some of the letter sounds and ask the students to write the different spellings for each one.

Read, write, and review (See page 181)

- The students go to page 66 of their books and say the alphabet. They point to each letter as they say it, pausing between the sections: A–E; F–M; N–S; T–Z.
- Call out some of the letters. The students find them and say whether they are red, yellow, green, or blue.
- Review how to write the capital letters F, G, H, and I. Remind the students that all the capital letters are tall, that they start at or near the top, and that none of them go down under the line.
- The students trace inside the outline lower-case letters and write the capital letters F, G, H, I, using a yellow pencil.

Yes or no

- Write the following words on the board and read them with the class: *sleeping, rabbits, five, socks, three, dragon, eggs, magpie*. Pay particular attention to the double letters, alternative spellings, and the schwa in *drag**o**n*.
- Show the students the six pictures on their lesson page and the sentence under each one. Read the first sentence with the class: *The cat is sleeping.* Look at the picture and discuss whether it is true or not. The students write over the dotted word *yes* in their books.
- The students read the other sentences on their own and decide whether they are true or not. They write *yes* if the sentence is true and *no* if it is not.

Answers

Words and Sentences

Is it true? Write **yes** or **no** underneath each statement.

The cat is sleeping. yes

Rabbits are good at hopping. yes

There are five red socks. no

It is three o'clock. yes

The dragon has ten eggs. no

The magpie has a hat. no

32

Extension activity

- The students could write a short story about a cat.
- Go around the class and ask the students to say something about the cat: its name, what it looks like, where it lives, who it lives with, and what it likes to do. Discuss what the title of the story should be and write it on the board.
- The students copy the title onto a sheet of paper and write as much as they are able. The spelling will not always be accurate but it can be read.

FURTHER PRACTICE

It is important to practice the skills needed for reading and writing on a regular basis.

Blending and segmenting

club, fill, laid, see, pie,
phew, dolphin, unlock, typhoon, broomstick

- Call out each word. The students say the sounds, holding up a finger for each one. Write the letters on the board as they do so and blend the word.
- Practice blending the words with the class (as well as in pairs or individually, if extra practice is needed).

Reading sentences

- Write these sentences on the board for the class to read. Point out the tricky words and blend any unknown words with the students:
  1. Did you get the parcel I sent?
  2. The circus clowns are very funny.
  3. There is some more rice in the jar.
  4. We must paint the fence before it rains.

Unit 3: Alternatives

Review

- Use flashcards to review soft ‹c›, ‹ph›, ‹ck›, and some of the alternative vowel spellings: ‹ai›, ‹a_e›, ‹ay›; ‹ee›, ‹e_e›, ‹ea›; ‹ie›, ‹i_e›, ‹y›, ‹igh›; ‹oa›, ‹o_e›, ‹ow›; ‹ue›, ‹u_e›, ‹ew›; ‹ou›, ‹ow›; ‹oi›, ‹oy›; ‹er›, ‹ir›, ‹ur›; ‹aw›, ‹au›, ‹al›. Point out that ‹y› can say /y/, /ee/, or /ie/.
- Call out some of the letter sounds and ask the students to write the different spellings for each one.

Vowel hand (See page 182)

- The students use the vowel hand at the back of their books (Student Book 2, page 72) to practice saying the short and long vowel sounds.
- They then use their finger to trace inside the outline letters for each sound.

Alternatives: soft <g>

- Say the words *gem, margin,* and *energy,* and write them on the board. Ask the class which letter is making the /j/ sound in each one *[‹g›].* Explain that when the letter ‹g› is followed by ‹e›, ‹i›, or ‹y›, it usually makes the /j/ sound. When this happens it is called a soft ‹g›.
- Read the words on the board again with the class. Underline the soft ‹g› in each one, along with the ‹e›, ‹i›, or ‹y› that influences it.

<ge>, <gi>, or <gy>?

- Read the soft ‹g› words with the students. Point out the two soft ‹g›s in the word *ginger* and remind the class that letters shown in light type are silent and have no influence on the rest of the word.
- The students find the soft ‹g› in each word, together with the ‹e›, ‹i›, or ‹y› that follows it, and underline them.

Answers

Step 3
Unit 3

Soft g

When the letter ‹g› is followed by ‹e›, ‹i›, or ‹y›, it usually makes a /j/ sound. Read the words and write each one in the vegetable with the same spelling pattern.

germ | margin | large | dingy | engine
allergy | ginger | magic | page | energy

ge: germ, large, ginger, page

gi: margin, engine, magic, ginger

gy: allergy, dingy, energy

Read the words and draw pictures for them.

giraffe | orange

33

- They then write each word in the vegetable with the same spelling.

Read and draw

- The students read the words *giraffe* and *orange* and draw pictures for each one.

Decodable books

Send the students home with a book that matches their independent reading level.

FURTHER PRACTICE

It is important to practice the skills needed for reading and writing on a regular basis.

Blending and segmenting

art, hill, shed, toaster, drum,
bounce, choice, fence, city, price

- Call out each word. The students say the sounds, holding up a finger for each one. Write the letters on the board as they do so and blend the word.
- Practice blending the words with the class (as well as in pairs or individually, if extra practice is needed).

Reading sentences

- Write these sentences on the board for the class to read. Point out the tricky words and blend any unknown words with the students:
  1. She is an engineer.
  2. Dad is allergic to dogs.
  3. Will you accept my apology?
  4. He has made a huge mistake.

Unit 3: Tricky Words

Flashcards

- Review the tricky words *little, down, what, when, why, where, who, which, any, many, more, before.*

Tricky words: other, were

- Show the students the words in the green flowers at the top of their lesson page. Say each one and ask the students to blend the sounds. Then help the class to work out the tricky parts:
  - The ‹o› in *other* is tricky because it makes the sound /u/. Saying it as it sounds (to rhyme with *bother*) helps the students remember the spelling.
  - In *were*, the final ‹e› is tricky because it is silent.
- The students write inside the outline letters using a green pencil and underline the tricky parts in purple.

Tricky word spelling routine (See page 28)

- The students practice writing the new tricky words on a separate sheet of paper.

Fill in the gaps

- The students write inside the outline letters, write over the dotted letters, and fill in the missing letters.

Other or were?

- Read the sentences with the class and discuss which tricky word should be used in each one.
- Read each sentence back to the students, using their chosen word, and ask them if it makes sense.
- The students complete the sentences, writing the correct word in each one.

Dictation

- Say the following sentences. The students listen carefully and write them in their books:
  - There were six fish in the pond.
  - My other boot was under the bed.

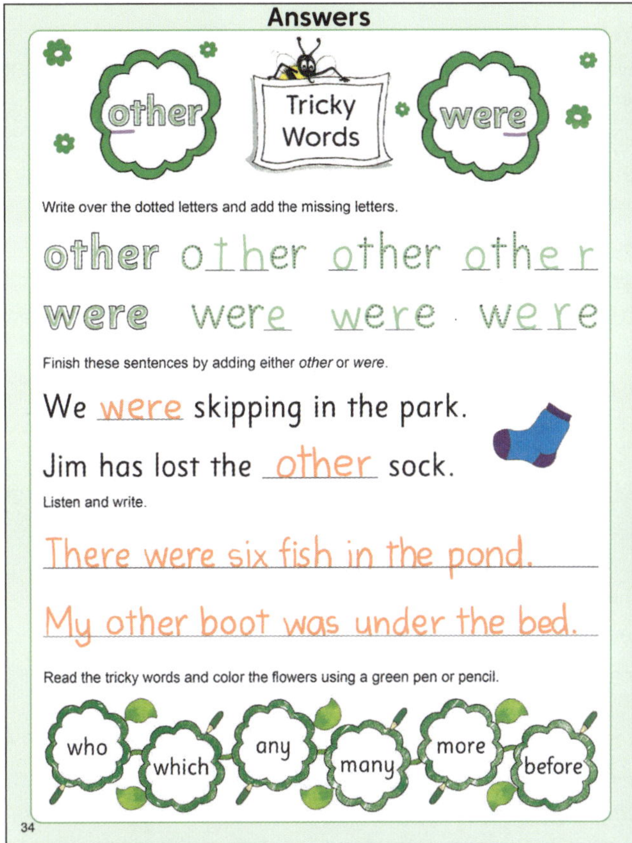

Answers

other Tricky Words were

Write over the dotted letters and add the missing letters.

other other other other

were were were were

Finish these sentences by adding either *other* or *were*.

We were skipping in the park.

Jim has lost the other sock.

Listen and write.

There were six fish in the pond.

My other boot was under the bed.

Read the tricky words and color the flowers using a green pen or pencil.

who which any many more before

34

Reading the tricky words

- The students read the tricky words in the flowers and color the edge of the flowers green.

FURTHER PRACTICE

It is important to practice the skills needed for reading and writing on a regular basis.

Blending and segmenting

wing, puff, flap, paint, shoot,
nice, mice, since, trace, space

- Call out each word. The students say the sounds, holding up a finger for each one. Write the letters on the board as they do so and blend the word.
- Practice blending the words with the class (as well as in pairs or individually, if extra practice is needed).

Reading sentences

- Write these sentences on the board for the class to read. Point out the tricky words and blend any unknown words with the students:
  1. The other boxes were much larger.
  2. His other shirt has orange stripes.
  3. Were there any giraffes at the zoo?
  4. The train passengers were waiting.

Unit 3: Words and Sentences

Review

- Use flashcards to review soft ‹g›, soft ‹c›, ‹ph›, ‹ck›, and some of the alternative vowel spellings.
- Call out some of the letter sounds and ask the students to write the different spellings for each one.

Read, write, and review (See page 181)

- The students go to page 66 of their books and say the alphabet. They point to each letter as they say it, pausing between the sections: A–E; F–M; N–S; T–Z.
- Call out some of the letters. The students find them and say whether they are red, yellow, green, or blue.
- Review how to write the capital letters J, K, L, and M. Remind the students that all the capital letters are tall, that they start at or near the top, and that none of them go down under the line.
- The students trace inside the outline lower-case letters and write the capital letters J, K, L, M, using a yellow pencil.

At the park

- Write the following words on the board and read them with the class: *carry, stone, looking, ducks, wall, bird, children, swinging*. Pay particular attention to the double letters, alternative spellings, and the schwa in *children*.
- Show the students the picture in their books and discuss what is happening in the park. Read the first incomplete sentence: *The dog is carrying a* _____. Point to the two words next to the sentence and ask the students whether the dog is carrying a *stone* or a *stick*. The students write *stick* in their books and complete the remaining sentences by themselves.

Answers

Extension activity

- The students could write a short story about a park. Go around the class and share ideas about what could be included, such as things happening in the picture or the students' own ideas. Discuss what the title of the story should be and write it on the board.
- The students copy the title onto a sheet of paper and write as much as they are able. The spelling will not always be accurate but it can be read.

FURTHER PRACTICE

It is important to practice the skills needed for reading and writing on a regular basis.

Blending and segmenting

cool, kiss, ground, step, street,
dice, face, place, grace, spice

- Call out each word. The students say the sounds, holding up a finger for each one. Write the letters on the board as they do so and blend the word.
- Practice blending the words with the class (as well as in pairs or individually, if extra practice is needed).

Reading sentences

- Write these sentences on the board for the class to read. Point out the tricky words and blend any unknown words with the students:
  1. The page has a wide margin.
  2. She has another food allergy.
  3. The mice were asleep in their cage.
  4. We had a magical time at the concert.

Unit 4: Alternatives

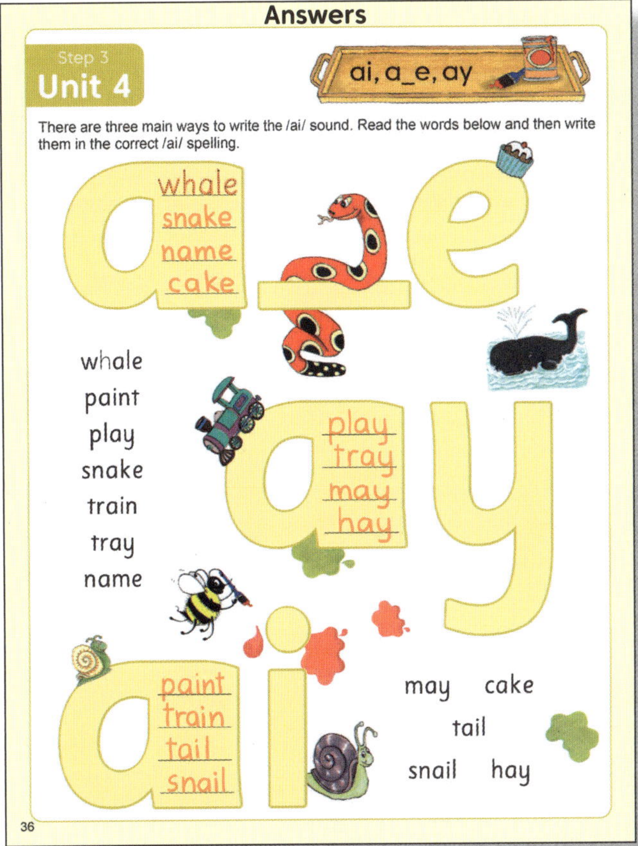

Review

- Use flashcards to review soft ‹g›, soft ‹c›, ‹ph›, ‹ck›, and some of the alternative vowel spellings: ‹ai›, ‹a_e›, ‹ay›; ‹ee›, ‹e_e›, ‹ea›; ‹ie›, ‹i_e›, ‹y›, ‹igh›; ‹oa›, ‹o_e›, ‹ow›; ‹ue›, ‹u_e›, ‹ew›; ‹ou›, ‹ow›; ‹oi›, ‹oy›; ‹er›, ‹ir›, ‹ur›; ‹aw›, ‹au›, ‹al›. Point out that ‹y› can say /y/, /ee/, or /ie/.
- Call out some of the letter sounds and ask the students to write the different spellings for each one.

Vowel hand (See page 182)

- The students use the vowel hand at the back of their books (Student Book 2, page 72) to practice saying the short and long vowel sounds.
- They then write inside the outline letters for the sounds /a/ and /ai/, and use their finger to trace inside the outline letters for the remaining sounds.

Alternatives: ‹ai›, ‹a_e›, ‹ay›

- Remind the students that there are three main ways to write the sound /ai/: ‹ai›, ‹a_e›, and ‹ay›. The ‹ay› spelling usually comes at the end of a word because the letter ‹i› is shy, so toughy ‹y› takes its place.
- Write the following words on the board and read them with the class: *faint, stay, made, brain, Sunday, cave, again, holiday, pancake, complain, crayons* and *lemonade.* Point out that *Sunday*, like all the days of the week, starts with a capital letter.
- Ask some students to come up and underline the letters making the sound /ai/ in each word.

‹ai›, ‹a_e›, or ‹ay›?

- Look at the word *whale* on the lesson page and read it with the class: Point out the silent letter ‹h› and remind the students of the tricky words *what, when, why, where,* and *which.* These words also use the letters ‹wh› to spell the sound /w/.
- Ask the class to write the word in the correct /ai/ spelling. The students write over the dotted word *whale* in the large yellow ‹a_e›.
- The students read the remaining /ai/ words and write them in the correct spelling.

Decodable books: Send the students home with a book that matches their independent reading level.

FURTHER PRACTICE

It is important to practice the skills needed for reading and writing on a regular basis.

Blending and segmenting

tail, rack, croak, blob, popcorn,
page, huge, gently, lounge, fringe

- Call out each word. The students say the sounds, holding up a finger for each one. Write the letters on the board as they do so and blend the word.
- Practice blending the words with the class (as well as in pairs or individually, if extra practice is needed).

Reading sentences

- Write these sentences on the board for the class to read. Point out the tricky words and blend any unknown words with the students:
    1. Do they travel by train or plane?
    2. The snakes were black and orange.
    3. We found a stray kitten in the lane.
    4. You can play some more games now.

Unit 4: Tricky Words

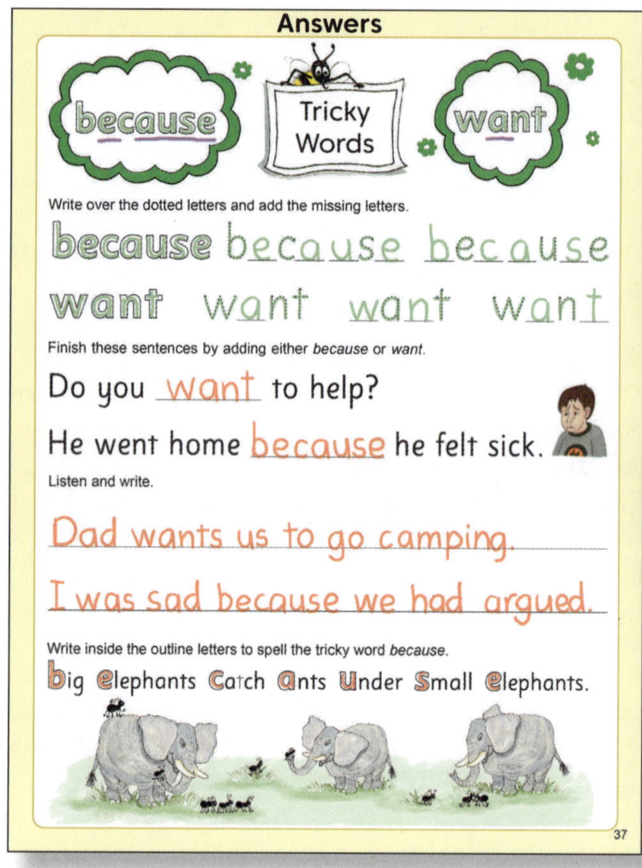
Answers

because

Tricky Words

want

Write over the dotted letters and add the missing letters.

because because because

want want want want

Finish these sentences by adding either *because* or *want*.

Do you want to help?

He went home because he felt sick.

Listen and write.

Dad wants us to go camping.

I was sad because we had argued.

Write inside the outline letters to spell the tricky word *because*.

big elephants catch ants under small elephants.

37

Flashcards

- Review the tricky words *what, when, why, where, who, which, any, many, more, before, other, were.*

Tricky words: because, want

- Show the students the words in the green flowers at the top of their lesson page. Say each one and ask the students to blend the sounds. Then help the class to work out the tricky parts:
  - The word *because* is mostly irregular, so the students can learn the mnemonic at the bottom of the page to help them spell it correctly: ***b**ig **e**lephants **c**atch **a**nts **u**nder **s**mall **e**lephants.*
  - In *want*, the ‹a› is tricky because it makes the sound /o/. Saying it as it sounds (to rhyme with *ant*) helps the students remember the spelling.
- The students write inside the outline letters using a green pencil and underline the tricky parts in purple.

Tricky word spelling routine (See page 28)

- The students practice writing the new tricky words on a separate sheet of paper.

Fill in the gaps

- The students write inside the outline letters, write over the dotted letters, and fill in the missing letters.

Because or want?

- Read the sentences with the class and discuss which tricky word should be used in each one.
- Read each sentence back to the students, using their chosen word, and ask them if it makes sense.
- The students complete the sentences, writing the correct word in each one.

Dictation

- Say the following sentences. The students listen carefully and write them in their books:
  - Dad wants us to go camping.
  - I was sad because we had argued.

Mnemonic

- The students read the sentence at the bottom of the page. Then they write inside the outline letter at the beginning of each word to spell the word *because*.

FURTHER PRACTICE

It is important to practice the skills needed for reading and writing on a regular basis.

Blending and segmenting

meet, list, vet, float, shopping,
large, magic, age, ginger, intelligent

- Call out each word. The students say the sounds, holding up a finger for each one. Write the letters on the board as they do so and blend the word.
- Practice blending the words with the class (as well as in pairs or individually, if extra practice is needed).

Reading sentences

- Write these sentences on the board for the class to read. Point out the tricky words and blend any unknown words with the students:
  1. I got wet because it was raining.
  2. Do you want to stay another night?
  3. We made lemonade because it was hot.
  4. They wanted some cake and ice cream.

Unit 4: Words and Sentences

Review

- Use flashcards to review soft ‹g›, soft ‹c›, ‹ph›, ‹ck›, and some of the alternative vowel spellings.
- Call out some of the letter sounds and ask the students to write the different spellings for each one.

Read, write, and review (See page 181)

- The students go to page 66 of their books and say the alphabet. They point to each letter as they say it, pausing between the sections: A–E; F–M; N–S; T–Z.
- Call out some of the letters. The students find them and say whether they are red, yellow, green, or blue.
- Review how to write the capital letters N, O, P, Q, R, and S. Remind the students that all the capital letters are tall, that they start at or near the top, and that none of them go down under the line.
- The students trace inside the outline lower-case letters and write the capital letters N, O, P, Q, R, S, using a green pencil.

Read and match

- Write the following words on the board and read them with the class: *waves, race, clean, dreaming, lying, shine, socks, sunny.* Look at the alternative spelling in each word, including the soft ‹c› in *race*.
- Show the students the six pictures in their books and ask them which words on the board go with which picture *[**boy:** race; **bed:** dreaming/lying; **sun:** shine/sunny; **sock:** socks; **soap:** clean; **boat:** waves].*
- Then ask the students to read each sentence and join it to the matching picture.

Extension activity

- The students could write a short story about a boat.

- Go around the class and ask the students to think of something they could say about the boat: for example, its name, what it looks like, who is sailing it, and where it is going. Discuss what the title of the story should be and write it on the board.
- The students copy the title onto a sheet of paper and write as much as they are able. The spelling will not always be accurate but it can be read.

FURTHER PRACTICE

It is important to practice the skills needed for reading and writing on a regular basis.

Blending and segmenting

loop, pest, argue, froth, mix,
cage, germ, charge, stage, energy

- Call out each word. The students say the sounds, holding up a finger for each one. Write the letters on the board as they do so and blend the word.
- Practice blending the words with the class (as well as in pairs or individually, if extra practice is needed).

Reading sentences

- Write these sentences on the board for the class to read. Point out the tricky words and blend any unknown words with the students:
  1. I paid for the paint in the sale.
  2. She came to see us on Saturday.
  3. We ate quickly because we were late.
  4. They want to visit you in the holidays.

Unit 5: Alternatives

Review

- Use flashcards to review soft ‹g›, soft ‹c›, ‹ph›, ‹ck›, and some of the alternative vowel spellings: ‹ai›, ‹a_e›, ‹ay›; ‹ee›, ‹e_e›, ‹ea›; ‹ie›, ‹i_e›, ‹y›, ‹igh›; ‹oa›, ‹o_e›, ‹ow›; ‹ue›, ‹u_e›, ‹ew›; ‹ou›, ‹ow›; ‹oi›, ‹oy›; ‹er›, ‹ir›, ‹ur›; ‹aw›, ‹au›, ‹al›. Point out that ‹y› can say /y/, /ee/, or /ie/.
- Call out some of the letter sounds and ask the students to write the different spellings for each one.

Vowel hand (See page 182)

- The students use the vowel hand at the back of their books (Student Book 2, page 72) to practice saying the short and long vowel sounds.
- They then write inside the outline letters for the sounds /e/ and /ee/, and use their finger to trace inside the outline letters for the remaining sounds.

Alternatives: ‹ee›, ‹e_e›, ‹ea›

- Remind the students that there are three main ways to write the sound /ee/: ‹ee›, ‹e_e›, and ‹ea›. Explain that the ‹e_e› spelling is not used as often as the ‹ee› and ‹ea› spellings.
- Show the students the words at the top of their lesson page. Read them with the class and ask the students to underline the spelling of /ee/ in each one. Point out the silent letter ‹e› at the end of the word *sneeze*.

‹ee›, ‹e_e›, or ‹ea›?

- Look at the other words on the page and ask the class to find the first one that uses the ‹ee› spelling *[bee]*. The students write over the dotted word *bee* in the large orange ‹ee›.
- They then read the remaining /ee/ words and write them in the correct spelling.

Answers

Step 3
Unit 5
ee, e_e, ea
As well as ‹y› at the end of a word, there are three main ways to write the /ee/ sound.
speed sneeze toffee three
evening complete extreme trapeze
teacher peanut peach teapot
Read the words below and write them in the correct /ee/ spelling.
tea bee these athlete
ee: bee, teeth, feet, sleep
eve seal read teeth
ea: tea, seal, read, beak
feet beak sleep theme
e_e: these, athlete, eve, theme
39

Decodable books

Send the students home with a book that matches their independent reading level.

FURTHER PRACTICE

It is important to practice the skills needed for reading and writing on a regular basis.

Blending and segmenting

wax, neck, tenth, perch, shell,
skates, tray, Spain, stale, playing

- Call out each word. The students say the sounds, holding up a finger for each one. Write the letters on the board as they do so and blend the word.
- Practice blending the words with the class (as well as in pairs or individually, if extra practice is needed).

Reading sentences

- Write these sentences on the board for the class to read. Point out the tricky words and blend any unknown words with the students:
  1. Steve likes to eat green beans.
  2. Have you seen Jean this evening?
  3. I had a bad dream when I was asleep.
  4. Do not feed the seagulls on the beach.

Unit 5: Tricky Words

Flashcards

- Review the tricky words *why, where, who, which, any, many, more, before, other, were, because, want.*

Tricky words: saw, put

- Show the students the words in the pink flowers at the top of their lesson page. Say each one and ask the students to blend the sounds. Then help the class to work out the tricky parts:
  - The ‹aw› in *saw* is tricky because it is an alternative spelling of /o/.
  - The ‹u› in *put* is tricky because it says /oo/. Saying it as it sounds (to rhyme with *hut*) helps the students remember the spelling.
- The students write inside the outline letters using a pink pencil and underline the tricky parts in purple.

Tricky word spelling routine (See page 28)

- The students practice writing the new tricky words.

Fill in the gaps

- The students write inside the outline letters, write over the dotted letters, and fill in the missing letters.

Saw or put?

- Read the sentences with the class and discuss which tricky word should be used in each one. Read each sentence back to the students, using their chosen word, and ask them if it makes sense. The students complete the sentences, writing the correct word in each one.

Dictation

- Say the following sentences. The students listen carefully and write them in their books:

Answers

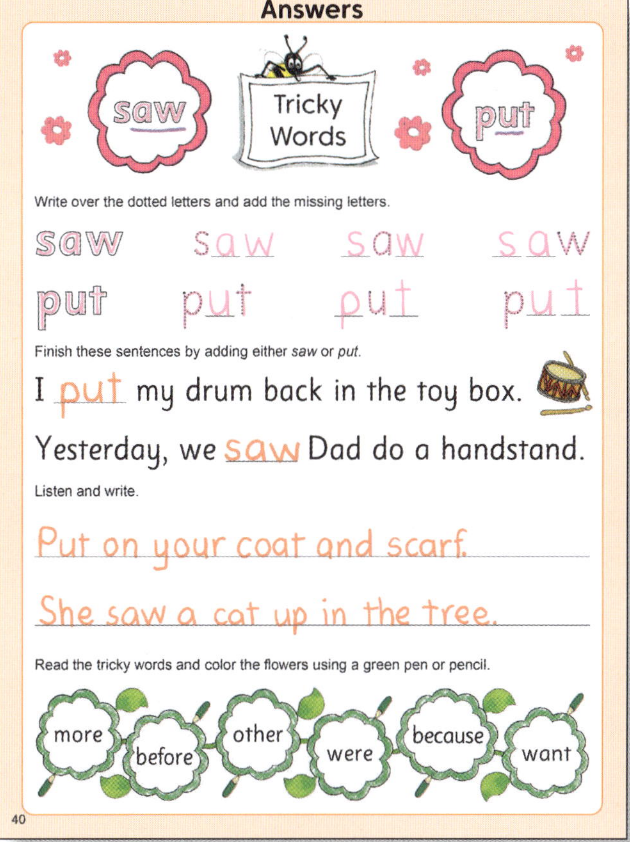

  - Put on your coat and scarf.
  - She saw a cat up in the tree.

Reading the tricky words

- The students read the tricky words in the flowers and color the edge of the flowers green.

Wordsearch (See page 181)

- The students go to page 69 of their books, write the tricky words and find them in the wordsearch.

FURTHER PRACTICE

It is important to practice the skills needed for reading and writing on a regular basis.

Blending and segmenting

long, hiss, stop, throat, shampoo,
spray, painting, shade, sway, player

- Call out each word. The students say the sounds, holding up a finger for each one. Write the letters on the board as they do so and blend the word.
- Practice blending the words with the class (as well as in pairs or individually, if extra practice is needed).

Reading sentences

- Write these sentences on the board for the class to read. Point out the tricky words and blend any unknown words with the students:
  1. Put your clean socks on now.
  2. I put the teabags in the teapot.
  3. Who saw the seals this evening?
  4. We saw the dog stealing some meat.

Unit 5: Words and Sentences

Review

- Use flashcards to review soft ‹g›, soft ‹c›, ‹ph›, ‹ck›, and some of the alternative vowel spellings.
- Call out some of the letter sounds and ask the students to write the different spellings for each one.

Read, write, and review (See page 181)

- The students go to page 66 of their books and say the alphabet. They point to each letter as they say it, pausing between the sections: A–E; F–M; N–S; T–Z.
- Call out some of the letters. The students find them and say whether they are red, yellow, green, or blue.
- Review how to write the capital letters T, U, V, and W. Remind the students that all the capital letters are tall, that they start at or near the top, and that none of them go down under the line.
- The students trace inside the outline lower-case letters and write the capital letters T, U, V, W, using a blue pencil.

Read and draw

- Write the following words on the board and read them with the class: *rabbit, black, boots, snails, some, stars, rainbow, sky.* Pay particular attention to the double letters, alternative spellings, and the tricky word *some.*
- Show the students the six phrases in their books and read the first one: *a rabbit in a hutch.* Point out the silent ‹t› in *hutch* and ask the students what they will draw: A rabbit? *[Yes]* In a rabbit hole? *[No]*
- The students read the rest of the phrases and draw a picture for each one, making sure the details match.

Extension activity

- The students could write about the weather and what kind they like best. Go around the class and share ideas: talk, for example, about the different types of weather; about how it makes people feel; and what they do or wear, depending on the weather. Discuss what the title should be and write it on the board.
- The students copy the title onto a sheet of paper and write as much as they are able. The spelling will not always be accurate but it can be read.

FURTHER PRACTICE

It is important to practice the skills needed for reading and writing on a regular basis.

Blending and segmenting

hard, pick, brick, spoon, drops,
plane, crayon, Sunday, faint, caveman

- Call out each word. The students say the sounds, holding up a finger for each one. Write the letters on the board as they do so and blend the word.
- Practice blending the words with the class (as well as in pairs or individually, if extra practice is needed).

Reading sentences

- Write these sentences on the board for the class to read. Point out the tricky words and blend any unknown words with the students:
  1. I need to see my teacher now.
  2. Put these toffees away in the jar.
  3. Dad put three peaches in the bowl.
  4. We saw you reading under the tree.

Unit 6: Alternatives

Review

- Use flashcards to review soft ‹g›, soft ‹c›, ‹ph›, ‹ck›, and some of the alternative vowel spellings: ‹ai›, ‹a_e›, ‹ay›; ‹ee›, ‹e_e›, ‹ea›; ‹ie›, ‹i_e›, ‹y›, ‹igh›; ‹oa›, ‹o_e›, ‹ow›; ‹ue›, ‹u_e›, ‹ew›; ‹ou›, ‹ow›; ‹oi›, ‹oy›; ‹er›, ‹ir›, ‹ur›; ‹aw›, ‹au›, ‹al›. Point out that ‹y› can say /y/, /ee/, or /ie/.
- Call out some of the letter sounds and ask the students to write the different spellings for each one.

Vowel hand (See page 182)

- The students use the vowel hand at the back of their books (Student Book 2, page 72) to practice saying the short and long vowel sounds.
- They then write inside the outline letters for the sounds /i/ and /ie/, and use their finger to trace inside the outline letters for the remaining sounds.

Alternatives: ‹ie›, ‹i_e›, ‹y›, ‹igh›

- Remind the students that there are four main ways to write the sound /ie/: ‹ie›, ‹i_e›, ‹y›, and ‹igh›.
- Write the following words on the board and read them with the class: *by, size, bright, bike, fries, crying, dried, thigh, spies, flying, bedtime* and *lightning.*
- Ask some students to come up and underline the letters making the sound /ie/ in each word.

‹ie›, ‹i_e›, ‹y›, or ‹igh›?

- Read the first word on the lesson page with the students and ask them to write it in the correct /ie/ spelling. The students write over the dotted word *light* in the large green ‹igh›.
- The students read the remaining /ie/ words and write them in the correct spelling.

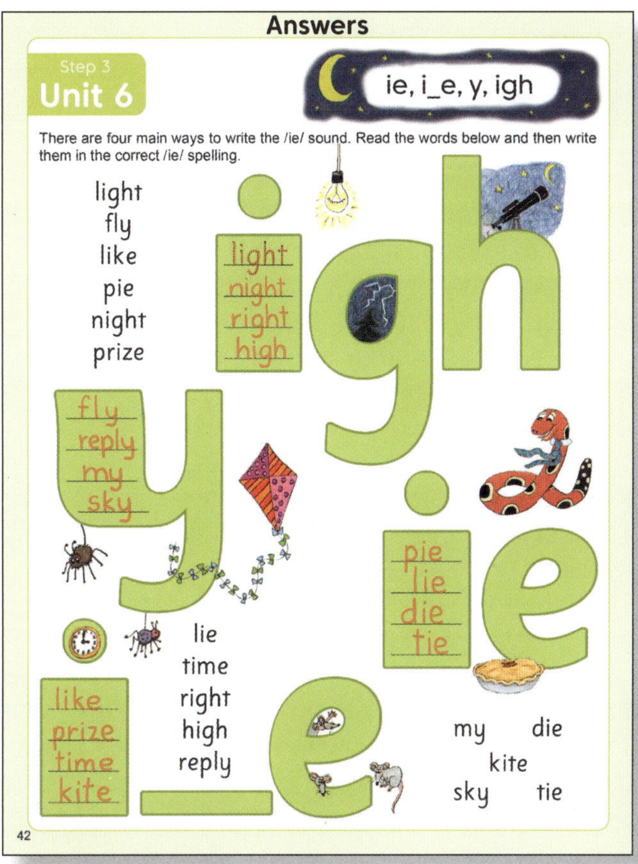

Decodable books

Send the students home with a book that matches their independent reading level.

FURTHER PRACTICE

It is important to practice the skills needed for reading and writing on a regular basis.

Blending and segmenting

boo, tent, from, better, sprain,
sleep, heap, theme, cleaner, underneath

- Call out each word. The students say the sounds, holding up a finger for each one. Write the letters on the board as they do so and blend the word.
- Practice blending the words with the class (as well as in pairs or individually, if extra practice is needed).

Reading sentences

- Write these sentences on the board for the class to read. Point out the tricky words and blend any unknown words with the students:
  1. Do moths fly around at night?
  2. We saw a bright light in the sky.
  3. I tied a red ribbon around the prize.
  4. You might like to try my blackberry pie.

Unit 6: Tricky Words

Flashcards

- Review the tricky words *who, which, any, many, more, before, other, were, because, want, saw, put.*

Tricky words: could, should, would

- Show the students the words in the pink flowers at the top of their lesson page.
- Say each one and ask the students to blend the sounds. Then help the class to work out the tricky parts. In these words, the first and last sound are regular, but the ‹oul› is tricky because it makes the little /oo/ sound.
- To help the students remember the spelling, point out that the only difference is the first letter in each word. They can remember the rest as the ***o u** lucky **d**uck* spelling.
- The students write inside the outline letters using a pink pencil and underline the tricky parts in purple.

Tricky word spelling routine (See page 28)

- The students practice writing the new tricky words on a separate sheet of paper.

Fill in the gaps

- The students write inside the outline letters, write over the dotted letters, and fill in the missing letters.

Could, should, or would?

- Read the sentences with the class and discuss which tricky word should be used in each one.
- Read each sentence back to the students, using their chosen word, and ask them if it makes sense.
- The students complete the sentences, writing the correct word in each one.

Answers

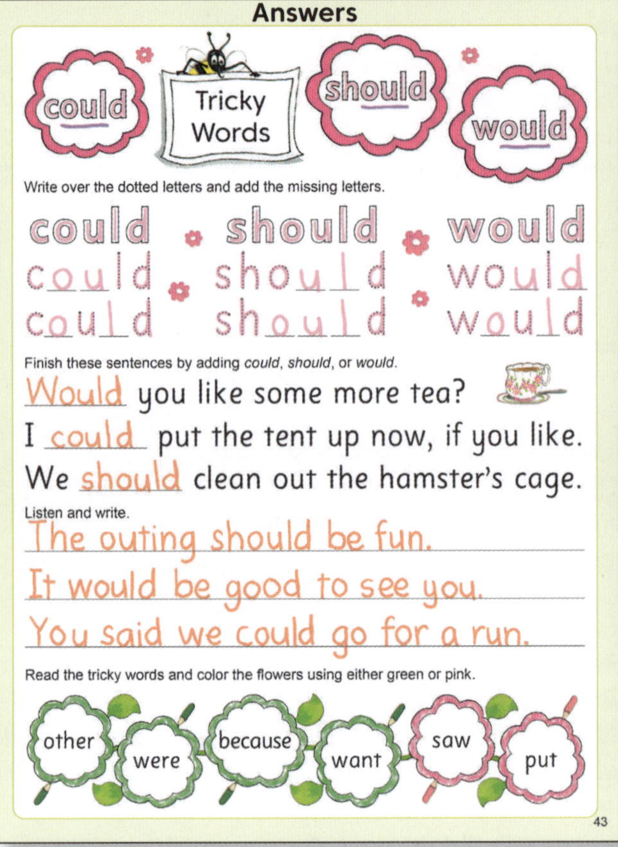

could Tricky Words should would

Write over the dotted letters and add the missing letters.

could should would
could should would
could should would

Finish these sentences by adding *could*, *should*, or *would*.

Would you like some more tea?
I could put the tent up now, if you like.
We should clean out the hamster's cage.

Listen and write.

The outing should be fun.
It would be good to see you.
You said we could go for a run.

Read the tricky words and color the flowers using either green or pink.

other were because want saw put

43

Dictation

- Say the following sentences. The students listen carefully and write them in their books:
  - The outing should be fun.
  - It would be good to see you.
  - You said we could go for a run.

Reading the tricky words

- The students read the tricky words in the flowers and color the edge of the flowers green or pink.

FURTHER PRACTICE

It is important to practice the skills needed for reading and writing on a regular basis.

Blending and segmenting

dust, goat, prim, chain, splash,
stream, keeper, teapot, meaning, athlete

- Call out each word. The students say the sounds, holding up a finger for each one. Write the letters on the board as they do so and blend the word.
- Practice blending the words with the class (as well as in pairs or individually, if extra practice is needed).

Reading sentences

- Write these sentences on the board for the class to read. Point out the tricky words and blend any unknown words with the students:
  1. Should we reply right away?
  2. The lightning is quite frightening.
  3. Could you give me a bit more time?
  4. I would like to ride my bike outside.

Unit 6: Words and Sentences

Review

- Use flashcards to review soft ‹g›, soft ‹c›, ‹ph›, ‹ck›, and some of the alternative vowel spellings.
- Call out some of the letter sounds and ask the students to write the different spellings for each one.

Read, write, and review (See page 181)

- The students go to page 66 of their books and say the alphabet. They point to each letter as they say it, pausing between the sections: A–E; F–M; N–S; T–Z.
- Call out some of the letters. The students find them and say whether they are red, yellow, green, or blue.
- Review how to write the capital letters X, Y, and Z.
- Remind the students that all the capital letters are tall, that they start at or near the top, and that none of them go down under the line. The students trace inside the outline lower-case letters and write the capital letters X, Y, Z, using a blue pencil.

Sentence matching

- Write the following words on the board and read them with the class: *tall, boys, play, like, brown, they, beak, yellow.* Pay particular attention to the double letters, alternatives, and tricky words.
- Show the students the six pictures in their books and explain that each one has two sentences that describe it. Read the first sentence with the class and then find the corresponding sentence in the next column *[I can see a hen. Her beak is yellow]*. Ask the students to join them, writing over the dotted line.
- The students read and match the other sentences.

Extension activity

- The class could write a short story, based on one of the six pictures. The students think of a title, write it at the top of a sheet of paper, and copy the two sentences that describe the picture underneath. Then they write as much as they are able to finish the story. The spelling will not always be accurate but it can be read.

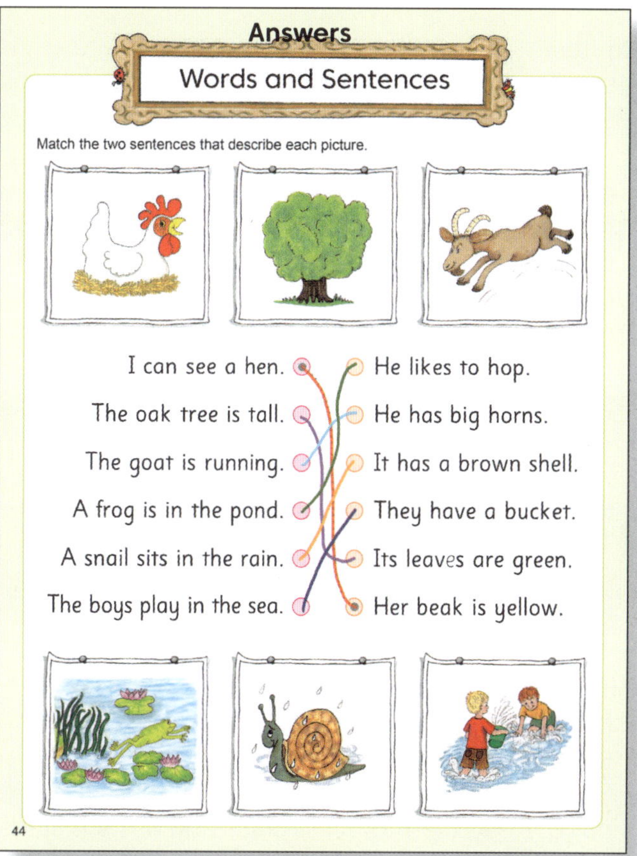

Answers

Words and Sentences

Match the two sentences that describe each picture.

I can see a hen.	He likes to hop.
The oak tree is tall.	He has big horns.
The goat is running.	It has a brown shell.
A frog is in the pond.	They have a bucket.
A snail sits in the rain.	Its leaves are green.
The boys play in the sea.	Her beak is yellow.

44

FURTHER PRACTICE

It is important to practice the skills needed for reading and writing on a regular basis.

Blending and segmenting

swim, broom, chick, quit, sack,
creepy, peanuts, evening, teacher, extreme

- Call out each word. The students say the sounds, holding up a finger for each one. Write the letters on the board as they do so and blend the word.
- Practice blending the words with the class (as well as in pairs or individually, if extra practice is needed).

Reading sentences

- Write these sentences on the board for the class to read. Point out the tricky words and blend any unknown words with the students:
  1. We could fly to Ireland tonight.
  2. It took five days for the letter to arrive.
  3. When should we put the logs on the fire?
  4. Would you like any more ice in your drink?

Unit 7: Alternatives

Review

- Use flashcards to review soft ‹g›, soft ‹c›, ‹ph›, ‹ck›, and some of the alternative vowel spellings: ‹ai›, ‹a_e›, ‹ay›; ‹ee›, ‹e_e›, ‹ea›; ‹ie›, ‹i_e›, ‹y›, ‹igh›; ‹oa›, ‹o_e›, ‹ow›; ‹ue›, ‹u_e›, ‹ew›; ‹ou›, ‹ow›; ‹oi›, ‹oy›; ‹er›, ‹ir›, ‹ur›; ‹aw›, ‹au›, ‹al›. Point out that ‹y› can say /y/, /ee/, or /ie/.
- Call out some of the letter sounds and ask the students to write the different spellings for each one.

Vowel hand (See page 182)

- The students use the vowel hand at the back of their books (Student Book 2, page 72) to practice saying the short and long vowel sounds.
- They then write inside the outline letters for the sounds /o/ and /oa/, and use their finger to trace inside the outline letters for the remaining sounds.

Alternatives: ‹oa›, ‹o_e›, ‹ow›

- Remind the students that there are three main ways to write the sound /oa/: ‹oa›, ‹o_e›, and ‹ow›.
- Show the students the words at the top of their lesson page. Read them with the class and ask the students to underline the spelling of /oa/ in each one.

‹oa›, ‹o_e›, or ‹ow›?

- Look at the word *those* on the lesson page and read it with the class. Point out that the letter ‹s› makes the sound /z/, as it does in other words like *is, as, his,* and *has* (as well as in many plural words). The saying *If one way does not work, try the other* is a useful strategy for blending such words.
- Ask the class to write the word in the correct /oa/ spelling. The students write over the dotted word *those* in the large purple ‹o_e›. Then they read the remaining /oa/ words and write them in the correct spelling.

Answers

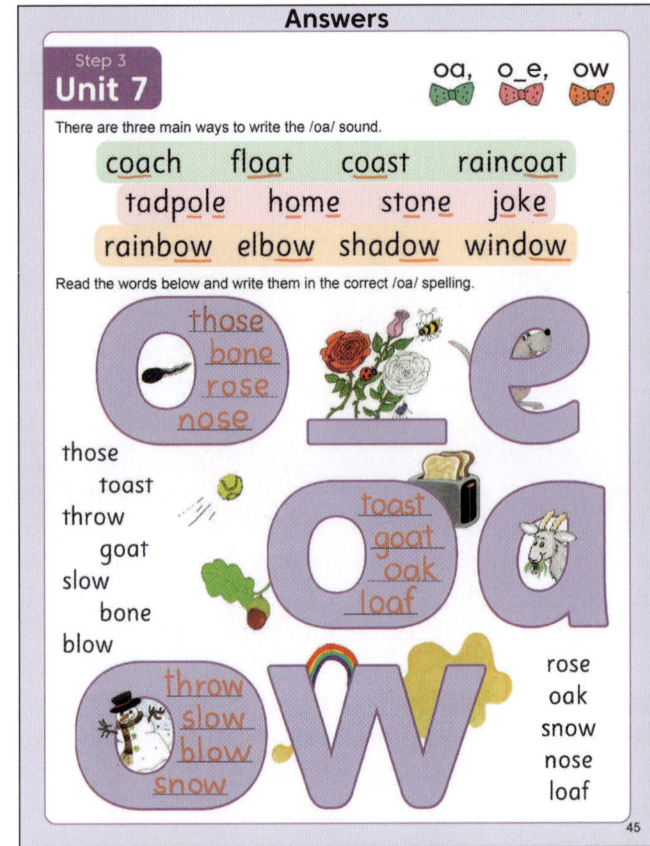

Step 3
Unit 7

oa, o_e, ow

There are three main ways to write the /oa/ sound.

coach float coast raincoat
tadpole home stone joke
rainbow elbow shadow window

Read the words below and write them in the correct /oa/ spelling.

o_e: those, bone, rose, nose
oa: toast, goat, oak, loaf
ow: throw, slow, blow, snow

those, toast, throw, goat, slow, bone, blow, rose, oak, snow, nose, loaf

45

Decodable books

Send the students home with a book that matches their independent reading level.

FURTHER PRACTICE

It is important to practice the skills needed for reading and writing on a regular basis.

Blending and segmenting

jump, next, skip, thump, strain, nylon, fight, quite, frying, playtime

- Call out each word. The students say the sounds, holding up a finger for each one. Write the letters on the board as they do so and blend the word.
- Practice blending the words with the class (as well as in pairs or individually, if extra practice is needed).

Reading sentences

- Write these sentences on the board for the class to read. Point out the tricky words and blend any unknown words with the students:
  1. I wish the snow would melt.
  2. We should go home tomorrow.
  3. Do not throw stones at the window.
  4. You could follow the road along the coast.

Unit 7: Tricky Words

Flashcards

- Review the tricky words *many, more, before, other, were, because, want, saw, put, could, should, would*.

Tricky words: right, two, four

- Show the students the words in the pink flowers at the top of their lesson page. Say each one and ask the students to blend the sounds. Then help the class to work out the tricky parts:
  - The ‹igh› in *right* is tricky because it is an alternative spelling of the sound /ie/.
  - The ‹wo› in *two* is tricky because it makes the long /oo/ sound.
  - The ‹our› in *four* is tricky because it makes the sound /or/.
- The students write inside the outline letters using a pink pencil and underline the tricky parts in purple.

Tricky word spelling routine (See page 28)

- The students practice writing the new tricky words on a separate sheet of paper.

Fill in the gaps

- The students write inside the outline letters, write over the dotted letters, and fill in the missing letters.

Right, two, or four?

- Read the sentences with the class and discuss which tricky word should be used in each one.
- Read each sentence back to the students, using their chosen word, and ask them if it makes sense.
- The students complete the sentences, writing the correct word in each one.

Answers

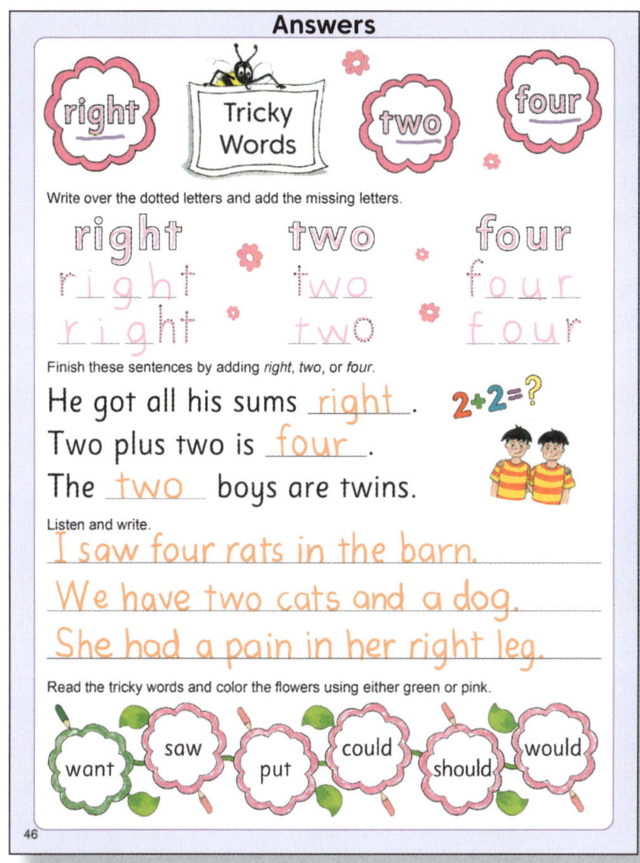

right · Tricky Words · two · four

Write over the dotted letters and add the missing letters.

right two four
right two four
right two four

Finish these sentences by adding *right, two,* or *four.*

He got all his sums right.
Two plus two is four.
The two boys are twins.

Listen and write.

I saw four rats in the barn.
We have two cats and a dog.
She had a pain in her right leg.

Read the tricky words and color the flowers using either green or pink.

want saw put could should would

46

Dictation

- Say the following sentences. The students listen carefully and write them in their books:
  - I saw four rats in the barn.
  - We have two cats and a dog.
  - She had a pain in her right leg.

Reading the tricky words

- The students read the tricky words in the flowers and color the edge of the flowers green or pink.

FURTHER PRACTICE

It is important to practice the skills needed for reading and writing on a regular basis.

Blending and segmenting

soft, sound, flag, cloud, river,
bedtime, myself, driveway, magpie, butterfly

- Call out each word. The students say the sounds, holding up a finger for each one. Write the letters on the board as they do so and blend the word.
- Practice blending the words with the class (as well as in pairs or individually, if extra practice is needed).

Reading sentences

- Write these sentences on the board for the class to read. Point out the tricky words and blend any unknown words with the students:
  1. Stop moaning and groaning.
  2. Those dogs stole two large bones.
  3. Four toads were croaking in the pond.
  4. We rode right around the moat in a boat.

Unit 7: Words and Sentences

Review

- Use flashcards to review soft ‹g›, soft ‹c›, ‹ph›, ‹ck›, and some of the alternative vowel spellings.
- Call out some of the letter sounds and ask the students to write the different spellings for each one.

Read, write, and review (See page 181)

- Recite the alphabet with the class. Any students who need some support can look at page 66 in their books.
- Review how to write the digraphs ‹oa› and ‹ng›. The students go to page 67 of their books and practice writing the digraphs.
- Model this sentence: *The king had a red cloak.* Encourage the class to call out the sounds of each word before you write it and to blend the word afterward.
- Dictate the following sentences: *It is a long road; She hung up her coat on the peg; A bee stung the goat on its throat.* The students write the sentences on a separate sheet of paper.

Read, write, and color

- Write the following words on the board and read them with the class: *oak, my, stripes, collar, little, night, garden, back.* Pay particular attention to the alternative spellings, the schwas in *gard**e**n* and *coll**a**r*, and the tricky words *my* and *little*.
- Show the students the description of each picture on their lesson page. Read the first one with the class and work out which word is missing: *The tall oak [tree] is green.* The students write in the word and color the tree green. There is a line for each sound in the word. A longer line shows that a digraph is needed.
- The students complete the remaining sentences and color in the pictures appropriately.

Answers

Words and Sentences

Read the sentences and fill in the gaps. Color the pictures to match.

The tall oak t r ee is green.

My t ie is long. It has red and black stripes.

My brown c oa t has a big collar.

The little green f r o g jumped into the pond.

The m oo n shines in the night.

I found a s n ai l in the garden. It had a yellow shell on its back.

47

Extension activity

- The class could write a short story about a little green frog. The students think of a title and write it at the top of a sheet of paper. Then they write as much as they are able. The spelling will not always be accurate but it can be read.

FURTHER PRACTICE

It is important to practice the skills needed for reading and writing on a regular basis.

Blending and segmenting

bump, thick, fluff, brush, kick,
untie, terrify, bright, beehive, nightdress

- Call out each word. The students say the sounds, holding up a finger for each one. Write the letters on the board as they do so and blend the word.
- Practice blending the words with the class (as well as in pairs or individually, if extra practice is needed).

Reading sentences

- Write these sentences on the board for the class to read. Point out the tricky words and blend any unknown words with the students:
  1. I stroked the horse's nose.
  2. He fell right into the hole.
  3. Could we borrow four pillows?
  4. They have broken two windows.

Unit 8: Alternatives

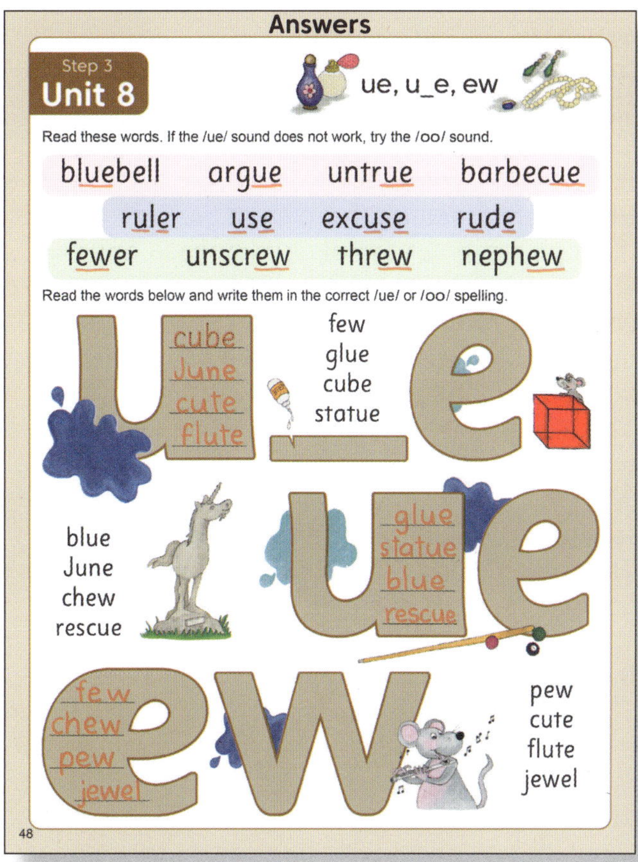

Review

- Use flashcards to review soft ‹g›, soft ‹c›, ‹ph›, ‹ck›, and some of the alternative vowel spellings: ‹ai›, ‹a_e›, ‹ay›; ‹ee›, ‹e_e›, ‹ea›; ‹ie›, ‹i_e›, ‹y›, ‹igh›; ‹oa›, ‹o_e›, ‹ow›; ‹ue›, ‹u_e›, ‹ew›; ‹ou›, ‹ow›; ‹oi›, ‹oy›; ‹er›, ‹ir›, ‹ur›; ‹aw›, ‹au›, ‹al›. Point out that ‹y› can say /y/, /ee/, or /ie/.
- Call out some of the letter sounds and ask the students to write the different spellings for each one.

Vowel hand (See page 182)

- The students use the vowel hand at the back of their books (Student Book 2, page 72) to practice saying the short and long vowel sounds.
- They then write inside the outline letters for the sounds /u/ and /ue/, and use their finger to trace inside the outline letters for the remaining sounds.

Alternatives: ‹ue›, ‹u_e›, ‹ew› as long /oo/

- Write the words *barbecue, use,* and *fewer* on the board and read them with the students. Remind them that there are three main ways to write the sound /ue/: ‹ue›, ‹u_e›, and ‹ew›.
- Now say the words *clue, rule,* and *flew.* Add them to the board and ask what sound the spellings are making now *[long /oo/].*
- Explain that ‹ue›, ‹u_e›, and ‹ew› can make one of two sounds: /ue/ or long /oo/. When blending an unknown word, the students need to try both sounds to see which one is right.
- Show the students the words at the top of their lesson page. Read them with the class and identify which sound is used in each word. Ask the students to underline the alternative spelling in each one.

‹ue›, ‹u_e›, or ‹ew›?

- Look at the other words on the page and ask the students to find the first word with the hop-over ‹e› digraph *[cube].* The students work out which sound the digraph is making *[/ue/]* and write over the dotted word *cube* in the large brown ‹u_e›. They read the remaining words, decide which sound the alternative spelling is making in each one, and write them in the correct spelling.

FURTHER PRACTICE

It is important to practice the skills needed for reading and writing on a regular basis.

Blending and segmenting

shop, roast, cliff, wedding, toffee,
tightrope, sparrow, tadpole, snowman, raincoat

- Call out each word. The students say the sounds, holding up a finger for each one. Write the letters on the board as they do so and blend the word.
- Practice blending the words with the class (as well as in pairs or individually, if extra practice is needed).

Reading sentences

- Write these sentences on the board for the class to read. Point out the tricky words and blend any unknown words with the students:
  1. We rescued four brown newts.
  2. The two twins were born in June.
  3. Can she play a tune on the flute?
  4. You must stir the stew right now.

Unit 8: Tricky Words

Flashcards

- Review the tricky words *other, were, because, want, saw, put, could, should, would, right, two, four.*

Tricky words: goes, does

- Show the students the words in the pink flowers at the top of their lesson page. Say each one and ask the students to blend the sounds. Then help the class to work out the tricky parts. In both words, it is the ‹oes› that is tricky because it says /oaz/ in *goes* and /uz/ in *does*.
- The students write inside the outline letters using a pink pencil and underline the tricky parts in purple.

Tricky word spelling routine (See page 28)

- The students practice writing the new tricky words on a separate sheet of paper.

Fill in the gaps

- The students write inside the outline letters, write over the dotted letters, and fill in the missing letters.

Goes or does?

- Read the sentences with the class and discuss which tricky word should be used in each one.
- Read each sentence back to the students, using their chosen word, and ask them if it makes sense.
- The students complete the sentences, writing the correct word in each one.

Dictation

- Say the following sentences. The students listen carefully and write them in their books:
  - She does not need a hat.
  - He goes to the pool by bus.

Answers

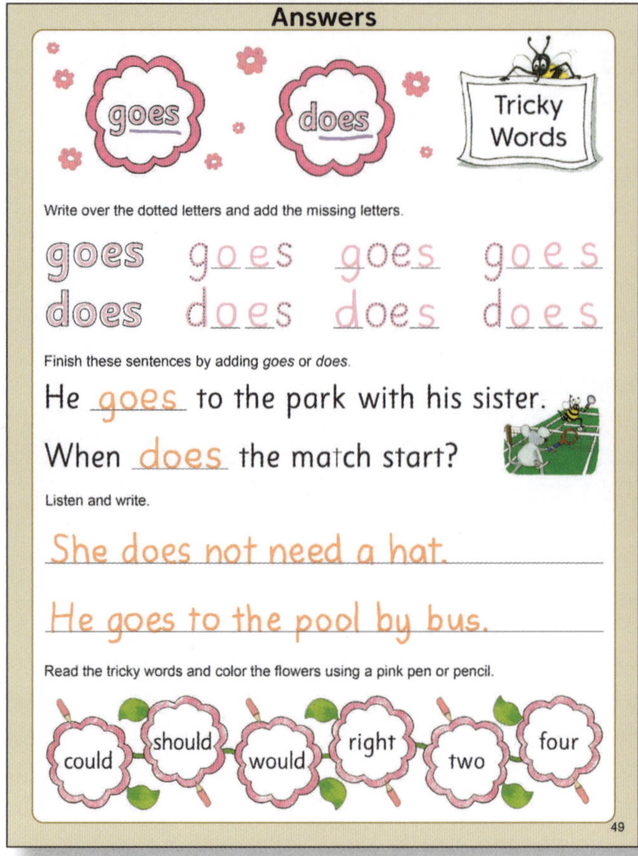
goes does
Tricky Words
Write over the dotted letters and add the missing letters.
goes goes goes goes
does does does does
Finish these sentences by adding *goes* or *does*.
He goes to the park with his sister.
When does the match start?
Listen and write.
She does not need a hat.
He goes to the pool by bus.
Read the tricky words and color the flowers using a pink pen or pencil.
could should would right two four
49

Reading the tricky words

- The students read the tricky words in the flowers and color the edge of the flowers pink.

Decodable books

Send the students home with a book that matches their independent reading level.

FURTHER PRACTICE

It is important to practice the skills needed for reading and writing on a regular basis.

Blending and segmenting

wind, sing, must, morning, frost,
cloak, throw, rainbow, lonely, snowstorm

- Call out each word. The students say the sounds, holding up a finger for each one. Write the letters on the board as they do so and blend the word.
- Practice blending the words with the class (as well as in pairs or individually, if extra practice is needed).

Reading sentences

- Write these sentences on the board for the class to read. Point out the tricky words and blend any unknown words with the students:
  1. Dad goes fishing on Tuesdays.
  2. When does the barbecue start?
  3. I put the new blue quilt on the bed.
  4. We saw many bluebells in the wood.

Unit 8: Words and Sentences

Review

- Use flashcards to review soft ‹g›, soft ‹c›, ‹ph›, ‹ck›, and some of the alternative vowel spellings.
- Call out some of the letter sounds and ask the students to write the different spellings for each one.

Read, write, and review (See page 181)

- Recite the alphabet with the class. Any students who need some support can look at page 66 in their books.
- Review how to write the digraphs ‹oo› and ‹or›. The students go to page 67 of their books and practice writing the digraphs.
- Model this sentence: *She needs a fork and a spoon.* Encourage the class to call out the sounds of each word before you write it and to blend the word afterward.
- Dictate the following sentences: *This popcorn is good; He had a good morning at the zoo; Our goat stood under a tree in the storm.* The students write the sentences on a separate sheet of paper.

In the zoo

- Write the following words on the board and read them with the class: *how, which, animal, trunk, what, where, who, two.* Pay particular attention to the alternative spellings, the schwa in *anim**a**l,* the ‹nk› saying /ngk/ in *trunk* and the tricky words.
- Show the students the picture of the zoo in their books, and read the names of the animals. Blend any unknown words, pointing out the schwas, silent letters, alternative spellings, vowel letters saying their long sounds, and minor irregularities, like the ‹o› in *monkey* making an /u/ sound.
- Read the questions and discuss the answers with the class. The students write them in their books, using one-word answers, as above.
- The students write over the dotted word *sleep* and think of six other words that can be made from the word *elephants*. Other examples include *he, she, lap, tap, hen, pen, pan, let, net, pet, set, peel, then, than, help, plan, snap, sent, sheep, sea, peas, sale.*

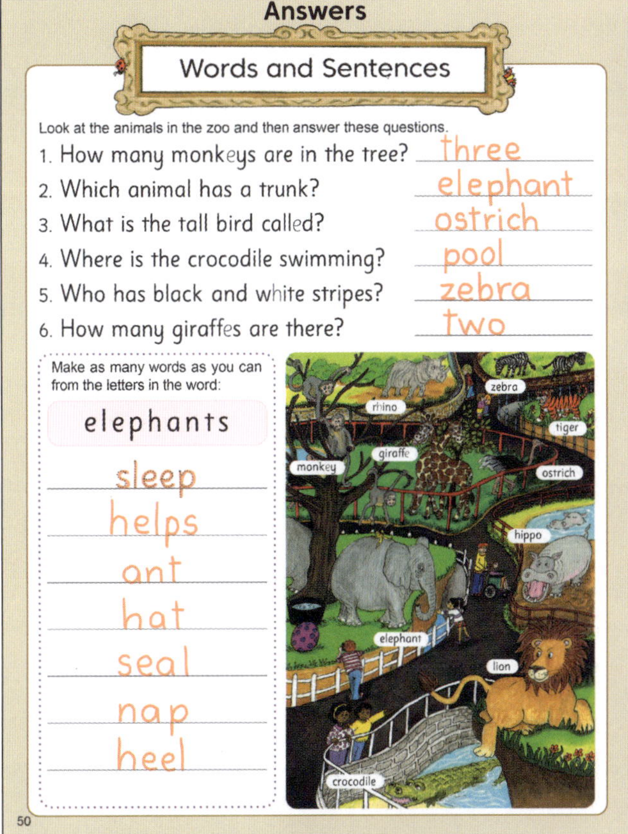

Answers

Words and Sentences

Look at the animals in the zoo and then answer these questions.

1. How many monkeys are in the tree? three
2. Which animal has a trunk? elephant
3. What is the tall bird called? ostrich
4. Where is the crocodile swimming? pool
5. Who has black and white stripes? zebra
6. How many giraffes are there? two

Make as many words as you can from the letters in the word:

elephants

sleep
helps
ant
hat
seal
nap
heel

50

Extension activity

- The students could write a short story about a trip to the zoo.

FURTHER PRACTICE

It is important to practice the skills needed for reading and writing on a regular basis.

Blending and segmenting

corn, duck, flick, charm, butter,
yellow, choke, foam, bowling, moaning

- Call out each word. The students say the sounds, holding up a finger for each one. Write the letters on the board as they do so and blend the word.
- Practice blending the words with the class (as well as in pairs or individually, if extra practice is needed).

Reading sentences

- Write these sentences on the board for the class to read. Point out the tricky words and blend any unknown words with the students:
  1. Did you read the news today?
  2. Can you tell me where he goes?
  3. My nephew does all the shopping.
  4. The moth flew too close to the flame.

Unit 9: Alternatives

Review

- Use flashcards to review soft ‹g›, soft ‹c›, ‹ph›, ‹ck›, and some of the alternative vowel spellings: ‹ai›, ‹a_e›, ‹ay›; ‹ee›, ‹e_e›, ‹ea›; ‹ie›, ‹i_e›, ‹y›, ‹igh›; ‹oa›, ‹o_e›, ‹ow›; ‹ue›, ‹u_e›, ‹ew›; ‹ou›, ‹ow›; ‹oi›, ‹oy›; ‹er›, ‹ir›, ‹ur›; ‹aw›, ‹au›, ‹al›. Point out that ‹y› can say /y/, /ee/, or /ie/.
- Call out some of the letter sounds and ask the students to write the different spellings for each one.

Vowel hand (See page 182)

- The students use the vowel hand at the back of their books (Student Book 2, page 72) to practice saying the short and long vowel sounds.
- The students then look at the first two panels below the vowel hand. Each one has a picture and two words *[ran/rain* and *cot/coat]*. The students read the words and write the one that matches the picture on the line *[rain/coat]*.

Alternatives: ‹ou› and ‹ow›

- Remind the students that there are two main ways to write the sound /ou/: ‹ou› and ‹ow›.
- Show the students the words at the top of their lesson page and read them with the class. Ask the students to underline the spelling of /ou/ in each one.
- Remind the students that the ‹ow› digraph can also make the sound /oa/. The students must try both sounds when blending an unknown word with the ‹ow› spelling.

‹ou› or ‹ow›?

- Look at the other words on the page and ask the class to find the first one that uses the ‹ou› spelling

Answers

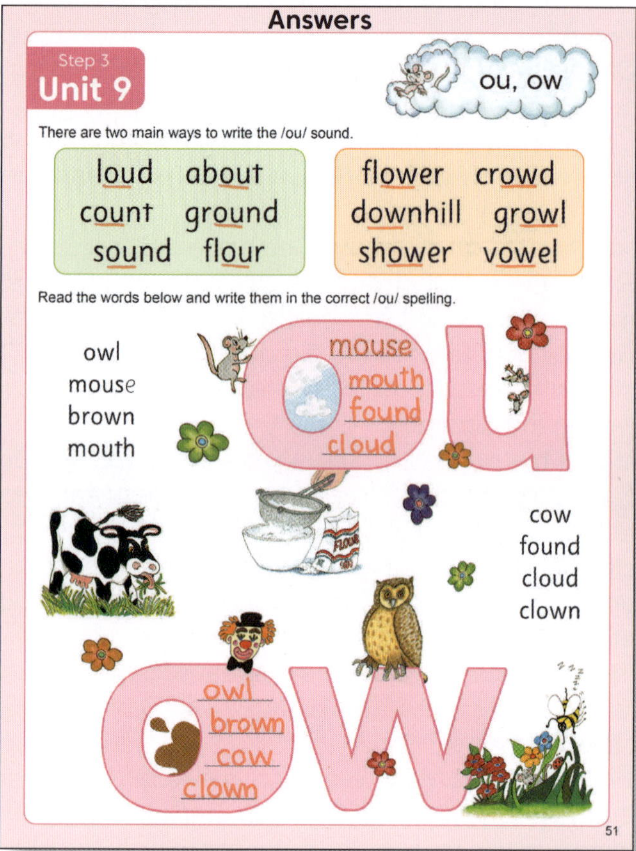

[mouse]. Remind the students that the ‹e› in *mouse* is shown in light type because it is silent. The students write over the dotted word *mouse* in the large pink ‹ou›. Then they read the remaining /ou/ words and write them in the correct spelling.

Decodable books

Send the students home with a book that matches their independent reading level.

FURTHER PRACTICE

It is important to practice the skills needed for reading and writing on a regular basis.

Blending and segmenting

sent, held, glad, never, crunch,
new, rescue, June, Tuesday, bluebell

- Call out each word. The students say the sounds, holding up a finger for each one. Write the letters on the board as they do so and blend the word.
- Practice blending the words with the class (as well as in pairs or individually, if extra practice is needed).

Reading sentences

- Write these sentences on the board for the class to read. Point out the tricky words and blend any unknown words with the students:
  1. She reads the letter out loud.
  2. The bus goes around the town.
  3. The prince's crown has many jewels.
  4. Why does the puppy bounce about so much?

Unit 9: Tricky Words

Flashcards
- Review the tricky words *because, want, saw, put, could, should, would, right, two, four, goes, does*.

Tricky words: made, their
- Show the students the words in the pink flowers at the top of their lesson page. Say each one and ask the students to blend the sounds. Then help the class to work out the tricky parts:
  - The ‹a_e› in *made* is tricky because it is an alternative spelling of the sound /ai/.
  - The ‹eir› in *their* is tricky because it says /air/.
- The students write inside the outline letters using a pink pencil and underline the tricky parts in purple.

Tricky word spelling routine (See page 28)
- The students practice writing the new tricky words on a separate sheet of paper.

Fill in the gaps
- The students write inside the outline letters, write over the dotted letters, and fill in the missing letters.

Made or their?
- Read the sentences with the class and discuss which tricky word should be used in each one. Read each sentence back to the students, using their chosen word, and ask them if it makes sense. The students complete the sentences, writing the correct word in each one.

Dictation
- Say the following sentences. The students listen carefully and write them in their books:
  - I made a card for my sister.

Answers

Tricky Words

made

their

Write over the dotted letters and add the missing letters.

made made made made

their their their their

Finish these sentences by adding *made* or *their*.

We made some cakes yesterday.

They played with their dog.

Listen and write.

I made a card for my sister.

They left their coats in the car.

Read the tricky words and color the flowers using a pink pen or pencil.

would right two four goes does

52

  - They left their coats in the car.

Reading the tricky words
- The students read the tricky words in the flowers and color the edge of the flowers pink.

Wordsearch (See page 182)
- The students go to page 70 of their books. They write over the dotted words in the tricky word flowers and then find them in the wordsearch.

FURTHER PRACTICE
It is important to practice the skills needed for reading and writing on a regular basis.

Blending and segmenting
mend, died, slip, freezing, waist,
threw, mule, cruel, costume, excuse
- Call out each word. The students say the sounds, holding up a finger for each one. Write the letters on the board as they do so and blend the word.
- Practice blending the words with the class (as well as in pairs or individually, if extra practice is needed).

Reading sentences
- Write these sentences on the board for the class to read. Point out the tricky words and blend any unknown words with the students:
  1. The clowns made the crowd smile.
  2. They took their towels to the beach.
  3. We made the sauce with some flour.
  4. The twins want new bikes for their birthday.

Unit 9: Words and Sentences

Review

- Use flashcards to review soft ‹g›, soft ‹c›, ‹ph›, ‹ck›, and some of the alternative vowel spellings.
- Call out some of the letter sounds and ask the students to write the different spellings for each one.

Read, write, and review (See page 181)

- Recite the alphabet with the class. Any students who need some support can look at page 66 in their books.
- Review how to write the digraphs ‹ie›, ‹ee›, and ‹ue›. The students go to page 67 of their books and practice writing the digraphs.
- Model this sentence: *I rescued the pie from three dogs.* Encourage the class to call out the sounds of each word before you write it and to blend the word afterward.
- Dictate the following sentences: *Do not argue with the queen; Lie on the bed and go to sleep; The beef is fried on the barbecue.* The students write the sentences on a separate sheet of paper.

Having a party

- Write the following words on the board and read them with the class: *party, cake, birthday, balloons, games, play, ate, family.*
- Discuss different types of celebration with the class, such as carnivals, festivals, family events, and birthday parties. Talk about the reasons for celebrating, who might be there, what food (if any) would be eaten, and what would be likely to happen.
- Show the students the four story sections in their books and read the unfinished sentence in the first one: *We had a party for* ____. Go around the class and ask for ideas on how to finish the sentence: for example, a student might say *my new sister* or *my birthday*. Do

the same with the second section: We ate some ____.
- The students finish the sentences in their books and add their own ideas to sections three and four. The spelling will not always be accurate but it can be read. They then draw a picture for each part of the story.

Extension activity

- The students could write a short letter saying thank you for being invited to a party. Show them how to begin and end the letter and discuss what they might say.

FURTHER PRACTICE

It is important to practice the skills needed for reading and writing on a regular basis.

Blending and segmenting

pond, dark, plug, shark, chimp,
flew, flute, chewing, screw, include

- Call out each word. The students say the sounds, holding up a finger for each one. Write the letters on the board as they do so and blend the word.
- Practice blending the words with the class (as well as in pairs or individually, if extra practice is needed).

Reading sentences

- Write these sentences on the board for the class to read. Point out the tricky words and blend any unknown words with the students:
    1. Their dogs are growling outside.
    2. The farmer has a little brown cow.
    3. We found some pretty blue flowers.
    4. Dad made us clean our muddy boots.

Unit 10: Alternatives

Review

- Use flashcards to review soft ‹g›, soft ‹c›, ‹ph›, ‹ck›, and some of the alternative vowel spellings: ‹ai›, ‹a_e›, ‹ay›; ‹ee›, ‹e_e›, ‹ea›; ‹ie›, ‹i_e›, ‹y›, ‹igh›; ‹oa›, ‹o_e›, ‹ow›; ‹ue›, ‹u_e›, ‹ew›; ‹ou›, ‹ow›; ‹oi›, ‹oy›; ‹er›, ‹ir›, ‹ur›; ‹aw›, ‹au›, ‹al›. Point out that ‹y› can say /y/, /ee/, or /ie/.
- Call out some of the letter sounds and ask the students to write the different spellings for each one.

Vowel hand (See page 182)

- The students use the vowel hand at the back of their books (Student Book 2, page 72) to practice saying the short and long vowel sounds.
- The students then look at the third and fourth panels below the vowel hand. Each one has a picture and two words *[bat/bait* and *rid/ride]*. The students read the words and write the one that matches the picture on the line *[bat/ride]*.

Alternatives: ‹oi› and ‹oy›

- Remind the students that there are two main ways to write the sound /oi/: ‹oi› and ‹oy›. The ‹oy› spelling usually comes at the end of a word because the letter ‹i› is shy, so toughy ‹y› takes its place.
- Show the students the words at the top of their lesson page. Read them with the class and ask the students to underline the spelling of /oi/ in each one.

‹oi› or ‹oy›?

- Look at the other words on the page and ask the class to find the first one that uses the ‹oi› spelling *[coin]*. The students write over the dotted word *coin* in the large grey ‹oi›. Then they read the remaining /oi/ words and write them in the correct spelling.

Answers

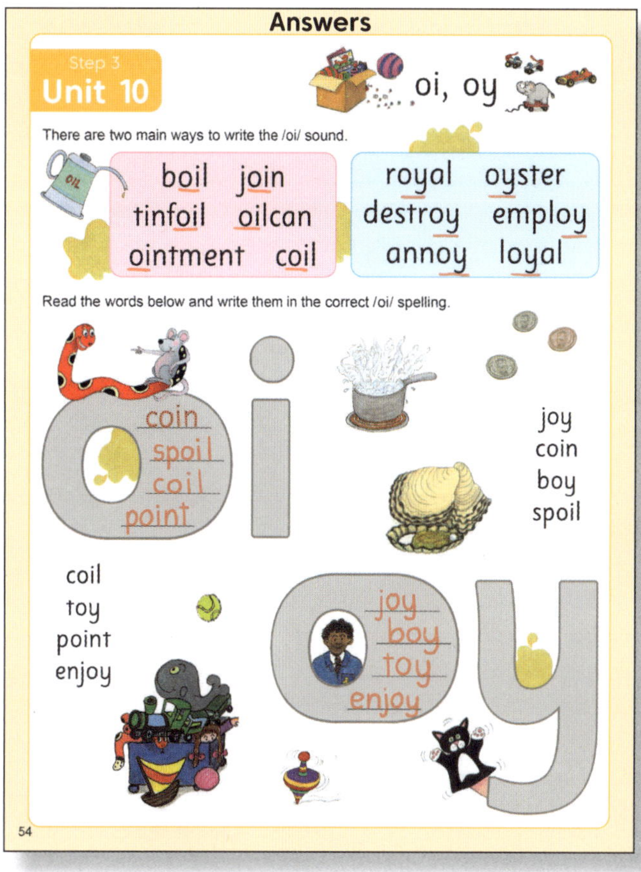
Step 3
Unit 10
oi, oy
There are two main ways to write the /oi/ sound.
boil join tinfoil oilcan ointment coil
royal oyster destroy employ annoy loyal
Read the words below and write them in the correct /oi/ spelling.
coin spoil coil point
joy coin boy spoil
coil toy point enjoy
joy boy toy enjoy
54

Jolly Phonics readers

- Students who have finished the Green Level Readers and who know the alternative spellings and tricky words taught so far can now start the Blue Level.

FURTHER PRACTICE

It is important to practice the skills needed for reading and writing on a regular basis.

Blending and segmenting

left, card, blend, cracker, ever,
pouch, tower, cowshed, flower, shouting

- Call out each word. The students say the sounds, holding up a finger for each one. Write the letters on the board as they do so and blend the word.
- Practice blending the words with the class (as well as in pairs or individually, if extra practice is needed).

Reading sentences

- Write these sentences on the board for the class to read. Point out the tricky words and blend any unknown words with the students:
    1. Those boys were very noisy.
    2. Dad dug the soil with a spade.
    3. They put their toys back in the box.
    4. We really enjoy swimming in the pool.

Unit 10: Tricky Words

Flashcards

- Review the tricky words *saw, put, could, should, would, right, two, four, goes, does, made, their.*

Tricky words: once, upon, always

- Show the students the words in the brown flowers at the top of their lesson page. Say each one and ask the students to blend the sounds. Then help the class to work out the tricky parts:
  - The ‹o› in *once* is tricky because it says /wu/. The ‹ce› is also tricky because it is an example of how the letter ‹c› says /s/ when it is followed by the letter ‹e›, ‹i›, or ‹y›.
  - The ‹u› in *upon,* is tricky because it makes the neutral schwa sound.
  - The word *always* is tricky because the ‹a› says /o/, the ‹ay› is an alternative spelling of the sound /ai/, and the ‹s› says /z/.
- The students write inside the outline letters using a brown pencil and underline the tricky parts in purple.

Tricky word spelling routine (See page 28)

- The students practice writing the new tricky words on a separate sheet of paper.

Fill in the gaps

- The students write inside the outline letters, write over the dotted letters, and fill in the missing letters.

Once, upon, or always?

- Read the beginning of the story with the class and discuss which tricky word is missing each time. Children's stories often begin with the words *Once upon a time*, so the students should be able to work this part out, with a bit of encouragement. This leaves *always* for the final word.
- The students add the missing words and finish the story, writing as much as they are able. Their spelling will not always be accurate but it can be read.

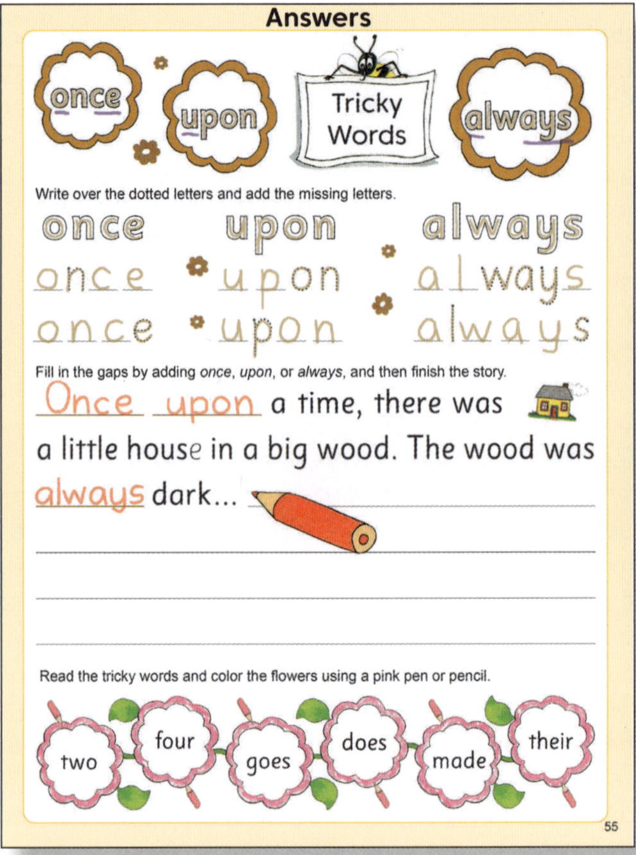
Answers

once upon Tricky Words always

Write over the dotted letters and add the missing letters.

once upon always

once upon always

once upon always

Fill in the gaps by adding *once*, *upon*, or *always*, and then finish the story.

Once upon a time, there was a little house in a big wood. The wood was always dark...

Read the tricky words and color the flowers using a pink pen or pencil.

two four goes does made their

55

Reading the tricky words

- The students read the tricky words in the flowers and color the edge of the flowers pink.

FURTHER PRACTICE

It is important to practice the skills needed for reading and writing on a regular basis.

Blending and segmenting

pump, found, scrub, farmer, under,
crowd, cloudy, powder, growl, sunflower

- Call out each word. The students say the sounds, holding up a finger for each one. Write the letters on the board as they do so and blend the word.
- Practice blending the words with the class (as well as in pairs or individually, if extra practice is needed).

Reading sentences

- Write these sentences on the board for the class to read. Point out the tricky words and blend any unknown words with the students:
  1. I once put oysters in the stew.
  2. My sister is always annoying me.
  3. There were row upon row of old coins.
  4. Once upon a time there was a lonely boy.

Unit 10: Words and Sentences

Review

- Use flashcards to review soft ‹g›, soft ‹c›, ‹ph›, ‹ck›, and some of the alternative vowel spellings.
- Call out some of the letter sounds and ask the students to write the different spellings for each one.

Read, write, and review (See page 181)

- Recite the alphabet with the class. Any students who need some support can look at page 66 in their books.
- Review how to write the digraphs ‹sh›, ‹ch›, and ‹th›. The students go to page 68 of their books and practice writing the digraphs.
- Model this sentence: *Thank him for the fish and chips.* Encourage the class to call out the sounds of each word before you write it and to blend the word afterward.
- Dictate the following sentences: *I can fix the bench in the shed; She had lunch on the ship with her dad; I think she has three fish in her pond.* The students write the sentences on a separate sheet of paper.

Moat Farm

- Read the story of Moat Farm to the class.
- Afterward, show the students the story in their books and point out that some of the words are missing. The missing words are at the top of the page.
- Read these words with the class and then read the first part of the story. Discuss why *Farm* is the right word to put there and ask the students to add it to the story, writing over the dotted letters.
- The students then read the rest of the story on their own and write in the missing words. They might find it useful to cross off each word as it is added.
- If copies of Moat Farm (Red Level) are available, the students could read the story for themselves.

Answers

Words and Sentences

Complete the story of Moat Farm, using the words below.

lives Neb Ben Farm sheep
Green sheepdogs hill truck

1 This is Moat Farm.

2 Farmer Green lives on Moat Farm.

3 Ben and Neb are sheepdogs.

4 Neb and Ben help on the farm.

5 This morning, Ben and Neb run up the hill...

6 ...and help round up the sheep.

7 Farmer Green checks that the sheep are well.

8 Neb and Ben rest in the back of the truck.

56

- **Note:** The tricky word *of* in the last sentence is taught in the next unit, but it is not so difficult to read.

Extension activity

- Discuss the story from the point of view of the sheepdogs. The students can then retell the story in their own words under the title *Ben and Neb*, adding as much detail as possible.

FURTHER PRACTICE

It is important to practice the skills needed for reading and writing on a regular basis.

Blending and segmenting

song, yard, smell, clever, vain,
town, clown, counter, without, flowerpot

- Call out each word. The students say the sounds, holding up a finger for each one. Write the letters on the board as they do so and blend the word.
- Practice blending the words with the class (as well as in pairs or individually, if extra practice is needed).

Reading sentences

- Write these sentences on the board for the class to read. Point out the tricky words and blend any unknown words with the students:
  1. Do not boil the oil in the pan.
  2. The old shaggy dog is very loyal.
  3. Put some ointment on your finger.
  4. Why do you always spoil things?

Unit 11: Alternatives

Review

- Use flashcards to review soft ‹g›, soft ‹c›, ‹ph›, ‹ck›, and some of the alternative vowel spellings: ‹ai›, ‹a_e›, ‹ay›; ‹ee›, ‹e_e›, ‹ea›; ‹ie›, ‹i_e›, ‹y›, ‹igh›; ‹oa›, ‹o_e›, ‹ow›; ‹ue›, ‹u_e›, ‹ew›; ‹ou›, ‹ow›; ‹oi›, ‹oy›; ‹er›, ‹ir›, ‹ur›; ‹aw›, ‹au›, ‹al›. Point out that ‹y› can say /y/, /ee/, or /ie/.
- Call out some of the letter sounds and ask the students to write the different spellings for each one.

Vowel hand (See page 182)

- The students use the vowel hand at the back of their books (Student Book 2, page 72) to practice saying the short and long vowel sounds.
- The students then look at the last two panels on the second row. Each one has a picture and two words *[hug/huge* and *rod/road]*. The students read the words and write the one that matches the picture on the line *[hug/road]*.

Alternatives: ‹er›, ‹ir›, ‹ur›

- Remind the students that there are three main ways to write the sound /er/: ‹er›, ‹ir›, and ‹ur›.
- Show the students the words at the top of their lesson page. Read them with the class and ask the students to underline the spelling of /er/ in each one.

‹er›, ‹ir›, or ‹ur›?

- Look at the word *dinner* on the lesson page and read it with the class. Ask the class to write the word in the correct /er/ spelling. The students write over the dotted word *dinner* in the large blue ‹er›. Then they read the remaining /er/ words and write them in the correct spelling.

- **Note:** Remind the students that the ‹e› in *purple* and *purse* is shown in light type because it is silent.

Decodable books

Send the students home with a book that matches their independent reading level.

FURTHER PRACTICE

It is important to practice the skills needed for reading and writing on a regular basis.

Blending and segmenting

arm, socks, count, swimmer, slug,
joy, toil, tomboy, oyster, spoilsport

- Call out each word. The students say the sounds, holding up a finger for each one. Write the letters on the board as they do so and blend the word.
- Practice blending the words with the class (as well as in pairs or individually, if extra practice is needed).

Reading sentences

- Write these sentences on the board for the class to read. Point out the tricky words and blend any unknown words with the students:
  1. Turn your shirt inside out.
  2. The little bird's wing was hurt.
  3. My family once flew in a helicopter.
  4. You are always better at singing than me.

Unit 11: Tricky Words

Answers

also · of · Tricky Words · eight

Write over the dotted letters and add the missing letters.

also · of · eight

Finish these sentences by adding *also*, *of*, or *eight*.

There are lots of sheep on the farm.

I also saw some cows in the barn.

I counted eight chickens in the yard, too.

Listen and write.

I also have a green tie.

Her dog had eight pups.

We saw a herd of goats.

Read the tricky words and color the flowers using either pink or brown.

does · made · their · once · upon · always

58

Flashcards

- Review the tricky words *should, would, right, two, four, goes, does, made, their, once, upon, always*.

Tricky words: also, of, eight

- Show the students the words in the brown flowers at the top of their lesson page. Say each one and ask the students to blend the sounds. Then help the class to work out the tricky parts:
  - The word *also* is tricky because the ‹a› says /o/ and the ‹o› makes its long vowel sound.
  - The ‹f› in *of* is tricky because it says /v/.
  - The ‹eigh› in *eight* is tricky because it makes the sound /ai/.
- The students write inside the outline letters using a brown pencil and underline the tricky parts in purple.

Tricky word spelling routine (See page 28)

- The students practice writing the new tricky words on a separate sheet of paper.

Fill in the gaps

- The students write inside the outline letters, write over the dotted letters, and fill in the missing letters.

Also, of, or eight?

- Read the sentences with the class and discuss which tricky word should be used in each one. Read each sentence back to the students, using their chosen word, and ask them if it makes sense. The students complete the sentences, writing the correct word in each one.

Dictation

- Say the following sentences. The students listen carefully and write them in their books:
  - I also have a green tie.
  - Her dog had eight pups.
  - We saw a herd of goats.

Reading the tricky words

- The students read the tricky words in the flowers and color the edge of the flowers pink or brown.

FURTHER PRACTICE

It is important to practice the skills needed for reading and writing on a regular basis.

Blending and segmenting

hump, click, bunch, spill, sixteen,
toy, spoil, boiler, tinfoil, cowboy

- Call out each word. The students say the sounds, holding up a finger for each one. Write the letters on the board as they do so and blend the word.
- Practice blending the words with the class (as well as in pairs or individually, if extra practice is needed).

Reading sentences

- Write these sentences on the board for the class to read. Point out the tricky words and blend any unknown words with the students:
  1. The carpet is really dirty.
  2. I saw eight ducklings by the river.
  3. A flock of birds flew across the sky.
  4. We will also see my sister on Thursday.

Unit 11: Words and Sentences

Review

- Use flashcards to review soft ‹g›, soft ‹c›, ‹ph›, ‹ck›, and some of the alternative vowel spellings.
- Call out some of the letter sounds and ask the students to write the different spellings for each one.

Read, write, and review (See page 181)

- Recite the alphabet with the class. Any students who need some support can look at page 66 in their books.
- Review how to write the digraphs ‹er›, ‹ar›, and ‹ai›. The students go to page 68 of their books and practice writing the digraphs.
- Model this sentence: *The snail left a trail on the tree bark.* Encourage the class to call out the sounds of each word before you write it and to blend the word afterward.
- Dictate the following sentences: *She can start her painting soon; The nails are in the jar under the shelf; This winter we had sharp frosts with rain and hail.*

Crossword clues

- Write these words on the board and read them with the class: *doctor, find, small, wash, water, year, cold, blue.* Point out the schwa in *doct**o**r*, the long vowel sounds in *find* and *cold*, minor irregularities, such as the ‹a› saying /o/ in *was* and *water,* and the pronunciation of *year* needing to be adjusted after blending.
- Show the students the crossword on their lesson page. Explain that the words around the grid are answers to the crossword clues. The students have to read the clues to work out where the words go.
- Read the words with the class, paying particular attention to the double letters and alternative spellings.
- Read the first clue with the students and discuss the possible answer *[map]*. Help them to find the crossword square with the number 1 in it, and ask the class to write over the dotted letters ‹m›, ‹a›, ‹p› in the squares going down. Go through the rest of the clues, helping the students to work out the answers, and write a few more. Then let them finish on their own.

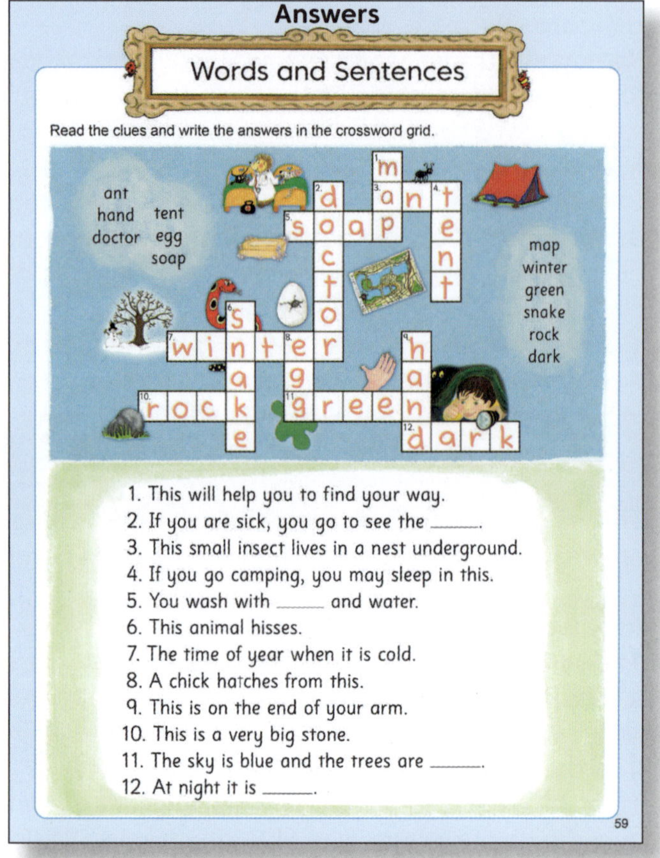

Answers

Words and Sentences

Read the clues and write the answers in the crossword grid.

ant
hand
doctor
tent
egg
soap

map
winter
green
snake
rock
dark

1. This will help you to find your way.
2. If you are sick, you go to see the ______.
3. This small insect lives in a nest underground.
4. If you go camping, you may sleep in this.
5. You wash with ______ and water.
6. This animal hisses.
7. The time of year when it is cold.
8. A chick hatches from this.
9. This is on the end of your arm.
10. This is a very big stone.
11. The sky is blue and the trees are ______.
12. At night it is ______.

59

Extension activity

- The students make up their own clues for zoo animals. Working in pairs, they read their clues to each other and try to guess the answers.

FURTHER PRACTICE

It is important to practice the skills needed for reading and writing on a regular basis.

Blending and segmenting

road, sick, twin, vest, fort,
boy, soil, joint, boiling, toybox

- Call out each word. The students say the sounds, holding up a finger for each one. Write the letters on the board as they do so and blend the word.
- Practice blending the words with the class (as well as in pairs or individually, if extra practice is needed).

Reading sentences

- Write these sentences on the board for the class to read. Point out the tricky words and blend any unknown words with the students:
  1. Eight is my lucky number.
  2. They also swim on Saturday.
  3. Thank you for the bunch of flowers.
  4. What is the first letter of the alphabet?

Unit 12: Alternatives

Review

- Use flashcards to review soft ‹g›, soft ‹c›, ‹ph›, ‹ck›, and some of the alternative vowel spellings: ‹ai›, ‹a_e›, ‹ay›; ‹ee›, ‹e_e›, ‹ea›; ‹ie›, ‹i_e›, ‹y›, ‹igh›; ‹oa›, ‹o_e›, ‹ow›; ‹ue›, ‹u_e›, ‹ew›; ‹ou›, ‹ow›; ‹oi›, ‹oy›; ‹er›, ‹ir›, ‹ur›; ‹aw›, ‹au›, ‹al›. Point out that ‹y› can say /y/, /ee/, or /ie/.
- Call out some of the letter sounds and ask the students to write the different spellings for each one.

Vowel hand (See page 182)

- The students use the vowel hand at the back of their books (Student Book 2, page 72) to practice saying the short and long vowel sounds.
- The students then look at the first two panels on the third row. Each one has a picture and two words *[net/neat* and *kit/kite]*. The students read the words and write the one that matches the picture on the line *[net/kite]*.

Alternatives: ‹aw›, ‹au›, ‹al›

- Remind the students that there are three main alternative spellings for the sound /o/: ‹aw›, ‹au›, and ‹al›.
- Show the students the words at the top of their lesson page. Read them with the class and ask the students to underline the alternative spelling for /o/ in each one.

‹aw›, ‹au›, or ‹al›?

- Look at the word *saw* on the lesson page and read it with the class. Ask the class to write the word in the correct alternative spelling. The students write over the dotted word *saw* in the large ‹aw›. Then they read the remaining words and write them in the correct spelling.

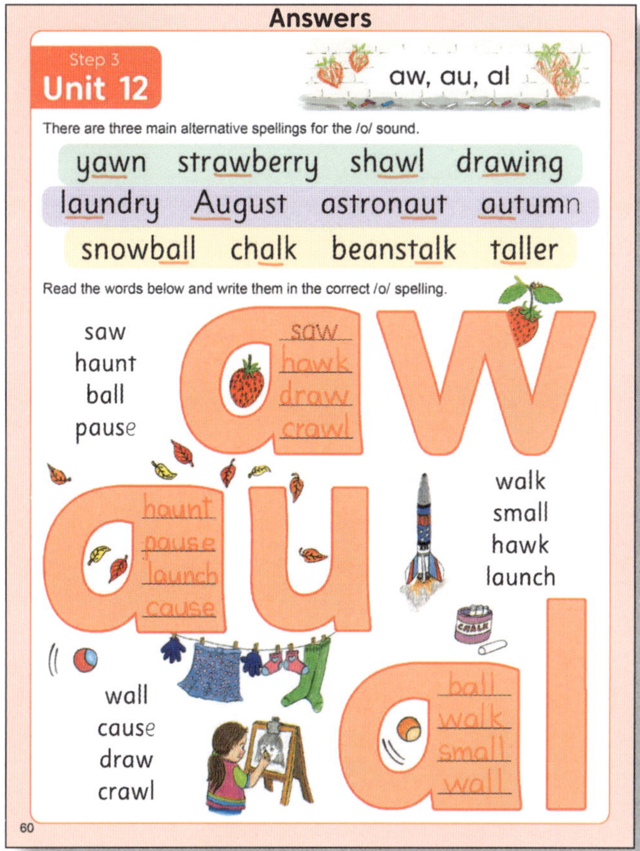

- **Note:** Remind the students that the ‹n› in *autumn* and the ‹e› in *pause* and *cause* are shown in light type because they are silent.

Decodable books

Send the students home with a book that matches their independent reading level.

FURTHER PRACTICE

It is important to practice the skills needed for reading and writing on a regular basis.

Blending and segmenting

damp, summer, groan, cheek, chill,
purr, thirsty, thunder, hamster, sunburn

- Call out each word. The students say the sounds, holding up a finger for each one. Write the letters on the board as they do so and blend the word.
- Practice blending the words with the class (as well as in pairs or individually, if extra practice is needed).

Reading sentences

- Write these sentences on the board for the class to read. Point out the tricky words and blend any unknown words with the students:
  1. Who threw that snowball?
  2. Do a drawing of an astronaut.
  3. The rocket launches into space.
  4. I found a box of chalks on the shelf.

Unit 12: Tricky Words

Flashcards

- Review the tricky words *two, four, goes, does, made, their, once, upon, always, also, of, eight*.

Tricky words: love, cover, after

- Show the students the words in the brown flowers at the top of their lesson page. Say each one and ask the students to blend the sounds. Then help the class to work out the tricky parts:
  - In the words *love* and *cover,* the ‹o› is tricky because it says /u/.
  - The final ‹e› in *love* is also tricky because it is silent.
  - The ‹a› in *after* is tricky only for those students who say /ar/ rather than /a/ in words like *grass*.
- Point out that *love* shares a similar spelling to the tricky words *live, give,* and *have.* These words all end in ‹ve› because English words rarely end in the letter ‹v›.
- The students write inside the outline letters using a brown pencil and underline the tricky parts in purple.

Tricky word spelling routine (See page 28)

- The students practice writing the new tricky words on a separate sheet of paper.

Answers

love cover Tricky Words after

Write over the dotted letters and add the missing letters.

love cover after
love cover after
love cover after

Finish these sentences by adding *love, cover,* or *after.*

I love to go swimming.
After lunch, we can play some games.
The cover of the book was torn.

Listen and write.

We love to sing songs.
Cover the pot with a lid.
Dad had a nap after you left.

Read the tricky words and color the flowers using a brown pen or pencil.

once upon always also of eight

61

Fill in the gaps

- The students write inside the outline letters, write over the dotted letters, and fill in the missing letters.

Love, cover, or after?

- Read the sentences with the class and discuss which tricky word should be used in each one. Read each sentence back to the students, using their chosen word, and ask them if it makes sense. The students complete the sentences, writing the correct word in each one.

Dictation

- Say the following sentences. The students listen carefully and write them in their books:
  - We love to sing songs.
  - Cover the pot with a lid.
  - Dad had a nap after you left.

Reading the tricky words

- The students read the tricky words in the flowers and color the edge of the flowers brown.

FURTHER PRACTICE

It is important to practice the skills needed for reading and writing on a regular basis.

Blending and segmenting

lift, crab, oilcan, tuck, jeep,
burn, shower, burger, thirty, birthday

- Call out each word. The students say the sounds, holding up a finger for each one. Write the letters on the board as they do so and blend the word.
- Practice blending the words with the class (as well as in pairs or individually, if extra practice is needed).

Reading sentences

- Write these sentences on the board for the class to read. Point out the tricky words and blend any unknown words with the students:
  1. We love talking to our granny.
  2. Who does the laundry at home?
  3. I will feed the dog after his walk.
  4. She covers her arms with a shawl.

Unit 12: Words and Sentences

Review

- Use flashcards to review soft ‹g›, soft ‹c›, ‹ph›, ‹ck›, and some of the alternative vowel spellings.
- Call out some of the letter sounds and ask the students to write the different spellings for each one.

Read, write, and review (See page 181)

- Recite the alphabet with the class. Any students who need some support can look at page 66 in their books.
- Review how to write the digraphs ‹oi› and ‹ou›. The students go to page 68 of their books and practice writing the digraphs.
- Model this sentence: *The scout cooks the trout in foil.* Encourage the class to call out the sounds of each word before you write it and to blend the word afterward.
- Dictate the following sentences: *The oil drips on the ground; We count the coins; She points to the clouds.* The students write the sentences on a separate sheet of paper.

On the beach

- Write the following words on the board and read them with the class: *beach, does, doing, seagull, octopus, animal, umbrella, sandcastle.* Pay particular attention to the double letters and alternative spellings, the schwas in *octo**pu**s, ani**ma**l,* and *umbrell**a**,* the silent letters ‹t› and ‹e› in *sandcastle,* and the tricky words *does* and *do(ing)*.
- Show the students the picture in their books and discuss what is happening on the beach.
- Read the first question with the class and discuss what the answer might be *[They are fishing]*. The students write either the full sentence or just the word *fishing* in their books.

Answers

Words and Sentences

What is happening on the beach? Look carefully and answer the questions below.

1. What are the children doing on the rocks?
   They are fishing.
2. What can you see in the tide pool?
   I can see a fish.
3. What is on the top of the sandcastle?
   There are three green flags.
4. How many legs does an octopus have?
   An octopus has eight legs.
5. How many beach umbrellas are there?
   There are four umbrellas.
6. What sort of animal is a seagull?
   A seagull is a bird.

62

- Go through the remaining questions with the class and discuss the answers. Then the students read the questions again by themselves and write the answers in their books.

Extension activity

- The students could write a short story about a day at the beach. They think of a title, write it at the top of a sheet of paper, and write as much as they are able.

FURTHER PRACTICE

It is important to practice the skills needed for reading and writing on a regular basis.

Blending and segmenting

roof, lick, swell, teeth, stick,
fur, first, church, dirty, blackbird

- Call out each word. The students say the sounds, holding up a finger for each one. Write the letters on the board as they do so and blend the word.
- Practice blending the words with the class (as well as in pairs or individually, if extra practice is needed).

Reading sentences

- Write these sentences on the board for the class to read. Point out the tricky words and blend any unknown words with the students:
  1. A small dog ran after the ball.
  2. We love to go camping in August.
  3. The caterpillar crawls along the wall.
  4. The bed cover has a strawberry pattern.

Unit 13: Alternatives

Review

- Use flashcards to review soft ‹g›, soft ‹c›, ‹ph›, ‹ck›, and some of the alternative vowel spellings: ‹ai›, ‹a_e›, ‹ay›; ‹ee›, ‹e_e›, ‹ea›; ‹ie›, ‹i_e›, ‹y›, ‹igh›; ‹oa›, ‹o_e›, ‹ow›; ‹ue›, ‹u_e›, ‹ew›; ‹ou›, ‹ow›; ‹oi›, ‹oy›; ‹er›, ‹ir›, ‹ur›; ‹aw›, ‹au›, ‹al›. Point out that ‹y› can say /y/, /ee/, or /ie/.
- Call out some of the letter sounds and ask the students to write the different spellings for each one.

Vowel hand (See page 182)

- The students use the vowel hand at the back of their books (Student Book 2, page 72) to practice saying the short and long vowel sounds.
- The students then look at the last panel, which has a picture and two words *[bed/bead]*. The students read the words and write the one that matches the picture on the line *[bead]*.

Alternatives: ‹air›, ‹ear›, ‹are› for /air/

- Introduce the sound /air/ and the three main ways to write it. Start by calling out the words *air, tear* and *scare.* Then say the sounds in each word, holding up a finger as you say each sound: /air/, /t-ear/, /s-c-are/. Write the words on the board and blend them with the students. Underline each spelling of the sound.
- Show the students how to write the three spellings. The students form the letters in the air before writing inside the outline spellings in their books.

Reading words

- Read the /air/ words at the top of the lesson page with the class and discuss the spellings and meanings. The students underline the alternative in each word.

Answers

Word and picture matching

- Look at the pictures in the bears and discuss them with the class, Then read the words in the salmon with the class and point out the ‹y› saying /ee/ in *fairy* and the ‹ow› saying /oa/ in *scarecrow*.
- The students read the words again by themselves and join the salmon to the correct bears. When they have finished, they can color the pictures in.

FURTHER PRACTICE

It is important to practice the skills needed for reading and writing on a regular basis.

Blending and segmenting

belt, trail, skull, chart, insect,
claw, chalk, haunt, seesaw, falling

- Call out each word. The students say the sounds, holding up a finger for each one. Write the letters on the board as they do so and blend the word.
- Practice blending the words with the class (as well as in pairs or individually, if extra practice is needed).

Reading sentences

- Write these sentences on the board for the class to read. Point out the tricky words and blend any unknown words with the students:
    1. The fairy has magical powers.
    2. Farmer Green made a scarecrow.
    3. The little boy loves his old teddy bear.
    4. The story about the phantom scared me.

Unit 13: Tricky Words

Flashcards

- Review the tricky words *does, made, their, once, upon, always, also, of, eight, love, cover, after*.

Tricky words: every, mother, father

- Show the students the words in the brown flowers at the top of their lesson page. Say each one and ask the students to blend the sounds. Then help the class to work out the tricky parts:
  - The word *every* is tricky because the second ‹e› is silent and the students have to remember the ‹y› as /ee/ spelling.
  - In the other two words it is the second letter that is tricky. Saying them as they sound (so *mother* rhymes with *bother* and *father* rhymes with *gather)* will help them remember the spelling.
- The students write inside the outline letters using a brown pencil and underline the tricky parts in purple.

Tricky word spelling routine (See page 28)

- The students practice writing the new tricky words on a separate sheet of paper.

Fill in the gaps

- The students write inside the outline letters, write over the dotted letters, and fill in the missing letters.

Every, mother, or father?

- Read the sentences with the class and discuss which tricky word should be used in each one. Read each sentence back to the students, using their chosen word, and ask them if it makes sense. The students complete the sentences, writing the correct word in each one.

Dictation

- Dictate the sentences shown on the answer page.

Reading the tricky words

- The students read the tricky words in the flowers and color the edge of the flowers brown.

Wordsearch (See page 182)

- The class do the wordsearch on page 71 of their books.

FURTHER PRACTICE

It is important to practice the skills needed for reading and writing on a regular basis.

Blending and segmenting

fried, dress, crack, sunny, antler,
hawk, stalk, caller, laundry, sawdust

- Call out each word. The students say the sounds, holding up a finger for each one. Write the letters on the board as they do so and blend the word.
- Practice blending the words with the class (as well as in pairs or individually, if extra practice is needed).

Reading sentences

- Write these sentences on the board for the class to read. Point out the tricky words and blend any unknown words with the students:
  1. Do not stare out of the window.
  2. Father grows pears in his garden.
  3. He sits in the same chair every day.
  4. They went to the fair with their mother.

Unit 13: Words and Sentences

Review

- Use flashcards to review soft ‹g›, soft ‹c›, ‹ph›, ‹ck›, and some of the alternative vowel spellings.
- Call out some of the letter sounds and ask the students to write the different spellings for each one.

Read, write, and review (See page 181)

- Recite the alphabet with the class. Any students who need some support can look at page 66 in their books.
- Review how to put letters into alphabetical order. Write three letters from each alphabet section on the board and help the class to put them into alphabetical order.
- The students then go to page 66 of their books and put the following sets of letters in alphabetical order: R j E o; N z i U; t L a D.

The midnight feast

- Write the following words on the board and read them with the class: *called, hungry, cheese, crumbs, floor, mouse, quiet, reached*. Pay particular attention to the alternative spellings; the silent letters in *calle**d**, chees**e**, crum**b**s, fl**o**or, mous**e***, and *reache**d**;* the ‹s› saying /z/ in *cheese;* the ‹g› in ‹ng› making its own sound in *hungry;* and the pronunciation of *quiet,* which needs to be adjusted after blending.
- Read the story to the students, and encourage them to read along in their books. Check that they can read the tricky words unprompted and take care with the more challenging words, such as *quiet, castle,* and *sandwiches.* These words are not totally regular, but the spelling is close enough for the students to read them, especially if they are in the students' vocabulary.
- As you are reading, ask some questions to make sure the class are following the story. At the end, go through the questions on the page and elicit the answers, prompting if necessary. Give the students enough time to write the answers in their books.

Answers

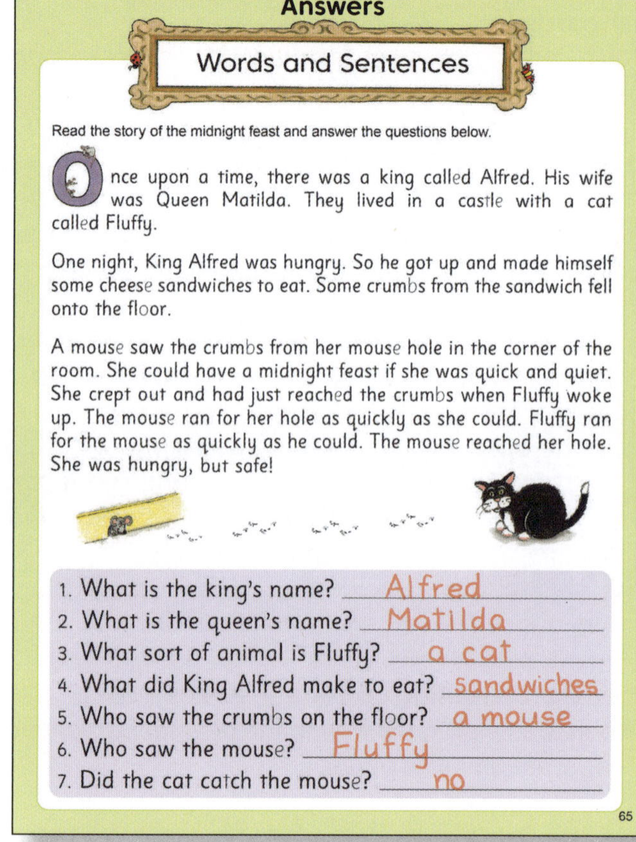

Words and Sentences

Read the story of the midnight feast and answer the questions below.

Once upon a time, there was a king called Alfred. His wife was Queen Matilda. They lived in a castle with a cat called Fluffy.

One night, King Alfred was hungry. So he got up and made himself some cheese sandwiches to eat. Some crumbs from the sandwich fell onto the floor.

A mouse saw the crumbs from her mouse hole in the corner of the room. She could have a midnight feast if she was quick and quiet. She crept out and had just reached the crumbs when Fluffy woke up. The mouse ran for her hole as quickly as she could. Fluffy ran for the mouse as quickly as he could. The mouse reached her hole. She was hungry, but safe!

1. What is the king's name? Alfred
2. What is the queen's name? Matilda
3. What sort of animal is Fluffy? a cat
4. What did King Alfred make to eat? sandwiches
5. Who saw the crumbs on the floor? a mouse
6. Who saw the mouse? Fluffy
7. Did the cat catch the mouse? no

65

Extension activity

- Discuss the story with the class and ask the students to imagine what it would feel like to be the little mouse. They could then retell some of the story from the mouse's point of view.

FURTHER PRACTICE

It is important to practice the skills needed for reading and writing on a regular basis.

Blending and segmenting

free, skill, quick, north, sister,
shawl, launch, walker, August, ballroom

- Call out each word. The students say the sounds, holding up a finger for each one. Write the letters on the board as they do so and blend the word.
- Practice blending the words with the class (as well as in pairs or individually, if extra practice is needed).

Reading sentences

- Write these sentences on the board for the class to read. Point out the tricky words and blend any unknown words with the students:
    1. The fox stared at the hare.
    2. Their father needs a haircut.
    3. Everyone went upstairs to bed.
    4. Mother is wearing her new scarf.

Further Unit Activities: Answers

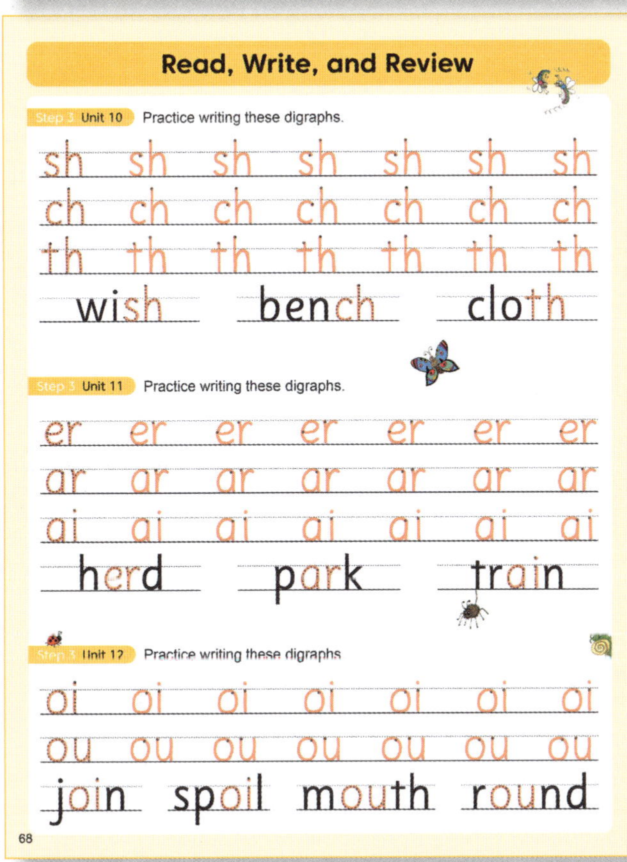

Further Unit Activities: Answers

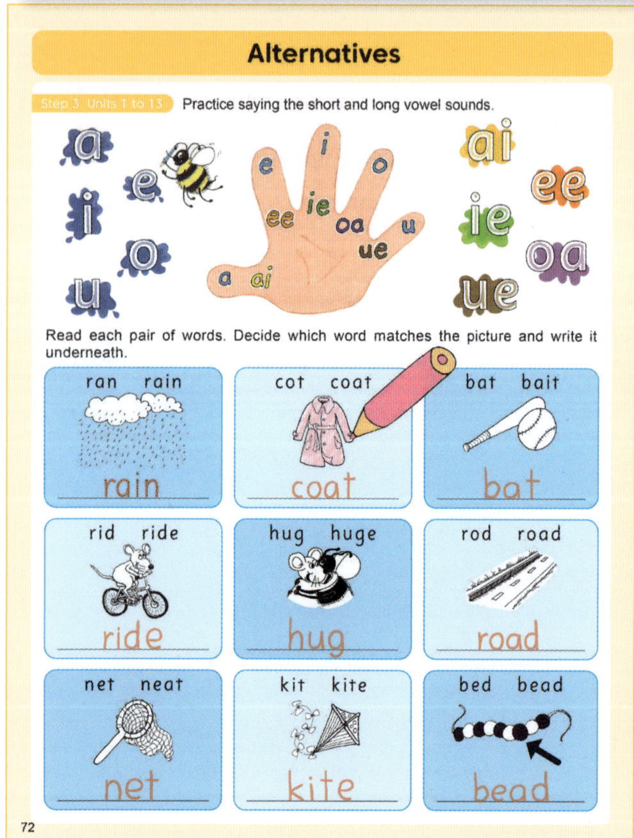

After Jolly Phonics

After a year of Jolly Phonics, most students will have mastered the five key skills required for reading and writing. The students will know the main letter sounds, have a good pencil grip, and be able to form letters correctly. They will know how to blend sounds together to read a word and be able to identify the sounds in a word in order to write it. They will have been taught the 72 tricky words and had lots of practice reading and writing simple sentences. In addition, the more able readers will have worked through different levels of decodable books that match their phonic knowledge. As a result, most students will be at the stage where they can write freely. This writing may not be spelled or punctuated correctly, but it should be easy to read and understand.

The next important stage in the students' literacy development is to hone their writing skills, by giving them a structured, systematic grounding in spelling, grammar, and punctuation. They will also need more advanced decodable readers to increase their fluency in reading before moving on to free reading when they are able.

Jolly Grammar

Jolly Grammar is a six-level program that gives young students the skills they need to be confident readers and enthusiastic writers. It builds on the teaching in Jolly Phonics and has the same multisensory, active, and fun approach. The systematic and cumulative syllabus enables students to spell and punctuate more accurately, use a wider vocabulary, and have a clearer understanding of how language works. Each level of Jolly Grammar has a write-in Student Book with a full set of lesson activities for the academic year. It also has a Teacher's Book providing step-by-step lesson plans and comprehensive support.

Jolly Grammar introduces complex grammatical concepts in an engaging and child-friendly way, and the program systematically reinforces the learning to ensure that no one is left behind. It teaches new spelling patterns, supports a greater understanding of sentence structure, expands vocabulary and comprehension, and cultivates dictionary and thesaurus skills.

The first level of Jolly Grammar extends the teaching of the Jolly Phonics Student Books. The students learn to spell, as well as read, words with the alternative vowel spellings, review the 72 tricky words, and develop the ability to put words in alphabetical order. They improve their understanding of sentence structure, learning how to punctuate speech and questions, and they are introduced to the spelling patterns ‹wh› and ‹nk›. At the same time, the students are taught the rudiments of grammar, focusing on the main parts of speech.

Alongside Jolly Grammar, the students can continue to develop their reading with the Blue and Purple Levels of the Jolly Phonics Readers.

Jolly Grammar

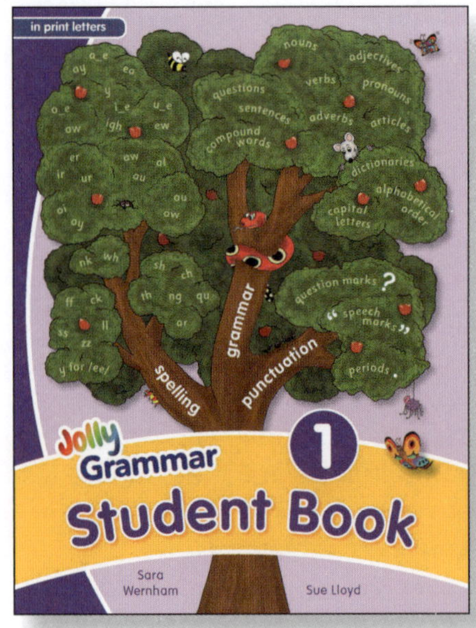

JL949
ISBN 978-1-84414-294-1

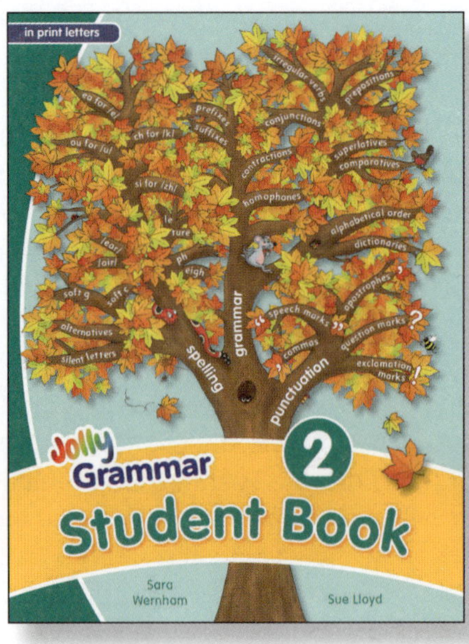

JL996
ISBN 978-1-84414-399-3

JL542
ISBN 978-1-84414-454-9

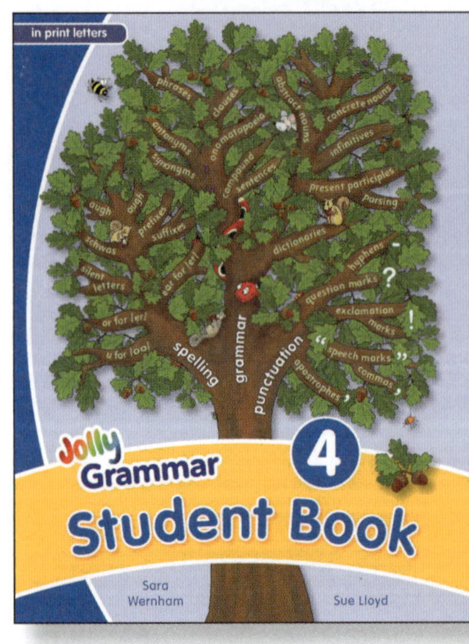

JL78X
ISBN 978-1-84414-478-5

JL844
ISBN 978-1-84414-484-6

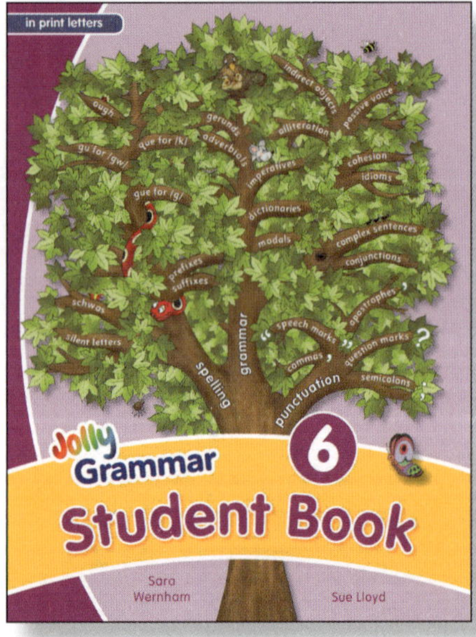

JL174
ISBN 978-1-84414-517-1

A six-level program that gets to grips with spelling, grammar, and punctuation